THE
MUTUAL
GAINS
ENTERPRISE

thomas a. kochan
paul osterman

THE MUTUAL GAINS ENTERPRISE

forging a winning
partnership among labor,
management,
and government

HARVARD BUSINESS SCHOOL PRESS
BOSTON, MASSACHUSETTS

98 97 96 95 94   5 4 3 2 1

Library of Congress Cataloging-in-Publication Data

Kochan, Thomas A.
    The mutual gains enterprise : forging a winning partnership
among labor, management, and government / Thomas A. Kochan,
Paul Osterman.
        p.   cm.
    Includes bibliographical references and index.
    ISBN 0-87584-394-8 (acid-free paper)
    1. Personnel management—Government policy—United
States.   2. Industrial relations—United States.   I. Osterman,
Paul.   II. Title.
HF5549.2.U5K63   1994
658.3—dc20   94-5930
                                                        CIP

The paper used in this publication meets the requirements of the
American National Standard for Permanence of Paper for Printed
Library Materials Z39.49-1984.

To
Henry and Esther Osterman
and
Kathryn Kochan

contents

acknowledgments

The Mutual Gains Enterprise brings together our recent work on labor market and employment policies with our work on the human resource strategies and labor management practices of individual firms. The book was prompted by our belief that these two domains are highly interrelated, yet too often treated separately in academic teaching and research, public policy making, and organizational decision making. Our hope is that it demonstrates the value of more direct interaction and dialogue among professionals in these domains.

We have accumulated a great many debts in the course of writing this book. For the past seeeveral years each of us has taught the core human resources class at MIT's Sloan School of Management. The experience of interacting with a very bright group of students has immensely sharpened our thinking. In addition, teaching this course jointly with our colleagues—including Thomas Barocci, Lisa Lynch, Bob McKersie, Jim Rebitzer, and Maureen Scully—has given us many opportunities to benefit from their ideas.

Many colleagues have read and provided helpful comments on portions of this book in either draft or article form. We wish to thank especially Phillip Beaumont, Peter Cappelli, Robert Crandall, Peter Doeringer, Lee Dyer, Harry Katz, Frank Levy, Richard Locke, Bob McKersie, Richard Murnane, Jeff Pfeffer, Michael Piore, Michael Porter, Maurice Segall, and Richard Walton.

We had the great benefit of assistance from several members of the MIT community. Rosemary Batt was a colleague in the research on state training programs that appears in several chapters. Brenda Lautsch did a wonderfully conscientious and thorough job as a research assistant for large portions of the book. Susan Wright played many roles, each of them well: she edited parts of the book, oversaw the production process, and kept track of numerous details, both large and small. Jody Hoffer-Gittel provided several background memos on specific company experiences. Karen Boyajian joined the project in its final stages and helped see it through to completion.

Carol Franco and Natalie Greenberg at the Harvard Business School Press have served as resourceful and excellent editors. We appreciate the help and advice they provided throughout this effort.

Paul Osterman's time was supported by the Spencer Foundation, which funded the establishment survey used throughout the book. Thomas Kochan's research was supported by the Alfred P. Sloan Foundation, the MIT Leaders for Management Program, and the MIT Industrial Performance Center. Kochan is also a member of the Commission on the Future of Workers Management Relations discussed in Chapter 8. The views expressed here are solely those of the authors and do not represent those of the commission or any of the research sponsors.

THE
MUTUAL GAINS ENTERPRISE

chapter one

INTRODUCTION

The past decade began with high expectations for human resource management research, practice, and policy. Human resource professionals and their academic colleagues would shed their "personnel management" orientation and adopt "strategic human resource management" theory and practice. According to *Business Week,* unionized firms were expected to trade in their traditional adversarial practices for new cooperative, high-trust ones built on a foundation of employee participation and labor and management partnership. As the decade progressed, various private and public "competitiveness" commissions added to the rhetoric by noting the link between human resource preparedness and development and macroeconomic performance. For American industry to be competitive in world markets, human resources would need to be a source of competitive advantage. Thus, human resource strategies moved to center stage in the business press, national policy debates, and corporate boardrooms. New human resource strategies promised to lead firms into a more prosperous and humane and cooperative era. Sparked by these efforts, the American economy would reemerge as a dominant competitor in world markets and the work force would share in the fruits of the resurgence.

For a while it looked as if these promises might be realized as the pressures from high inflation, sluggish productivity, and increasing international competition that were building gradually throughout the 1970s gave way to a period of rapid and unprecedented workplace innovations in the first half of the 1980s. These innovations were unleashed by the confluence of the deep economic recession of 1981–1983, the political climate that led to the election of Ronald

Reagan as president, and the visible impacts of international competition that eroded the markets of American firms.

But to date this rhetoric has had little impact on national policy and macroeconomic performance, and only limited and uneven effects on private practice. Some innovations such as quality circles proved to be short-lived management fads. Those innovations which proved to be more powerful and sustainable, such as teamwork in production and product development, have diffused unevenly across organizations. Instead, the leading firms, managers, and union leaders that advocate innovative human resource practices have become islands of innovation in a sea of traditional practices.

By the early 1990s the momentum seemed to have dissipated. The recession and sluggish recovery created a return to short-run economies: cost cutting, head-count reductions, and restructuring. Both *The Wall Street Journal* and *Business Week* reported that the culture-building CEOs of the 1980s were being replaced by hard-driving, cold-blooded executives who were not reluctant to eliminate jobs or reduce head count. Human resources, with a few exceptions, failed to take its expected place in the strategic decision-making chambers of top corporations or in national economic and social policy-making institutions. Even IBM, the company with perhaps the most highly professional and influential human resource staff in America, announced plans to decentralize, replacing much of its corporate staff with an external contracting unit from which the company's business units could purchase services "as needed."

In the same vein, despite the fact that many unions did work with managers to introduce significant innovations in labor-management relations, the labor movement continued to shrink and lose influence throughout the 1980s and into the 1990s. By 1993 union membership in the private sector had fallen to less than 12 percent, nearly as low as it was at the beginning of the Great Depression. Instead of building on its experience with innovation to produce a new vision or strategy for society or its own future, the labor movement remained mired in quiet internal debate, unable to articulate a viable long-term strategy for representing the changing American work force. Like their management counterparts, many leaders and professionals in the labor movement had advocated more proactive and innovative strategies for representing the changing nature and needs of the work force. But apparently formidable obstacles have kept this innovative approach from emerging as labor's dominant image or role in society and at the workplace.

New vigor was given to the debates about workplace innovations in the presidential election campaign of 1992. Each candidate had proposals to restore the long-term competitiveness of the American economy and to create good jobs at good wages. At the heart of these debates was the view that American workers are undertrained, and even when employees have skills, American workplaces lack the features needed to take full advantage of them. With the election of President Bill Clinton came the expectation that the federal government would work with business and labor to increase investment in training, workplace innovation, and other strategies to improve productivity and the standards of living of American workers.

The question, however, remains: What can or should the government do to help? Would a more active government role foster private sector investment in training or workplace reform? Many in the business community are considerably skeptical: Can government intervention avoid further regulations or reinforcing the traditional adversarial relationships between organized labor and the business community or between workers and managers?

American policy makers and firms and their workers are caught between two worlds—an old system that no longer meets their needs and a new order that seems unreachable and unstable. We need to ask, What keeps these new practices from taking hold and diffusing across the economy? We seek to address this puzzle by presenting the theoretical and empirical evidence that one or more new "models" of employment relations exist that outperform traditional systems. The features of these new models are described in the first section of the book. We explore why some firms adopt innovations and others do not and summarize the extent to which various workplace innovations have diffused across the economy. Then we analyze why these new approaches are not more widely adopted by identifying the systemic obstacles in the American economy, its institutions, and public policies that block widespread adoption and diffusion of human resource innovations. Many of these obstacles lie outside the control of any individual firm and can be overcome only with changes in national policies and through the concerted efforts of the business, labor, and policy-making communities.

But a simple call for more cooperation among labor, management, and government similar to the common pleas found in most competitiveness commission reports of the 1980s will not do the job. Instead, a new approach, one led by a national policy that endorses and facilitates innovation in employment relations—will be needed to structure the relationships among these parties. Thus, in the final section of the book, we propose a new framework with specific elements for national employment and human resource policy, as well as a new role for government, that can overcome these obstacles. We call this a mutual gains[1] policy framework because it proposes ways to go beyond the New Deal labor policies, which regulated conflicts, to policies that support practices which, if widely adopted, promise benefits for workers, firms, and the national economy. Finally, to implement this new strategy we call for a new coalition of workers and professionals within business, labor, government, and the academic community to promote mutual gains employment policies and practices.

Normative Debates and Positive Analysis

We move between normative argument and theoretical and empirical analysis. We do so in the belief that any viable national policy or enterprise strategy is only as strong as its intellectual foundations. But we also see a need for a debate about the current models that shape the "world views" of people in our field. In short, we need to construct a new intellectual foundation for national employment and human resource policy and firm-level human resource practice, one that shifts the way we teach human resources to managers, one that positions human resource strategies squarely within the governance system of American firms, one that provides a clearer vision and strategy for workers and their representatives, and one that redirects national employment policy.

The lack of a strong intellectual framework is reflected in how human resources are taught in business schools. The material is too restricted by the fads and the shifting priorities of top managers and fails to adequately challenge American management to look beyond its short-term business strategies. The prevailing view is that human resource strategies should be matched to business strategies and that human resource professionals should view executives and line managers as their most important "customers." While this perspective is understandable, we feel it perpetuates the low status and influence of human resource issues within organizations. In the majority of American firms, human resource considerations are a residual concern, to be dealt with after all other important strategic decisions are made. We argue that to change this state of affairs, human resource professionals need to take a broader, coalitional view of their task and work with their professional colleagues in government, labor, and the academic community to build *institutional* bases for articulating human resource concerns in strategic decision making. Then it will be their special responsibility to implement practices within their operations that demonstrate added value for integrating human resource issues into corporate and national strategies.

National policy making in turn depends on a too narrow laissez-faire model of the economy that fails to understand adequately how *real organizations* work. The competitiveness commissions and the stated policies of the Clinton administration tend to believe that more investment in research and development, plant and equipment, and human resources will automatically translate into sustained improvements in productivity growth and workers' wages. But, we argue, while greater investment in both hardware and human resources are necessary, they are far from sufficient to produce the desired results.

National policy makers need to find ways to *change organizations,* starting with the highest levels of the firm, where long-term strategic decisions are made. Again, this requires a broader and a more comparative analytical lens than is provided by standard economic theory. It requires a new focus on institutional and organizational theory—one that builds inductively on the experiences of managers and labor leaders to identify and apply a new model of employment relations. It also requires a comparative perspective—one open to learning whether practices or institutions that work in other countries can be adapted to American customs and institutions. Finally, we place human resource and labor-management practices in the enterprise in the larger debate over the governance structures of the firm and the relationship between individual firm policies and national labor and human resource and public policies. We seek to provide both a substantive agenda for a new national policy and organizational practices *and* an intellectual agenda for this field of inquiry.

Theoretical and Empirical Foundations

Our starting point is a model of the relationships between human resource practices and the economic performance of firms. This is combined with a framework that relates these same practices to the competitiveness and standards of living of the national economy.

Figure 1-1 illustrates the model we use to relate firm-level human resource practices to national economic performance. The key argu-

Figure 1-1
Human Resources and National Competitiveness

ment is that achieving competitiveness at high standards of living requires a high rate of growth in productivity, product innovation, and adaptability to changing markets. This in turn requires corporate strategies that give high priority to developing and fully utilizing the skills of the work force. Finally, the gains of improved productivity must be distributed in an equitable fashion to the multiple stakeholders who helped create them and reinvested in ways that ensure future generations improved standards of living.

At the heart of this model lies the need to improve productivity—the efficiency with which a firm and the economy use their scarce human, material, capital, and other resources—and the model reflects the traditional economics argument that real wages, a measure of the standard of living, in the long run are determined by the rate of productivity growth. So, to improve both the national economic performance and living standards, firms and society as a whole must make efficient use of the resources available.

But the concept of productivity must be broadened in a world where new technologies and innovations come quickly, consumer tastes are varied and uncertain, and breakthroughs introduced to the market by one firm are quickly copied or surpassed by rivals. To be competitive, firms must also produce goods and services of high—and continuously improving—quality, speed new products to market, discover and develop new market opportunities, and be able to adapt quickly and at low cost to changes in market conditions or demand. While a purist might argue that productivity, properly measured, would encompass all these considerations, in reality these performance objectives need not, and often do not, move together. Firms can, for example, improve quality by adding more repair or inspection personnel, but this increases costs and lowers productivity. Or firms can become very lean and mean by cutting excess personnel, reduce the time and resources available for training or research and development, and in the process reduce their ability to develop the next-generation product or transfer knowledge from one product line to another.

Similarly, national economies can increase their competitiveness by lowering the price of their products through holding down wages or devaluing their currencies. This increases the "competitiveness" of the nation's products in international markets but leads to a gradual decline in living standards. As we will see in Chapter 2, this has been precisely the experience of the American economy for the past decade.

Ultimately, the purpose of any economy is to improve the long-term welfare of its citizens. This is why most public and private studies of the competitiveness of the American economy in recent years have used a definition of competitiveness that has the two components central to our concept of mutual gains: high productivity and high wages or, stated more generally, competitiveness at high standards of living. It is these twin objectives that guide our review of the recent performance of the American economy and that we use to assess its prospects for the future.

The linking of human resource practices of a firm and national competitiveness and social welfare ensures that the work force is educated and trained adequately to contribute to productivity growth and that the organizational practices are such that this human potential is fully utilized on the job. Finally, firm policies also affect the distribution of gains from increased productivity to the various stakeholders who have a legitimate claim to these rewards: the owners or investors in the enterprise, the workers, and the larger public who provide the "public goods," or infrastructure, needed for any individual enterprise to prosper.

The Role of History

Any analysis that hopes to interpret and ultimately guide future behavior must be careful not to overlook the lessons of history. Chances are we have been in a similar position. We have, but we must return to the first two decades of this century to find the appropriate historical parallels. We probe the nature of the American corporation and its legal and normative underpinnings and evolution in order to understand why employees now find themselves at a distinct disadvantage vis-à-vis shareholder interests. We look at a similar period of management-led workplace innovation from World War I through the 1920s, when, as in the past two decades, the national government took a laissez-faire approach to labor-management relations that changed only in response to the economic and social crises of the 1930s. This will help us understand why government policy makers have been such passive actors in the labor-market events of the 1980s, even given the increasing evidence that our human resource and labor policies were not addressing the fundamental needs of a modern economy and a democratic society.

We analyze the role of personnel and human resource professionals to see why, despite calls for them to take up more strategic and powerful positions, they remain among the weakest of all managerial groups in corporate decision making. And we look at the politics of strategy formulation and leadership development in the American labor movement to understand why labor seems unable to create a new vision and strategy capable of sowing the seeds of its resurgence.

An International Perspective

Just as important as a historical perspective is an international one, especially given the speed at which today's technical and organizational innovations are transferable across national boundaries. Indeed, American managers have realized the hard way that perhaps we have more to learn from our competitors abroad than we have to teach them! In the 1980s Japan provided the key lessons. In the 1990s, however, growing attention is being given to Europe. Where applicable, these lessons need to be incorporated into American practice in ways that make them truly improve productivity.

A Bottom-Line Perspective

Finally, given the pragmatic character of Americans, we need to document the economic effects of alternative approaches to human resource and labor-management practice and policy. In short we need to show in concrete terms the empirical evidence relating human resource practices to economic performance.

The CEO as Change Agent?

Why can't we depend on a few good leaders to show the way and act as role models? The reason is that a top-down model ignores the constraints imposed by the system within which leaders operate. It also ignores the need to obtain the participation and commitment of all members of the organization.

In recent years there has been a tendency to glorify the role of the CEO as the key to transformation. Transformational leaders and leadership have been touted as the key to achieving change. Profiles of visionary leaders who navigated their companies through the painful and uncertain waters of the 1970s and early 1980s to restructured and more effective organizations dominated the business press.[2] But these profiles were followed by muckraking books about Wall Streeters who abused the power of their positions and engaged in the buying and selling of organizations as though they were simply bundles of financial assets rather than human beings.[3]

Then there was the view that outside members of boards of directors were not aggressive enough in insisting that CEOs represent shareholder interests. Finally, there are recent business books about the new, hard-nosed CEO who, perhaps in response to pressures from outside directors or other shareholder representatives, pares down corporate bureaucracies and decentralizes control to different business units in search of lean, cost-conscious, and flexible organizations.[4]

Unfortunately, there is a basic conceptual flaw in theories that take this top-down, CEO-leadership view of organizational change and transformation. No one denies the critical role that top leaders play in driving change. It is almost a cliché, but an accurate one, to say that top management commitment is a necessary condition for significant change to occur in an organization. Indeed, throughout this book we present data showing the importance of the values espoused by top executives. But models of organizational behavior that emphasize managerial values and culture too often are unaware of the legal foundations of the American corporation.

Corporate executives are agents of and are held accountable to their shareholders. This means that top executives are accountable not to the average shareholder but to the Wall Street analysts and advisers who shape the opinions of investors and have the greatest incentives to encourage firms to maximize short-term gains because their jobs depend on squeezing maximum gains out of the portfolios they manage before their account is up for its next review. But behind these analysts are the financial institutions and institutional investors that affect the time horizons of executives. Therefore, we explore the argument that American financial institutions bias managers toward short time horizons that lead them to avoid "intangible" investments, i.e., projects that have clear, visible short-term costs and only long-term, and somewhat invisible if not uncertain, benefits. Investments in training and human resource innovations clearly fit this description.

An additional limit on the strategies that rely entirely on CEO leadership is that such leadership cannot obtain sustained organizational change without the commitment of employees. This is the hard lesson that was demonstrated perhaps most dramatically by Frank Lorenzo's disastrous leadership of Continental and Eastern airlines. However, employee commitment cannot be maintained in the long run without the mutual gains enterprise.

Worker Voice and Action

If things are going poorly for American workers, why don't they revolt and change things for themselves? Why don't they join unions, organize spontaneously, or simply take advantage of the freedom in our labor markets by leaving jobs that are unacceptable and accepting only jobs that meet their expectations? A free and efficiently functioning labor market should solve this problem or, if it doesn't, indignant workers should organize to obtain their objectives. We explore the current state of the American labor movement and its attempt to reverse the decline in union membership and worker representation. Labor has indeed worked cooperatively with management in a large number of firms to introduce innovations. (By the mid-1980s unions ceased to be a significant force in impeding change.) At the same time, however, labor did not champion these new ways of empowering and representing workers, so in many settings unions simply became marginalized and at least served as junior partners in managing the change process. The inability of unions to adopt new strategies and structures meant that traditional labor union representation continued to decline. Further, government policy and American managerial ideology remained hostile to unionization and failed to support new roles for worker representatives.

Here one must be sensitive to the history of worker protest and unionization. While union decline has tended to follow a rather smooth path, as it did from 1920 to 1933, union growth tends to be abrupt and spontaneous. This happened to industrial workers in the 1930s and to public sector workers in the 1960s. Worker protest and labor conflict erupt when political or economic conditions begin to improve but significant groups see little prospect for improvement in their own welfare. If this is true, we may simply be experiencing the lull before the storm.

Academics and Ideas

At the outset we argued that academics can make significant contributions to national economic objectives and policy making if they broaden their analytical lens to incorporate a more powerful theory of the firm and link micro—firm-level—strategies to their macro-level counterparts. Thus, we end the book with a discussion of the implications of our approach for future theory and empirical research in the human resource management field. We suggest a new paradigm that takes a decidedly more international approach and integrates human resource management with organizational theory and internal and external labor market research.

Engaging the Debate: A Note to Readers

The arguments we advance in this book challenge a number of views that have come to be accepted as doctrine by some in the business, labor, and academic communities. We very much hope that readers will judge our discussion with a critical but open mind and bring to bear their own experience and analysis on our arguments. We expect, and indeed hope, that most readers will have questions, doubts, and amendments. Conversations with colleagues who have been exposed to our arguments suggest that three major questions are likely to come to many readers' minds. Although we address each of these points in greater detail in the chapters that follow, it seems useful to address them briefly here so that readers can be clear about our position.

We think that the following questions will occur to many readers:

1. If the ideas proposed in the book are so terrific, why will not the market naturally diffuse them? What will prevent these developments from occurring on their own?

2. At many points in the book we note the importance of employment continuity and security. Yet we live in an economy in which layoffs are both common and, according to many, necessary for competitiveness. Are not our arguments regarding the importance of employment security somewhat naive?

3. The book argues for the importance and active involvement of two institutions—government and unions—that have been in some disrepute in recent years. How can we justify our emphasis on these institutions?

Diffusion

We believe that there are two broad explanations for why the practices we propose will not adequately diffuse on their own. First, there are *market failures,* which make adoption of new practices more expensive and risky than they otherwise would be. A market failure occurs when the action of some economic actors, such as other firms, has an unintended but negative impact on the prospects of others and when the negatively affected party cannot seek redress through normal market mechanisms. Virtually all economists recognize that, in the presence of market failures, the case for public policy is strong.

Second, we recognize that firms, unions, and employees make decisions based on the context—the economic constraints and institutional settings—within which they operate. By "institutional settings" we mean the broader relationships among businesses, labor, government, and other key groups or actors that shape the environment in which individual firms operate. Decisions that are optimal in one market or institutional context may not be optimal in another. Yet we must recognize that the context itself is open for discussion and that social welfare might be enhanced if the context and constraints were changed so that a different set of decisions, or outcomes, emerge. Therefore practices that fail to diffuse in one context may very well do so in another.

We take up these points in detail throughout the book. A summary of some of the key issues might be:

1. Introduction of new ways of organizing work requires new skills, yet firms, particularly small and medium-size ones, face a classic market failure. If they train their employees, they run the risk

of losing them to their competitors. Hence there is systematic underprovision of training.

2. The incentives managers face, particularly from the stock market, emphasize short time horizons and limited investment in hard-to-measure activities such as work reorganization and training. The weakness of employee representation means that there are few countervailing pressures. Put differently, the current structure or context values the gains to only one of a firm's multiple stakeholders.

3. In contrast to our competitors overseas, employer associations are weak and employers are isolated from one another. The weakness of these cross-firm institutions limits the diffusion of knowledge and innovation in a wide range of areas, including work organization. It also limits the ability of industry representatives to discipline "free riders," i.e., ensure that all competitors that benefit from the availability of an adequate supply of skilled workers contribute their fair share to the development and maintenance of these skills.

4. Small and medium-size employers face special constraints. In addition to the training problem alluded to above, they are frequently capital constrained and operate on thin margins. They cannot take the risks inherent in changing work organization and they receive no support from government or business associations in doing so. They also lack the managerial time necessary to make these investments even though the changes might pay off handsomely.

5. High unemployment and a generally undertrained labor force combine to reduce incentives for employers to adopt mutual gains systems. This is because there is an abundant supply of relatively unskilled and low-wage labor. It is when labor markets are tight and employees skilled that employers seek to get the most out of their labor force by designing work systems which utilize their full potential.

6. Historically and currently, relationships between American business and labor and relationships between American business and government have been more adversarial than those of most of our trading partners and key international competitors. Operating in a low-trust institutional context adds significant costs to individual firms because they must absorb high transaction, negotiation, or litigation costs to protect their autonomy against hostile interests. Over time this low-trust context becomes self-reinforcing, making

it difficult for parties either to see the potential for or build institutions capable of achieving mutual gains outcomes.

Taken together, these market failures and institutional weaknesses limit the diffusion of mutual gains systems despite their benefits to the firm and to employees. Not surprisingly, when we turn to policy, many of our recommendations are aimed at overcoming the obstacles listed above.

Employment Security

It is difficult to introduce mutual gains systems in an environment characterized by high levels of economic insecurity. In subsequent chapters we lay out in detail why this is so and conclude that we need to find ways to make employment more secure. Yet this runs squarely into the commonly shared perception that many firms are overstaffed and that layoffs and restructuring are necessary to compete in today's markets. One might well argue, for example, that IBM waited too long before making the first layoffs in its history and that the firm and its current employees would have been better off had some of these layoffs taken place sooner.

By the same token, while many, including ourselves, often point to the so-called lifetime employment system of Japan as a model, we must also recognize the limitations of that approach. First, it applies to only roughly a third of the Japanese work force. Women, in particular, are systematically excluded from protection. Second, it is buttressed by a labor market in which young people leave school and immediately go to work for their "lifetime" employer and in which interfirm mobility is strongly discouraged. None of this seems acceptable in the American context.

We know that there is substantial truth in these arguments and that in the current environment it is very difficult, if not impossible, for any firm to promise its employees absolute protection from layoffs. This does not, however, diminish the importance of economic security. Instead, it has implications for employer and public policy.

Although employers cannot promise no layoffs, they can commit themselves to avoiding a knee-jerk hire/fire response to economic downturns. For many purposes it is enough that employers engage in a series of policies—reducing outsourcing, smoothing product demand where possible, retraining and reassigning employees—which mitigates layoffs. In addition, employers should share the pain. In the event of contraction, stockholders and managers should accept their fair share of sacrifice. We believe that the combination of creative personnel policies and shared sacrifice will help firms introduce and sustain mutual gains systems even in an insecure environment.

Although the foregoing strategy is a piece of the answer, it is not enough. The concept of economic security needs to be shifted from a firm-specific idea to the notion that employees should be able to navigate the labor market successfully should events force them to do so. In part this will also require action by employers, in this instance to ensure that an adequate level of training is provided. The problem, however, is that economic incentives do not point companies in this direction since, to the extent that training makes workers more mobile, firms run the risk of not capturing the returns on their investment. So active public policies with respect to training and job search will be important, and we spend considerable time laying these out.

The insecurity of the current economic environment is less than ideal for introducing mutual gains systems. We must remember, however, that it is precisely the economic turbulence that generates this insecurity which motivates the need for new ways of working. We believe that creative personnel policies, an atmosphere of shared sacrifice, and active public policy are the best answers to this dilemma.

The Role of Government and Unions

There are two vehicles available for overcoming market failures, both of which require external agents or actors to encourage cross-firm coordination and cooperation. One is the government, which can provide incentives, requirements, or resources supporting cross-firm coordinated action. The problem with government, however, is that it often lacks the practical or detailed knowledge required to tailor its interventions in ways that are, in the end, market enhancing. Instead, it uses blunt instruments that increase costs and divert managerial attention and resources to reporting or other compliance activities. Prior generations of labor economists often referred to government intervention in labor markets as akin to a cobbler trying to fit everyone into a "size 8 shoe." Or, as in the area of occupational safety and health, the economy is just too big and the number of regulations far too numerous to enforce effectively. Indeed, over the past twenty years the number of labor-market regulations and associated enforcement tasks have more than quadrupled—a recent count found more than

150 different laws and regulations currently affecting the American workplace!

So when we argue for a new role for government here, we do it cautiously and envision a very different role, one in which government policy is *informed* by private practices and serves as a catalyst for innovation through provision of information, technical resources and support, and enabling legislation that removes constraints which currently limit the ability of firms and employees to innovate. In some cases we do suggest new incentives such as matching contributions between state and federal agencies or between government agencies and private parties. The principle here is that both private and public actors must see an effort as a reasonable investment before committing our public or private resources.

In a few cases, such as changing labor laws, we propose changing the rules under which private parties operate. In these cases the evidence we present convinces us—and we suspect our readers as well—that current rules are outdated and need revision to better enable the private parties to take responsibility for improving the performance of American labor markets and labor-management relations. This is one example of changes designed to modify and improve the institutional context within which individual firms, employees, and unions make decisions.

The second vehicle for overcoming market failures is the collective voice of employees. In the United States, trade unions have traditionally served this function through collective bargaining and political lobbying for policies such as minimum wages, safety and health standards, equal employment opportunity protections, and so forth. Here America has a dilemma and perhaps even a crisis of its own making. As noted earlier, union membership has been declining for years and American management remains as hostile or vigorously opposed to a rebirth of unionism today as it has been historically. Indeed, we confront directly one of the most difficult and sensitive issues in our field, which is too often avoided in civil political discourse or even in academic research, namely, the fact that some of the firms which have been leading innovators in human resource practices over the past twenty years are among those most strongly opposed to unionization of their employees.

Yet, as we note later, most informed executives, and the vast majority of the American public, continue to believe that effective employee voice and representation are critical to a well-functioning democracy. Objective surveys and opinion polls continue to find that a substantial number of unrepresented workers prefer to have some form of representation in their workplaces. Thus, we have what some of our colleagues have begun to call a representation gap in the American labor force.

Our suggestion about how to close this representation gap is to encourage a variety of alternative forums for employee participation and representation that have considerable potential for producing and sustaining mutual gains to employees, firms, and the larger society. By doing so we hope to avoid the knee-jerk reaction of management advocates who reject any ideas that might strengthen employee voice or the equally knee-jerk reaction of labor advocates who prefer simply to reform labor law in ways that might recreate labor unions in their prior image and reject any new approaches to participation and/or representation as inherently "anti-union." To bolster our argument, we draw on experience with new forms of participation that have proved their value in specific American workplaces and supplement this with a look at approaches used in countries that are our major trading partners and competitors.

We develop these ideas in more detail in the chapters that follow. We present them here to open the minds of our readers to new ways of thinking about old problems and to encourage you to debate these ideas with us as we present the evidence. It is exactly this type of debate which we believe needs to be stimulated among the American public and in the management, labor, and policy-making communities if mutual gains solutions to the challenges we face are to be generated.

Chapter Outline

Chapter 2 provides a macro overview of the performance of the American economy during the past decade on the measures of critical concern to workers, firms, and national policy makers. Chapter 3 presents a model of the mutual gains enterprise derived inductively from the trial-and-error experimentation of leading firms and labor unions. In Chapter 4 we explore the factors that influence the choice of human resource strategies and policies within firms and use a variety of survey and case-study information to assess the extent to which workplace innovations have diffused across the economy to date. We also summarize the evidence explaining why only partial diffusion has occurred and is likely to occur in the absence of changes in national policy and the practices of business and labor. Chapter 5 is devoted to a special topic, one that is rather new to most human resource professionals and researchers: the influence of financial markets and corporate governance structures on human resource strategy and practice. This chapter allows us to take a decidedly comparative perspective on our work as we look carefully at Japanese and German corporations for clues to why these countries seem to do better at institutionalizing human resource practices that can gain strategic or competitive advantages for their firms.

Chapter 6 takes up the question of the role of unions and worker representation and reviews the efforts of the American labor movement to search for new ways to represent the diverse work force. Chapters 7 and 8 turn to the challenge of building a national employment and labor-management policy environment that encourages and supports the adoption of mutual gains strategies by private parties to employment relationships. Chapter 7 focuses on the employment, training, and broad human resource policies and institutions relevant to this task. Chapter 8 follows up with an analysis of the new labor-management policies and government role that we believe are necessary to support a mutual gains strategy. Finally, we end in Chapter 9 where our discussion started—with practical implications for the academic and professional communities that want to move from rhetoric to reality in making human resources a source of sustained competitive advantage for the American economy, work force, and society.

chapter two

HUMAN RESOURCES, NATIONAL COMPETITIVENESS, AND EMPLOYEE WELFARE

Ultimately, we judge the performance of a nation's economy and human resource policies and practices by the nation's ability to achieve two objectives simultaneously: to be competitive in international markets and to improve the working conditions and standards of living of its citizens. In this chapter we explore how the American economy and human resource system have performed against these goals in recent decades and how well we are positioning ourselves for the coming decade.

After disastrous competitiveness and a drop in living standards in the 1970s and early 1980s, some American industries have regained international market share. Productivity in manufacturing industries has improved in recent years, but Americans continue to experience stagnating real wages, increased inequality in the distribution of income, diminished job security, and an inadequate supply of good new jobs. The first part of this chapter briefly reviews these economic and social indicators.

In the second part of the chapter, when we look to the future, our concerns run even deeper. First we show that our education and training systems are not providing new entrants and current employees with the skills that will be required by employers seeking to transform their employment systems. Second, we show the tensions in American corporations: those responsible for human resource strategy and policies are being asked to increase productivity and enhance their firms' competitiveness while cutting staff, holding down wages and benefits, and reducing opportunities for promotion and long-term careers.

The Performance of the U.S. Economy, 1970–1990

The fact that the long-term rate of productivity growth fell in the 1970s and 1980s compared with the twenty-five years following World War II is one sign of economic trouble for America. According to Bureau of Labor Statistics (BLS) data shown in Figure 2-1, productivity grew by 2.5 percent between 1948 and 1973, but less than 1 percent in the subsequent period. Moreover, the rate of growth in productivity over the past two decades did not match that of some of our key international competitors. For example, productivity in Germany grew 3 percent and in Japan increased 3.2 percent between the early 1970s and 1980s.[1]

So while the United States remains the world's most productive economy, the gap has closed somewhat. Some of this narrowing is to be expected since other economies have shortened their learning curves and, over time, approached the leader's productivity level. Yet some macro economists worry that if the trends of the past two decades continue, U.S. productivity will be surpassed in the early twenty-first century by perhaps as many as nine other countries.[2] To avoid this,

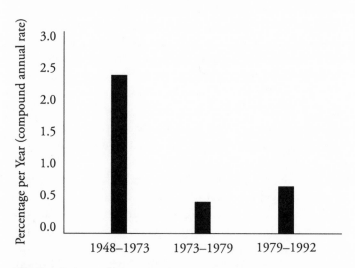

Figure 2-1

Labor Productivity Growth in U.S. Nonfarm Business for Selected Periods, 1948–1992

Note: Labor productivity is equal to output per hour at work.

Source: Bureau of Labor Statistics, report prepared for the Commission on the Future of Worker Management Relations, June 17, 1993.

William Baumol and colleagues estimate that we must raise our annual rate of productivity growth by almost 1 percent (0.8 percent is their precise estimate) to ensure that this country's long-term standard of living rises at the same rate as it has for the past hundred years. Others have shown that productivity growth produced a doubling of living standards in this country between 1950 and 1970. But if productivity grows at a rate of only 1 percent a year, as it has for the past decade, it will take seventy years to double American living standards.

Despite these disturbing trends, productivity growth in the manufacturing sector has improved considerably since the mid-1980s. While averaging approximately 1 percent growth from 1973 to 1979, manufacturing productivity grew 3.1 percent between 1979 and 1990.[3] Recent figures show further improvement, with 4.6 percent growth in 1992.[4]

If manufacturing productivity improved in recent years, the performance of the nonmanufacturing sector must have been abysmal to account for the overall stagnation of American productivity. The statistics confirm this. Table 2-1 shows that productivity actually declined in several key service industries between 1960 and 1987, growing on average less than 1 percent overall.

We should be careful not to make too much of these statistics since it is difficult to measure service sector output accurately. Productivity calculations are even less reliable because the only plausible output measure is price. And in industries such as banking, available measures

Table 2-1
Productivity Growth in Selected Service Industries, 1960–1987

Annual Service Productivity Growth	*1960s*	*1970s*	*1980s (1979–1987)*
Transportation	3.9	2.9	0.3
Communications	4.1	6.5	2.1
Utilities	4.7	0.5	−1.8
Wholesale Trade	3.6	1.5	2.4
Retain	3.1	1.6	1.3
Finance, Insurance, and Real Estate	2.2	0.7	−0.7
Other Services	3.3	0.9	−0.4

Source: Lester Thurow, *Toward a High-Wage, High-Productivity Service Sector* (Washington, D.C.: Economic Policy Institute, 1989), p. 5.

fail to capture such quality improvements as the spread of automatic teller machines. Moreover, the boundaries between the manufacturing and service sectors are becoming increasingly blurred, making sector-specific productivity numbers less reliable. This happens, for example, when work that was done by employees of a manufacturing firm is contracted out. So we are forced to fall back on the aggregate estimates as the more accurate indicator of the efficiency of the overall economy.

Other Measures of International Competitiveness

While aggregate productivity is the best summary measure of the performance of an economy, it does not tell the whole story. We need to know whether American firms are gaining or losing market share in ways that translate into improved working and living conditions for American workers. For example, are we maintaining our share of exports and manufacturing output?

In Figure 2-2 we see that most of the dip in both measures in the 1970s was recaptured in the 1980s. By neither measure is America losing its markets or its share of manufacturing output. While these numbers are encouraging, we need to remember that there are good ways and bad ways to maintain international competitiveness. The good way is by improving productivity and quality. The bad way is by making the product cheaper by cutting wages or by devaluing a country's currency. In the 1980s the United States followed all three strategies. The manufacturing data in Table 2-2 show the experience of the United States and its major Organization for Economic Cooperation and Development (OECD) competitors with respect to physical productivity, wage growth, and unit labor costs in both national currency and U.S. dollars. The latter figure reflects the impact of exchange rates.

Just as for exports and manufacturing output, numbers show that from the first oil shock in 1973 to the end of the 1970s productivity growth was abysmal for the United States, but a substantial rebound occurred in the 1980s.

But productivity gains are only a part of export success. The price of the product and hence wage costs are also important. Here again the turnaround is striking. In the 1970s the rate of increase of U.S. wage payments was in the middle range of that of our competitors, but in the 1980s only Japan had a slower rate of wage growth. Indeed,

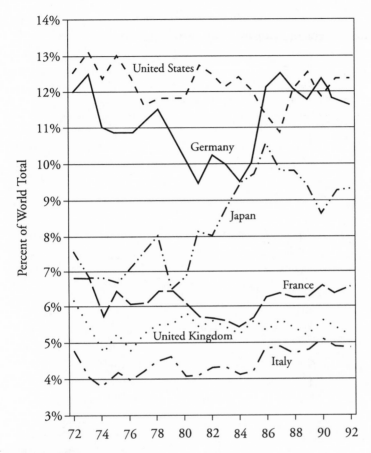

Figure 2-2
World Export Shares
Source: Christopher Heye, "Five Years After: A Preliminary Assessment of U.S. Industrial Performance Since Made in America," paper presented at the World Economic Forum Industry Summit Conference, Cambridge, Mass., September 1993.

despite the good productivity performance of the U.S. manufacturing sector, the average real wages of production workers in manufacturing declined. This fact illustrates an important point: productivity improvement is a necessary but far from sufficient condition for improving the welfare of employees in any sector or firm.

The impact of productivity gains and wage restraint shows up in unit labor costs. Again, only Japan exceeded our performance in the 1980s. Finally, when exchange rates are factored in, the rate of increase in U.S. unit labor-cost increases were the lowest. Therefore, it is not

Table 2-2
Manufacturing Statistics (percentage changes)

	Output per Hour	Hourly Compensation	Unit Labor Costs National Currency	Unit Labor Costs U.S. Currency
United States				
1960–1973	3.3	5.1	1.8	1.8
1973–1979	1.4	9.7	8.2	8.2
1979–1990	3.1	5.3	2.1	2.1
Canada				
1960–1973	4.5	6.2	1.6	1.3
1973–1979	2.1	12.0	9.8	6.9
1979–1990	1.5	6.9	5.4	5.4
Japan				
1960–1973	10.2	15.1	4.4	6.7
1973–1979	5.0	12.8	7.4	11.3
1979–1990	4.1	4.4	.3	4.1
France				
1960–1973	6.4	10.0	3.4	4.2
1973–1979	4.6	16.3	11.2	12.0
1979–1990	3.2	8.6	5.2	2.9
Germany				
1960–1973	5.6	10.3	4.4	8.1
1973–1979	4.2	9.3	5.0	11.6
1979–1990	2.1	5.5	3.3	4.5
United Kingdom				
1960–1973	4.2	9.2	4.8	3.7
1973–1979	1.2	19.4	18.0	15.2
1979–1990	4.4	9.8	5.1	3.5

Source: Arthur Neef and Christopher Kask, "Manufacturing Productivity and Labor Costs in 14 Economies," *Monthly Labor Review,* December 1991, 29–30.

surprising that U.S. export performance has improved since the latter half of the 1980s.

Those who paint an entirely negative picture of the performance of the American economy are being misleading. Signs of improvements in international competitiveness are visible, particularly in the manufacturing sector. While part of this improvement appears to be due to gains in productivity that may have long-term potential for raising living standards, some is due to the cheapening of American products abroad because of a lowering of the value of the dollar and a lowering of American wages. Whether these adjustments in the relative price of American goods and services are a foundation for long-term growth in market share remains to be seen.

None of these indicators provide a complete picture of the performance of the economy or its contribution to our standard of living. For this we need to look at trends in wages, benefits, employment security, and working conditions and at whether the firms are preparing the economy and the work force to be competitive in the future.

Worker Welfare

The most basic measure of the well-being of the labor force is wages. Earlier we hinted that some of the gain in American international competitiveness was bought at the expense of lower wages. A nation can always manage to sell its goods in the international market if the price is low enough. This low-wage strategy has been the only option for the least developed countries in the world. Is the United States following this path?

Table 2-3 contains the basic data on wage developments in the United States in the past decade. The table, using real dollars and

Table 2-3
Percentage Change in Real Wages and Salaries by Education Level

Education Level	1979–1989	1989–1991	1979–1991
High School Dropout	−17.3	−3.9	−20.5
High School Graduate	−9.8	−2.2	−11.8
Some College	−5.9	−1.2	−6.9
College Degree	2.0	−1.6	.3
More Than College Degree	7.6	.2	7.8
All	−2.7	−.9	−3.6

Source: Larry Mishel and Jared Bernstein, "Declining Wages for High School and College Graduates: Pay and Benefits Trends by Education, Gender, Occupation, and State, 1979–1991" (Washington, D.C.: Economic Policy Institute, May 1992), p. 8.

thereby eliminating the effects of inflation, shows the rate of increase or decrease in earnings for different educational groups.

Examination of the experience of all workers (bottom row), makes it apparent that the 1980s witnessed a decline in real earnings. Clearly the productivity gains discussed above did not translate into earnings gains.[5]

Even though real wage *levels* have fallen for the work force as a whole, there also has been a shift in the relative wages paid to different groups. In particular, the better educated have gained in relation to the less well educated. This twist in the wage structure has been the subject of a number of careful studies,[6] and various explanations for it have been offered. These include changing demographics, the decline of unions, the worsening of the quality of high school education, the loss of traditional manufacturing jobs, and shifts in the demand for skilled (educated) labor.

In the end, most analysts agree that an increased demand for skilled labor is the most important reason for the change in wage structure. Other factors may contribute but are of secondary importance. For example, the decline in high school quality cannot be the main cause because the same wage trends hold for older cohorts who graduated from high school many years ago. The loss of manufacturing employment is also not the entire reason because the same trends are apparent within manufacturing industries (for example, the wages of lesser skilled machine operators fell relative to those of more highly skilled maintenance workers and tool and die makers).

In short, for all groups below top executives and the most highly educated and paid professionals, wages either stagnated or went down. At the same time, there was a twist within the wage distribution. The wages of some groups decreased much more than those of other groups. So the paradox is that the economy which demands more skilled labor is not willing to pay more for it. Hence it is incorrect to associate a "low-wage" with a "low-skill" strategy, at least in the short run. In our view, the demand for skill partly reflects efforts to adopt new work systems for producing goods and services. However, the effort to get this skill without paying for it reflects the limited diffusion of these models and the downward pressure exerted on wage levels by the large number of employers that continue to compete only on the basis of cost.

Table 2-4 shows that other nations did not share the U.S. experience of declining wages. Each of the other large OECD nations experienced average earnings *gains* in manufacturing. In addition (not shown in the table), all European nations except Great Britain experienced much less of an increase in earnings inequality than America did.

Table 2-4
Index of Real Hourly Compensation in Manufacturing
(1982 = 100)

	United States	West Germany	Canada	Japan	France	Italy	United Kingdom
1980	98.0	99.9	97.9	96.0	92.3	96.9	97.1
1990	97.3	126.9	103.0	118.4	107.7	122.4	115.3

Source: Bureau of Labor Statistics, "International Comparison of Manufacturing Production and Unit Labor Cost Trends, 1990," August 20, 1991, Table 2, p. 26.

The labor-cheapening strategy of the 1980s was not limited to wages. Pension coverage, as David Bloom and Richard Freeman demonstrate, also fell sharply during this period.[7] Among all employees, the percentage of workers covered by pensions went from 63 percent in 1979 to 57 percent in 1988. All subgroups of workers, broken out by sex, age, and education, experienced declines, but the reduction was sharpest for less-well-educated males. For example, among men age 25 to 34 with less than 12 years of schooling, the percentage covered fell from 49 percent to 23 percent. Bloom and Freeman show that the most important factors contributing to this decline are falling wages and lower rates of unionization.

Health and safety are other important, albeit often overlooked, measures of employee welfare. Here too the recent U.S. record is unsatisfactory, and we seem to have performed worse than our major trading competitors. Figure 2-3 provides BLS data on injury and illness incidence in the U.S. private sector between 1972 and 1991. As these raw data show, total injury rates and nonlost day rates generally declined during the 1970s but remained stable or rose in the 1980s. In a more detailed study, which controlled for the business cycle, Robert Smith shows that the percentage of manufacturing workers experiencing lost workdays because of injuries was 5.3 in 1988–1990, up from 4.0 in 1972.[8] These data show the sharpest upward trend in the post-1981 period. This is true despite the implementation of the Occupational Safety and Health Act in 1970, which led to more than a million safety and health inspections.

American work injury rates are considerably higher than those of Germany and Japan although differing definitions make comparison difficult. This problem is eased if we examine rates of change, i.e., percentage reductions in injuries. Both Germany and Japan reduced

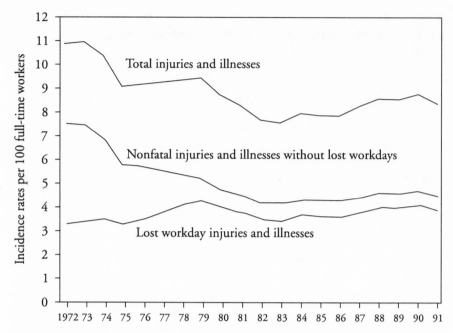

Figure 2-3

Occupational Injury and Illness Incidence Rates, Private Industry, 1972–1991

Source: Bureau of Labor Statistics, U.S. Department of Labor, *Annual Survey of Occupational Injuries and Illnesses, June 1993.*

work injury rates in the 1980s at a pace that considerably exceeded the U.S. rate.[9]

Finally, employment security has clearly worsened in recent years. The recession of the past few years has given way to a weak recovery, but unemployment remains very high. Furthermore, there are indications that the nature of unemployment has changed, a topic addressed by Harvard labor economist James L. Medoff in testimony prepared for the Joint Economic Committee. First, the ratio of job vacancies to job searchers has declined in recent years. In 1977, when the unemployment rate was 7.1 percent, the help wanted index was 118. In January 1991, when the unemployment rate was also 7.1 percent, the help wanted index was only 85.[10] This means that the average unemployed person looking for work has fewer opportunities for success than in the past.

Medoff also shows that the quality of new jobs found by searchers has declined: a much smaller fraction of firms offers pensions and health care coverage. Finally, the composition of unemployment has changed, with white-collar workers at much greater risk than in the past. In the two recessions of the early 1980s, white-collar unemployment accounted for between 13 percent and 22 percent of all new joblessness. By contrast, between 1990 and 1992 the comparable figure was 38 percent.

The degree of insecurity for employees cannot be overstated. Even those who do not lose their jobs have much to fear. Widely reported layoffs in such large and previously secure employers as Sears and IBM, as well as massive restructuring in manufacturing firms such as General Motors (GM) and Eastman Kodak, contribute to a pervasive sense of insecurity. The fact that a very large fraction of new jobs is temporary or contingent adds to the insecurity. This insecurity has consequences not only for the individuals, but also for the firms themselves. It is very difficult to adopt work reform in an environment of fear.

Are We Building a Secure Foundation for the Future?

What about the future, especially the future labor force? Will the negative trends in worker welfare correct themselves with the next generation of workers? If human capital is a strategic asset, we must start our discussion with an assessment of the education and training of the work force in response to the demands for skilled workers. We need to examine the future demand for skill and whether our public education, training systems, and private firms will generate enough skilled workers to match demand. And since the quality of the labor force is a relative phenomenon, we need to compare the American education and training systems to those of other nations.

The Demand for Skill

Is there a shortage of skilled workers in America? Many national commissions have asserted there is, yet we also read that low-skill jobs will be among the fastest growing occupations of the next decade. The widening dispersion of wages, described above, clearly suggests a growing demand for skill. Where does the truth lie?

To assess the demand for high skills we need to ask two questions. First, what is the expected demand if current human resource systems continue unchanged? Second, what would be the demand for skill if more firms adopted the mutual gains model discussed throughout this book?

29

Bureau of Labor Statistics occupational projections provide the most conventional approach to addressing the first question. These projections, based on data from the BLS *Dictionary of Occupational Titles* (DOT), show modest upskilling over time and a continuation of this modest upward trend to the year 2000.

The problem with these estimates, and others like them, is that they assume the content of each job is stable, and they provide data only about the mix of jobs in the economy. Such measures miss, for example, the fact that one strategy for upskilling machine operator jobs would be to include computer programming skills as numerically controlled machines are introduced.[11] They also miss employers' efforts to move to work teams and to introduce responsibility for quality control into production workers' jobs. Thus, the difference between the projections offered by the DOT and the surge of concern of employers about skills may be explained by the fact that some employers see the content of these jobs changing in ways not captured by conventional BLS measures.

Our case studies support the view that adoption of transformed human resource management and production systems requires significant increases in training and skills. Consider, for example, the investments in training made in new Japanese auto plants in the United States. Studies of the Mazda plant in Michigan and the Toyota plant in Kentucky suggest that training costs account for as much as 10 to 20 percent of the total capital required to bring these facilities on line.

Data from the Saturn Corporation of General Motors (GM) provide another example. This organization is perhaps the most extreme example of a transformed human resource system available in the United States today. It should not be surprising, therefore, that training is an integral part of the organization. Training policy was outlined in the initial memorandum of agreement between the United Auto Workers (UAW) and GM, and training targets are part of the company's strategic plan. Saturn's target is for each employee to spend 5 percent of his or her working hours in training. In the start-up stage, operating technicians received approximately 300 hours of training, while skilled trade technicians received between 450 and 700 hours. In 1992 Saturn and the UAW reinforced the importance of ongoing training by making a portion of each person's salary contingent on receiving a minimum of 92 hours' (approximately 5 percent of annual working hours) training per year.

Case study data from high-technology industries further support the hypothesis that moving to mutual gains human resource and production systems requires additional investments in training. In one plant of a computer company we studied, the decision to move from a conventional individual job-classification form of work organization to a team-based system required a major investment in cross-training. The plant's training budget more than doubled. As a result, nearly two-thirds of the work force was cross-trained within their teams. Furthermore, their skills were reinforced and utilized through job rotation within the teams. A substantial portion of the training focused on developing statistical process control and problem solving. Moreover, the highest-performing teams (measured against quality, cycle time, yield, delivery, and customer satisfaction measures) were those with the highest degree of cross-training, job rotation, and use of statistical process control techniques.[12]

A final source of evidence on the demand for skill comes from a survey we conducted of American business establishments. This national establishment survey, described in more detail in Chapter 4, is a representative national sample of all private sector establishments with fifty or more employees. Among the topics covered was the demand for skills among what we termed "core" employees, i.e., each establishment's largest and most important group of nonsupervisory employees. In some cases these core employees were blue-collar production workers, in others white-collar professionals.

Table 2-5 describes the respondents' assessment of the skill distribution of the core jobs and their description of how the skill content of the jobs is changing. The table includes data for the entire sample and distinguishes between blue-collar employees and professional/white-collar employees (together, professional/white-collar and blue-collar workers account for 77.1 percent of the observations).

It comes as no surprise that professional/white-collar jobs are considered higher skilled on average than blue-collar ones. Of greater note is the substantial fraction of blue-collar core jobs at the lower end of the skill spectrum. It is, however, not entirely clear how to interpret these data as they are not anchored in a common metric (in the sense that the DOT purports to measure months needed to learn a job or years of education a job requires). The information on skill change is less subject to this criticism.

For professional/white-collar employees the trend is clearly toward more complex work. For blue-collar employees the trend is also upward (in the sense that a larger fraction of enterprises indicate increase in complexity rather than decrease), but the upskilling is clearly less pronounced and more uneven. There is also a relationship between

Table 2-5
Skill Level and Skill Trends

	All	Blue-Collar	Professional/Technical
Skill Level			
Not skilled	1.8%	0.2%	0.0%
Slightly skilled	19.5	23.7	0.0
Moderately skilled	43.2	57.2	14.5
Very skilled	28.1	18.7	63.9
Extremely skilled	7.2	.05	21.5
Change in Skill			
No change	38.1%	37.4%	29.1%
Less complex	3.5	11.4	0.0
More complex	39.9	36.0	51.1
Same level, different skill	17.7	15.1	19.7

Note: The respondents were asked to reply to the question "Which best characterizes the skill level of core employees?" using a five-point scale ranging from not skilled to extremely skilled. They were also asked, "Have the skills involved in doing the core job changed in the past few years?" If the answer was yes, they were asked how. The responses were "more complex," "less complex," or "equally complex, different skills." They were also asked an open-ended question, "Would you briefly describe how the skills are different now?" This response was coded as described in the text.

Source: National Establishment Survey. Paul Osterman, "Skill, Training, and Work Organization in American Firms," *Industrial Relations,* forthcoming.

the level of skill and the direction of change. For example, among blue-collar workers whose job was very or extremely skilled, 56.1 percent were reported to experience an increase in complexity, whereas among the not skilled, slightly skilled, and moderately skilled, the figure was 33.0 percent. These two patterns suggest that there is a growing inequality in the skill distribution.

Table 2-6 provides information on the nature of the changes in job content in the jobs that became more complex.

For both blue- and white-collar jobs the shifts involved changes in job content more than changes in the qualities required for the job. Beyond this, however, there is a significant difference for the two occupational groups. While for both group shifts in technology and heightened use of computers are important, they are relatively less so for blue-collar workers. By contrast, more general shifts involving behavioral changes are more important for blue-collar employees. This

Table 2-6
Nature of Skill Change When Jobs Become More Complex

	Professional/Technical	*Blue-Collar*
Personality/responsibility	8.3%	14.4%
Cognitive	3.7	9.2
Job characteristics	59.1	55.9
Computer usage	28.8	20.3

Source: National Establishment Survey. Paul Osterman, "Skill, Training, and Work Organization in American Firms," *Industrial Relations,* forthcoming.

lends some support to the view that innovations such as team work and quality programs are transforming the nature of blue-collar work.

The survey collected information on whether the establishments had such innovative work practices as self-managed work teams, quality circles, job rotation, and total quality management. Respondents were also asked what percentage of core employees were involved in each of these practices (the distribution and determinants of these practices are examined in detail in Chapter 4). As the foregoing arguments suggest, there is a strong relationship between adoption of these practices and training and skill. When two of these practices were present and 50 percent or more of core employees were involved, the core job was described as highly skilled 57 percent of the time and an average of 42 percent of the core employees received formal off-the-job training. By contrast, in the establishments that did not meet this level of use of innovative work practices, the core job was highly skilled 42 percent of the time and only 23 percent of core employees on average were given formal training.[13] Clearly, a strong relationship exists between adoption of new work systems and skill development.

The Supply of Skill

In general, an American youth receives more years of education than youth in other countries. In 1986, 59.6 percent of 16- to 24-year-olds in this country attended post–high school educational institutions compared to 28.9 percent in Japan, 30.1 percent in Germany, and 31.4 percent in Sweden.[14] Indeed, these figures are an understatement: if we ask what percentage of the American high school class of 1980 received some form of postsecondary education within four years of graduation, the figure is 61.7 percent. A substantial part of this postsecondary education was vocational, with 37.9 percent of the class of 1980 entering vocational-oriented education programs.[15]

Although American youths receive more education than their foreign cohorts, there is cause for concern with respect to quality. Data on achievement scores of U.S. students point out two sources of concern. First, there appears to be wider variation in achievement levels of U.S. youth than in other countries. Our high school drop-out rate is 25 percent nationally and rises to as high as 45 percent among blacks and Hispanics in poor inner-city neighborhoods in cities like Boston.[16] We are developing an educational underclass disproportionately composed of minorities but with considerable numbers of white urban poor. When these data are combined with Lisa Lynch's finding that educational level is positively correlated with the amount of on-the-job training youth receive,[17] the projected effects of these drop-out rates are clear cause for concern.

Second, achievement test scores for U.S. students indicate that they learn much less than foreign students. Results from the Second International Math Study and the Second International Science Study show that U.S. high school students scored well below those of other nations in which a similar fraction of youth took the math and science exams.[18] Indeed, John Bishop reports that the 18 percent of Canadian youth taking the physics test scored nearly as well as the 1 percent of American youth who took the test. Hence, we can no longer make the excuse that more Americans than foreigners take these tests and hence the dismal American results simply reflect compositional issues.

Data of this kind refer to the relatively small fraction of American youth who take advanced placement math and science courses in high school and doubtlessly continue to higher education. How well are we preparing the far larger number who enter the work force after high school?

American high school–based vocational education programs are problematic at best. The average American high school student takes 4.35 vocational credits in courses such as home economics or typing, and 16.5 percent of high school graduates take 8 or more credits.[19] The number of students enrolling in post–high school vocational schools has been declining since 1982. The typical finding of evaluation evidence on vocational education has been that it has little payoff, although there can be gains from specialized programs. In any case, no observer believes that American high school vocational education programs compare well to their German equivalents (described below).

34

The United States does have a unique asset in its 1,400 community colleges. Approximately 5 million people are enrolled in degree programs in community colleges, and another 4.5 million participate in nondegree programs. These colleges represent an opportunity for individual firms to tailor training and development programs to their specific needs. In addition, evidence shows that there is an economic payoff for those who graduate.[20] Although community colleges are an important resource, they are, unfortunately, not widely available in all states. In addition, completion rates are a cause for concern. Looking at the high school class of 1980 four years after graduation, 19.4 percent went to some form of two-year college, but only 7.8 percent had acquired an academic associate, vocational associate, or certificate degree.[21]

Finally, this country's formal apprenticeship system is very weak. In 1990 only 39,411 registered civilian apprentices graduated, a decline from the already low 54,111 in 1978.[22]

The need to improve the link between school and work is clear when we compare the U.S. system with those of our major competitors. German students follow a well-marked route of part-time schooling and apprenticeship, which culminates in examinations and placement into a first adult job. They gain high levels of skills in the apprenticeship placements. Their academic program is motivated by the work experience, and they are required to pass a national standardized examination in academic and occupational skills. In Japan noncollege-bound high school students are placed into their first job by their teachers and are expected to remain there.[23]

The American process appears chaotic compared to these models, and there are important questions about the quality of the skills American youth obtain. Because students don't learn job skills in school, they go through an extended period of labor-market adjustment when they leave. This includes casual work and nonwork associated with aging and maturation as well as the search for an adult job.[24] The consequences of this period of search and job-hopping can be negative: survey data show that little more than a third of all men and women in their early thirties fail to find a job that lasts for at least a year and another 16 percent had their jobs for only a year.[25]

Human Resource Development for Adults

How does America compare with Germany and Japan in training its incumbent adult work force? Virtually all observers note that Japanese employers provide considerably more training than their American counterparts. This is what we would expect, given that the dominant Japanese human resource system resembles the mutual gains model. For example, Japanese firms tend to provide longer initial training and orientation to new employees, allocate more time for formal training of experienced employees, and perhaps most important, make greater use of job rotation to broaden and deepen skills. The following observation is typical:

> Production workers [in Japan] are given responsibility for solving routine and non-routine problems. These non-routine problems flowing from changes in product and labor mix and production methods are far more common than outsiders commonly recognize. The American solution generally speaking has been to turn over the disposition of these non-routine problems to specialized experts: skilled maintenance workers and engineers . . . In effect, Japanese manufacturing firms have created a large cadre of lower-level technicians who make enormous contributions to fine tuning the production system . . . A lot of the firefighting and job redesign that so bedevils management and engineering personnel in American plants is done in Japanese plants by production workers . . . This includes having production workers working closely with product and process engineers to design new products and processes.[26]

The importance of training in the Japanese enterprise is paralleled by the status given to the human resource function. As Ronald Dore and David Cairncross note, "Personnel Departments . . . are seen as key departments, likely to be manned, not by a company's more sluggish and unimaginative elements, but by some of its brightest and most ambitious spirits, many of whom have a good chance of ending up as Board members."[27]

The contrast between Japanese and American training is not limited to blue-collar production workers. In their comparison of U.S. and Japanese engineers, D. E. Westney and K. Sakakibara note that "in the United States it is the individual engineer who bears primary responsibility; in Japan it is the company. The greater company responsibility and control begin with the more extensive entry level training and extend to mid-career training, assignment to projects, and job rotation."[28]

Firm-level survey data tell a similar story. Among large Japanese firms with more than a thousand employees, 99 percent have a training manager and even in small firms with twenty to ninety-nine employees, 69 percent have a training manager, well above comparable American figures.[29]

International Comparisons: The Case of the Auto Industry

The evidence we have presented thus far is based on national surveys of firms and of individuals. More light could be shed on the issues by examining training and broader human resource systems in a specific industry with a common product and market. The best data of this kind are found in the MIT study of the international motor vehicle industry.[30]

Survey data on productivity, quality, manufacturing practices, human resource policies, and the amount of training were collected from a sample of fifty-six auto assembly plants located in North America, Japan, Europe, Australia, South America, and several newly industrialized countries of Asia. We focus here specifically on the data in this work that isolate the amount of training provided in U.S. plants compared with plants in other countries.[31]

Table 2-7 compares the amount of training provided new hires and experienced workers in plants located in different regions. North American plants are separated between those owned by U.S. and those owned by Japanese firms. The data show that U.S.-owned plants provide significantly less training to both new hires and experienced workers than plants owned by Japanese and European firms.

More sophisticated analysis of these data, which control for differences in plant size, level of investment in advanced technologies (robotics and other forms of automation), and the complexity of the cars produced found that these differences remain significant. Only when controls were added for whether these plants had adopted the flexible production and human resource systems discussed throughout this book did some, but not all, of these international differences go away.[32] Thus, these industry-specific comparisons reinforce the macro comparisons: on average, U.S. firms may be lagging behind their international competitors in training investments needed to be competitive in the future. Part of the reason is that American firms also lag in implement-

Table 2-7
Regional Means for Training Hours for Production Workers in Auto Assembly Plants

	Jpn/Jpn	Jpn/NA	US/NA	US/Eur	Eur/Eur	NIC	Aust
Newly Hired Production Workers (hours in first six months)	364	225	42	43	178	260	40
Experienced Production Workers (hours per year for those with more than one year of experience)	76	52	31	34	52	46	15
n	8	4	14	4	10	11	6

Jpn/Jpn = Japanese-owned plants in Japan
Jpn/NA = Japanese-owned plants in North America
US/NA = U.S.-owned plants in North America
US/Eur = U.S.-owned plants in Europe
Eur/Eur = European-owned plants in Europe
NIC = Newly industrialized countries (Korea, Mexico, Taiwan, Brazil)
Aust = Australia

Source: John Paul MacDuffie and Thomas A. Kochan, "Do U.S. Firms Underinvest in Human Resources? Determinants of Training in the World Auto Industry," unpublished manuscript, MIT Sloan School of Management, September 1993.

ing changes in production and human resource systems necessary to promote sustained mutual gains.

Sustainability Problems from the Demand Side

Some of the productivity gains we documented earlier in this chapter came from eliminating waste and introducing state-of-the-art technology. Examples include improved backroom operations in banking and insurance as well as manufacturing firms such as Tenneco, which have introduced new efficiencies.[33] However, as much as we may applaud gains based on cost savings, they have clearly diminishing returns.

The second source of progress is different in character. Firms that have introduced new work systems—the kind of mutual gains systems we are advocating here—have experienced continuous improvement whose source is not static—reducing staff for a given level of output— but rather dynamic—continuous improvement and increasing output per employee. This characterization is valid for many of the companies—for example, Xerox, Saturn, Cummins, Corning, Motorola, which we cite throughout this book. In principle, gains of this kind do not suffer from diminishing returns. However, it may prove to be very difficult in the current environment to sustain employment systems that underwrite these gains.

To see why these systems may be difficult to sustain, it is important to understand that much of the gain inherent in new work systems comes from a sense of mutual commitment or reciprocity on the part of firms and employees. Paul Adler conducted a series of intensive interviews in the General Motors–Toyota New United Motors Manufacturing Inc. (NUMMI) plant in California, and his findings illustrate this point nicely.[34] This plant implemented the Toyota system of team work, just-in-time inventories, continuous improvement, and employee responsibility for quality along the line. These production changes alone do not necessarily buy commitment, as Mazda learned in Flat Rock, Michigan, or as GM and Suzuki learned in a similar joint effort to implement the Toyota production system in Canadian Automotive Manufacturing Inc. (CAMI), a Canadian plant. In contrast, NUMMI's new system was combined with shifts in management behavior and in the nature and quality of union-management relations. For example, one of Adler's interviewees says,

> NUMMI's managers are generally pretty good at considering suggestions when workers make them. They respect workers' ideas. NUMMI's managers always get back with: "It's a great idea" or "It's a good idea but . . ." This is what we like to see. At GM, you were lucky if they wrote the idea down; as soon as you left the room you knew the idea was headed for the garbage can.

NUMMI also explicitly offered strong job security pledges and respected worker power along the assembly line (the line could be stopped to correct quality problems). Consequently NUMMI is judged to have made tremendous gains on productivity and quality, gains that cannot easily be attributed to traditional systems of management and control.[35]

Adler gives numerous examples of workers making small suggestions that cumulate into substantial savings, such as color coding of circuit breakers or replacing chrome water fountains with metal, as well as behavior such as voluntarily picking up cigarette butts from the work area floor. Haruo Shimada and John Paul MacDuffie use the phrase borrowed from other Japanese scholars, "giving wisdom to the machine," to characterize employee contributions in transformed systems.[36] Adler's quotes demonstrate the explicit *reciprocal* nature of these actions: they are in response to management demonstrations of commitment to the labor force.

The danger facing firms that have adopted these systems, and those considering adoption, is that other trends in the labor market, especially the high level of layoffs and job insecurity, make reciprocity uncertain. In addition, companies are increasingly using contingent or temporary employees. For example, in our survey of firms, 44 percent of employers with 500 or more workers expect their use of temporary and contingent employees to increase in the next five years. Obviously it is difficult to implement or sustain high-commitment work systems with temporary employees.

This kind of confusion is reflected in the experiences of firms such as Boeing Aircraft and Eastman Kodak. Boeing included in its 1989 labor contract a number of provisions aimed at increasing employee involvement in decisions about work organization and technology and established a joint training fund to prepare workers for changing job requirements. But it took more than four years, a major downturn in business and large layoffs, and a change in union leadership before agreement was reached on how to use these funds. In this case the labor-management relationship did not change significantly, and the disagreement over the new training fund became another arena for the low-trust relationship between the parties to play itself out. This low-trust syndrome is not, however, limited to the union sector. Eastman Kodak, a well-known nonunion firm, has repeatedly swung back and forth between a strategy of building commitment and employee participation and widespread layoffs.

The absence of a credible, public labor-market policy exacerbates these problems. We recognize that it may not be possible for some American firms to maintain all the elements of mutual gains work systems. In recent years we have witnessed one company after an-other—IBM, Digital Equipment Corporation, Delta Air Lines—retreat from employment continuity and in so doing undermine the goodwill and commitment they had built up with their labor force.[37] In some industries the forces of market competition may simply require that firms have numerical flexibility with respect to their work force. Even in these cases, this need not undermine transformed work systems, provided that mechanisms are in place to find new jobs for displaced employees. With these mechanisms, layoffs would not necessarily undermine the commitment of the remaining employees. However, as is well known, the United States lacks such a policy.

Finally, to the extent that new work systems require higher levels of skill, the low level of training America provides its work force imposes additional costs on those firms seeking to adopt new systems.

In short, a number of aspects of the environment, taken together, lead us to be concerned about the sustainability of the rebound in productivity and international competitiveness of the late 1980s.

Tensions Facing Human Resource Professionals

Considering the difficulties facing firms with respect to the skill level of their labor force as well as the pressures caused by a turbulent and uncertain environment, we might expect internal contradictions and confusion as they seek to transform themselves. This is just what was found in a recent "Delphi survey" of the leading human resource management professionals in the country conducted by Lee Dyer and his colleagues.[38]

This survey of experts illustrates the problems that professionals in organizations have in acting on the knowledge that human resource investments and innovations in practices are critical to the future. The survey asked respondents to project changes in the organizational and human resource practices that will occur between now and the year 2000. The results show a rather conflicted profession. There was agreement on the need for dramatic improvements in productivity by the year 2000—projected by these professionals to be on the order of 7 percent per year! How would firms produce such dramatic improvements? These professionals accepted the need to transform practices in ways discussed in this book: significant increases in expenditures for work force training and development, greater use of teamwork and flexible work systems, more employee participation at the workplace, and more flexible compensation systems such as profit and gains sharing.

But there was a contradiction. Although these professionals accepted the need to innovate in these ways, they reported a corresponding need to control compensation costs, downsize the organization, reduce the layers of management and supervision, and hire more temporary and contract workers, thereby lowering the average tenure of the work force. They also saw fewer opportunities for career progression within the firm and little increase in union influence or worker participation in critical decisions.

These latter tendencies are exactly the forces that hold back investments in innovations and lower trust in organizations. Thus, from these data we conclude that the need to innovate faces serious countervailing pressures and obstacles. Unless advocates of human resource innovations overcome the pressures on organizational decision makers to behave in ways that discourage investments and innovations in human resources, the sustained improvements in performance and standards of living these innovations promise are not likely to be realized.

If we combine recognition of these dual pressures with the fact that human resource issues traditionally take a back seat to financial concerns in American corporations, the reasons to worry about the eventual outcome are obvious. This is why we argue that changes will be needed in American corporations, institutions, and public policies to elevate the influence of human resource considerations and employee interests if we are to realize the mutual gains of improved competitiveness at high standards of living.

Summary and Conclusions

This chapter shows that macro concerns over competitiveness and social welfare can be successfully addressed only if we improve the micro-level performance of our human resource systems. It also shows that we must be careful to look beyond the simple macroeconomic indicators for two reasons. First, the rise in manufacturing productivity in recent years may lull us into a complacent view that the economy has righted itself and, if it is left alone, all will be well. Only by looking more carefully at the full range of productivity, quality, employment, education and skill development trends, and social welfare indicators do we see a deeper problem. Second, the simple view that it was just a conservative Republican administration that kept workers' wages and living conditions down and that we just need to recreate the institutional arrangements of the 1960s and 1970s is equally incorrect. The 1970s were as bad, if not worse, as now because of sluggish productivity, declining international competitiveness, and high rates of inflation. Therefore, we need to find a new solution—one that creates wealth and distributes it in a way that is fair to current stakeholders and future generations. This is the macroeconomic and social welfare argument for a mutual gains strategy. In the remaining chapters we turn to an examination of what is required to implement a mutual gains strategy at the micro level of the economy.

chapter three

THE MUTUAL GAINS ENTERPRISE

What kind of enterprise can help restore the American economy? There is remarkable consensus among a wide range of scholars, management writers, consultants, labor leaders, and human resource professionals regarding the fundamental principles needed to achieve competitiveness in individual enterprises.

One reason for this consensus is that these principles are not derived only from academic theory or from the mistaken glorification of a single organization's economic success. The consensus is the product of both theoretical and empirical research and more than a decade of trial and error and comparison of traditional and transformed human resource and organizational practices. What sets this consensus apart is that no single practice is seen as the silver bullet or simple solution. Rather, it is the combined and mutually reinforcing effects of *a broad-based and deep commitment to these principles followed by effective implementation* that add up to a new system of employment relations. We review these principles in this chapter by drawing on the experiences of a variety of companies that have led the way in this experimental phase and whose valuable experience sharpened our understanding. We demonstrate that the foundations for this new system have already been laid in practice.

Generic Principles of Mutual Gains Enterprises

Many terms have been used to describe firms that treat human resources as a source of competitive advantage and do so in a manner that preserves high standards of living: "high commitment,"[1] "excellent,"[2] "best practice,"[3] "high performance,"[4] "salaried,"[5] or "transformed."[6] We use the term "mutual gains"[7] because it conveys a key message: achieving and sustaining competitive advantage from human resources require the strong support of multiple stakeholders in an organization. Employees must commit their energies to meeting the economic objectives of the enterprise. In return, owners (shareholders) must share the economic returns with employees and invest those returns in ways that promote the long-run economic security of the work force. And everyone involved in decision making must behave in ways that build and maintain the trust and support of the work force.

Exhibit 3-1 summarizes the generic principles that characterize the mutual gains approach. It is important to realize that these are broad principles applied differently in different settings. They do not translate into a universal set of "best practices," but rather stand as generic requirements that can be met in ways that conform to particular cultural or organizational realities.

Exhibit 3-1 organizes the principles according to the three-tiered model developed in some of our research.[8] We distinguish among the workplace, personnel policy making, and the strategic levels of enterprise activity. The central argument is that policies at these different levels must reinforce one another to produce sustained support

Exhibit 3-1
Principles Guiding the Mutual Gains Enterprise

Strategic Level
   Supportive business strategies
   Top management commitment
   Effective voice for human resources in strategy making and governance

Functional (Human Resource Policy) Level
   Staffing based on employment stabilization
   Investment in training and development
   Contingent compensation that reinforces cooperation, participation, and
      contribution

Workplace Level
   High standards of employee selection
   Broad task design and teamwork
   Employee involvement in problem solving
   Climate of cooperation and trust

---

for a mutual gains enterprise and for the system to achieve the benefits necessary to be competitive at high standards of living.

Workplace Policies

We start at the bottom of the model with workplace policies because this is where most organizations began experimenting with new employment practices. This should not be surprising because introducing change at this level doesn't threaten the existing power structure of top management or, in unionized settings, of the collective bargaining process and contract.

By the workplace level we mean the day-to-day interactions of employees with their co-workers, supervisors, and jobs. Here we see several principles as critical. Clearly, a mutual gains workplace system starts with high recruitment standards. Potential employees must be selected not only for their education, skills, and training, but also for their ability and willingness to engage in further training and development and to work effectively with others in group settings. Thus both objective indicators of skill and subjective evidence of new recruits' attitudes are important. In fact, Peter Cappelli's review of surveys of what employers are looking for suggests that among blue-collar workers these subjective attitudes are as strong as or, in some cases, even more important than specific technical skills.[9]

Chapter 2 showed that employers who adopt workplace innovations are more likely to offer highly skilled work and provide more training than other firms do. In addition, we also observed that there is strong corroborating evidence of the importance employers attach to school completion and development of good cognitive skills in school. For example, in the past decade the gap between the earnings of college graduates relative to high school graduates grew substantially, as did the gap between high school graduates and high school dropouts.[10] Recent data analyzed by Frank Levy and Richard Murnane showed that the earnings gain that young people received from doing well on simple math tests increased substantially during the 1980s. This is additional evidence that returns for skill have grown.[11]

The implications are clear. Future labor force entrants must have these skills to compete effectively in the labor market. Little wonder that employers have shown renewed interest in the performance of our public education system, and there is a growing recognition that new and better school-to-work transition institutions are needed to prepare people for these jobs. Michael Useem found, for example, among firms surveyed by the Conference Board in 1991, that only 50 percent of the applicants with high school degrees were judged qualified for the entry-level jobs these firms had to offer. Moreover, firms that were adopting the mutual gains model reported more difficulty finding qualified applicants than did firms that relied on traditional work practices.[12] These findings again reinforce those reported from our survey data on training introduced in Chapter 2: mutual gains firms will require of future recruits a higher level of technical, analytical, and behavioral skills and attitudes toward work. If we fail to supply new entrants with the characteristics needed for mutual gains systems to function effectively, we will make this approach too expensive to adopt in this country and these jobs will migrate to countries that do provide entry-level talent.

The second essential principle for a mutual gains workplace system is that the education and skills of employees be fully utilized on the job. The job design principles that continue to dominate in too much of American industry were developed around the turn of the century for an uneducated immigrant labor force undisciplined in the ways of mass production. It was Frederick Taylor whose principles of industrial engineering and supervision separated the conception of how to do a job from the execution of specific tasks. While these principles may have fitted the requirements of that era, they are completely out of date today. A mutual gains enterprise requires job and career structures that eschew narrow, Tayloristic job assignments in favor of a flexible work organization that allows for the free-flowing movement of employees across tasks and functional boundaries.

These new conceptions of how to design jobs grew out of the 1950s and 1960s behavioral science models of job enlargement, job rotation, and sociotechnical design principles.[13] Not surprisingly, given their substantial departures from existing arrangements, these approaches were most often adopted in greenfield facilities that were opened in the 1960s and 1970s.[14] Early research on these new approaches to job design showed that the results were mixed. Quantitative studies of small-scale experiments in existing facilities demonstrated that while job satisfaction increased for a majority of, but not all, employees, there was little consistent evidence that productivity increased. Yet case studies in new plants reported more positive performance results. What accounts for this difference? The explanation most often cited, and one that research on which we report later supports, is that job designs in new plants were implemented by a totally new system rather than by incremental changes that left the rest of the traditional employment practices and policies intact.

A third principle at the workplace level deals with opportunities for employees and their representatives to engage in problem solving and decision making in matters that involve their jobs and their work environment—what Edward Lawler referred to as job involvement, and what more recently has been referred to as employee "empowerment."[15]

There is a long and checkered history of employee involvement efforts in the United States, dating back to the early experiments with job enlargement and rotation in the 1960s and through the quality of work life and quality circle fads of the late 1970s and early 1980s to the more recent popularity of total quality management (TQM) programs. Each cycle of innovation brings new labels and new approaches to employee involvement, but over time none have survived, even though some have been quite widely adopted. For example, a 1985 survey showed that more than 50 percent of large firms and one-third of all employees in a nationally representative survey had some experience with employee involvement at their workplace. A 1990 survey suggested that the number of firms with some experience had increased to 70 percent; however, within these firms, on average, less than a third of the work force actually participated in involvement programs.[16] Chapter 4 presents the results of our own survey on the spread and adoption of these practices, in which we found considerable use of these innovations.

One reason that various participation programs have faltered is that they place too much emphasis on the social or democratic functions of participation and not enough on building the technical knowledge needed for job-related problem solving and decision making. Consider the differences between the notion of an autonomous work group and the kind of problem solving and participation that occurs at NUMMI under the Toyota production system. NUMMI uses the concept of standardized work, or what Paul Adler calls humanized Taylorism.[17] That is, each job is studied in minute detail, the way to perform individual tasks is recorded, and each job is defined relatively narrowly. The difference is that individual workers move among the different jobs frequently and they, rather than industrial engineers, provide the ideas for continuous improvement and modification of the standardized procedures for performing the work. In that fashion, they acquire the technical knowledge necessary to do their jobs, and they are expected to use that knowledge to improve the designs of those jobs. But they do not have the autonomy to change work procedures unilaterally, because any individual change may affect the way other jobs are performed. However, empowerment should not be confused with pure autonomy or democracy.

Indeed, in our own fieldwork at the Saturn Corporation we saw the importance of this consideration. While from the beginning Saturn has had in place considerable joint labor-management structures for consultation and governance, its shop-floor employees and engineers lacked good processes for working together to solve technical problems bearing directly on manufacturing costs and productivity. Recognizing this, a new, focused technical problem-solving process was instituted to channel ideas for continuous improvement in manufacturing from the shop-floor workers to the product engineers who can authorize design changes. But in its effort to introduce new social systems, Saturn's initial design may inadvertently have given too little consideration to technical issues.

As suggested, the employee participation movement has gained new momentum in recent years as interest in TQM practices has spread throughout American industry. A major impetus for this interest in TQM is the phenomenal visibility achieved by the U.S. Department of Commerce Baldrige Award program. Instituted in 1988 and named after former Secretary of Commerce Malcolm Baldrige, this award is given to companies that demonstrate exemplary practices for meeting customer quality and satisfaction criteria. By 1992, seventeen awards had been issued—for different size businesses and sectors—to companies ranging from Xerox, Motorola, IBM, AT&T, Federal Express, the Ritz-Carlton, and Cadillac Motor Division of GM to such smaller and lesser-known names as Zytec, Solectron, Granite Rock, and Wallace Marlow Industries. More than 500 firms completed the detailed applications, and more than 240,000 firms requested information about the award criteria!

Although not all approaches to TQM give a major role to employee participation, we present evidence in the next chapter that TQM practices are stronger and more likely to be sustained over time in settings where they incorporate principles of teamwork and employee involvement. It is ironic, therefore, that the Baldrige Award gives so little weight—less than 5 percent of the total number of points considered in judging applicants—to this aspect of workplace innovation. Indeed, there is an active debate under way among representatives of the departments of Commerce and Labor about giving more weight to employee participation and other human resource and labor-management innovations. We are likely to see modifications of the weighting scheme in the future and possibly new award programs designed to promote more widespread diffusion of employee participation and empowerment.

The fourth and final workplace principle relates to the quality of relationships between employees, their representatives, and managers. A high-conflict/low-trust relationship[18] is incompatible with the task of building and maintaining the psychological and social climate needed to produce and sustain mutual gains. This does not mean that all conflicts between employees and employers wither away. Indeed, we assume that conflicting interests are a natural part of the employment relationship. But such conflicts cannot be so all encompassing that they push out the potential for effective problem solving and negotiations. It is not conflict per se that matters, it is how effectively and efficiently the parties resolve conflicts which naturally occur that really matters.

Xerox provides a case in point. At a recent meeting a former Xerox manager, now employed at another corporation, described the difference in the cultures of the two firms.

> Xerox has always been known for its confrontational culture. Conflict was aired and people challenged each other at meetings. It was expected. At [this executive's current company] everyone just smiles at each other and avoids open confrontation. The result is nobody really trusts that what somebody says reflects their real views or feelings and we never get to the heart of problems.

Or consider our experience at Saturn, where decision making is not conflict-free. Because Saturn institutionalizes employee voice in decision making across a wide array of issues, conflicts that in most organizations lie suppressed below the surface can be and are more openly expressed. The reason is that the union representatives have sufficient independence to challenge the views of higher-level managers while their management-level counterparts are more reticent to do so. One example was observed by a colleague, Robert McKersie, at a 1990 meeting of the Saturn Strategic Action Council, where "the only individuals who were willing to take issue and to 'tell it like it is' were the UAW representatives. Other participants in the meeting did not speak their minds as freely and tended to back off when the CEO expressed a point of view."[19] This forthright communication puts more pressure on decision makers to address their differences by searching for mutual gains solutions.

Some industrial relations specialists and union leaders view employment relationships in which employees have independent union representation or other sources of independent voice or protection as an inherent competitive advantage. Although formal union representation may not be the only means by which conflicts can be aired openly and conflict resolution achieved expeditiously, some surrogate for this traditional form may be needed in settings where employees lack formal representation.

The Personnel Policy Level

Moving to the personnel policy level, we suggest three additional principles that are critical to a mutual gains enterprise. First, staffing policies must be designed and managed so that they reinforce the principle of employment security and thus promote the commitment, flexibility, and loyalty of employees. This does not imply guarantees of lifetime employment, but it does imply that the first instinct in good times and bad is to build and protect the firm's investment in human resources, not indiscriminately add and cut people as knee-jerk responses to short-term fluctuations in business conditions. Put differently, the firm—and its stockholders—should be willing to incur significant costs before resorting to layoffs.

Lee Dyer, Felecian Foltman, and George Milkovich of Cornell University surveyed firms that avoided such knee-jerk reactions in the 1970s and 1980s.[20] Exhibit 3-2 lists the practices they followed in coping with declines in product demand or technological change without resorting to layoffs. Clearly, implementing such strategies as avoiding certain contracts or business opportunities of short duration requires organizational discipline that can be achieved only through a strong concern for human resource issues at the top of the firm. This condition was present at firms such as Control Data Corporation, IBM, Hewlett-Packard, Eli Lilly, and others included in the Dyer-Foltman-Milkovich study, until some of them experienced significant losses in market share and profitability.

This last point deserves more discussion. Many of the firms known for their use of the employment stabilizing techniques listed in Exhibit 3-2 have had to resort to layoffs in the 1980s or 1990s as their market share shrunk, competition from lower-cost producers in maturing markets took its toll, and Wall Street analysts intensified their criticism of these "full employment practices."

We do not believe that it is possible or feasible for any firm to guarantee lifetime job security, nor do we necessarily advocate that firms make iron-clad pledges of employment continuity (although, as noted, we believe that firms and their stockholders should be willing

Exhibit 3-2
Actions to Maintain Employment Security

When Output Is Increasing	When Output Is Variable	When Output Is Declining
Avoid business that appears to be short run or cyclical.	Call in vendored work.	Call in vendored work.
Gear up slowly.	Move work to people.	Produce for inventory.
Vendor some work.	Stretch productivity improvement programs.	Create work.
Add new jobs as a last resort.	Pressure suppliers for more reliable deliveries.	Freeze hiring.
Use overtime.	Move people to work.	Cut overtime.
Hire temporaries.		Share work.
Increase training.		Encourage voluntary leaves, retirements, and severance.
		Cut pay.
		Tighten performance standards.

Source: Lee Dyer, George Milkovich, and Felician Foltman, "Contemporary Employment Stabilization Practices," in Thomas A. Kochan and Thomas A. Barocci, eds., *Human Resource Management and Industrial Relations* (Boston: Little, Brown, 1985), pp. 207–209.

to incur costs before laying off employees). Instead, we later emphasize that we have what is sometimes referred to as a "market failure" or "public goods problem." Individual firms find it extremely difficult and perhaps too costly to provide long-term employment security if surrounded by or competing with firms that follow short-term employment practices. Yet, if a sufficient number of firms adopt long-term employment practices, the costs of these practices to individual firms decline, making them more economically efficient and likely to endure. We return to this point in discussing the role of government in economic policy.

Closely related to employment security practices are employee training and development strategies. Indeed, recognition that iron-clad employment security guarantees are seldom feasible makes training all the more important. Long-term employment security in today's economy lies not with a lifetime job in a single firm but in procuring and keeping current general skills that can transfer across firms as needed over the course of a career. Similarly, firms that seek competitive advantage through human resources must make the necessary investments to ensure that their employees have the appropriate skills and training not only to meet short-term job requirements, but also to anticipate changing job requirements over time. Both employers and employees must be prepared to adopt the concept of lifelong learning.

The third critical principle at the human resource policy level concerns compensation. It is very simple: if we are to stabilize employment (quantity of labor), we must have greater flexibility regarding the price of labor. Achieving this is far from simple.

One thing is clear, and has been as far back as the 1940s, when Joseph Scanlon invented one of the best known and most enduring forms of contingent compensation, known as the Scanlon Plan. Scanlon, an official of the United Steelworkers of America, joined the MIT faculty at the invitation of Douglas McGregor. Scanlon developed an organizationwide gain-sharing plan that seeks to provide all employees with incentives to search for ways to reduce the overall costs of goods sold. He was clear on one thing, a basic point he passed on to Fred Leiseur, another proponent of the plan, who joined the MIT faculty in 1956. An effective gain-sharing plan must be a supplement to, not a substitute for, a fair, competitive base wage.[21] Scanlon and Leiseur's instincts about worker reactions to incentives were based on years of direct experience with blue- and white-collar workers. Their instincts, sound then, are just as sound today.

Beyond this basic point there is little agreement among experts or little convincing empirical evidence to indicate that there is a single, best contingent compensation program or strategy. Profit sharing, employee stock ownership, stock options, and other equity- or profit-based plans may work better for higher-level executives who can see directly the relationship between their efforts and these outcomes; however, one must be careful not to warp management incentives in ways that lead people to maximize their own short-run compensation at the expense of overall organizational goals or long-term interests. Group incentives obviously make more sense than individual incentive plans when team work, task interdependence, and internal mobility across jobs and departments are critical to a firm's success. But where individuals work alone or their performance is not dependent on others—for example, salespersons with separate districts or products—or lawyers or consultants with separate clients, or athletes in individual sports such as tennis or golf (but not basketball!), individual incentive plans may still be appropriate. Suffice it to say that the number of settings where individuals work independently in organizations appears to be declining and, therefore, so too does the scope for individual incentive pay systems or contracts.

Strategic-level Requirements

A third group of mutual gains principles relates to decisions that traditionally were thought to lie beyond the legitimate domain of human resource professionals, employees, or labor union leaders. This is no longer the case, since these high-level or "strategic" decisions have a profound effect on employment relations; they are part of the domain of human resource and labor-management relations practitioners.

Of all the important considerations at this level, perhaps the most central are a firm's competitive strategies. It is essential that the firm not depend solely on low costs, especially not on low wages, salaries, and benefit levels, but rather on such sources of competitive advantage as affordable quality, innovation, flexibility, speed, and customer service. Consider, for example, the difference between the strategies adopted after industry deregulation by Continental and Delta airlines. In 1983, Frank Lorenzo, the CEO of Continental, announced that the company was shifting its competitive strategy. It was determined to become the low-cost carrier and compete on the basis of low fares. Lorenzo used loopholes in Chapter 11 bankruptcy proceedings (later closed by Congress, partly in response to Lorenzo's actions) to cancel labor contracts with his employees, cut wages by 25 to 50 percent for different work groups, decertify his employees' unions, and thereby achieved the low labor costs needed to implement his strategy. Clearly this did little to build employee commitment or trust and obviously did not include employee participation or labor-management cooperation.

Compare this strategy to Delta's. Delta was known in the industry for its conservative financial strategies, its commitment to high-quality service to customers, and its commitment to its employees. For example, Delta was the only major U.S. airline to avoid layoffs during the steep recession the industry experienced in the early 1970s. In return, its employees pooled their funds to purchase a Boeing 767 for the company! Consistent with its historical approach, Delta decided not to push for lower labor costs in the wake of industry deregulation and as a result retained its reputation for both quality of service and quality of employee relations. Over time, however, it did end up in the unhappy position of being the carrier with the highest labor costs, but at the

same time it achieved the most consistent service quality and profitability record in the industry.

Delta is not, however, free of problems. In fact, in 1993 it had to
resort to layoffs of pilots because they refused to take pay cuts to
help cover losses the company, like most other airlines, experienced
following the fare wars of 1992. But this merely serves to reinforce
the point we are making: conflict with its employees, which may
threaten the high level of trust and commitment Delta built up with
them, emerged precisely when the company was forced to give greater
weight to price and wage reduction as competitive weapons.

The lesson is clear. High employee commitment is impossible to
sustain over time unless a company has a competitive strategy that
requires the commitment and loyalty and motivation of its employees
to succeed. The resulting differences in employee relations at Continental and Delta over the first ten years following airline deregulation are
evident. Indeed, in airlines or other service industries where employee
interactions with customers are so crucial to customer satisfaction,
these differences may be essential to long-term competitiveness.

Key decision makers must also be guided by organizational values
and traditions that view employees as valued stakeholders in the organization, not as mere cogs in the machine. For reasons that perhaps
are best left to future business historians, many successful high-tech
entrepreneurs of the 1940s through the 1960s seemed to espouse
these values more than their predecessors or their successors. Thomas
Watson, Jr., at IBM, Edwin Land at Polaroid, Kenneth Olsen at Digital
Equipment, David Packard and William Hewlett, to name only a
visible few, were all strong-minded founders or early leaders who
nurtured their rapidly growing companies with a culture and values
that encouraged mutual commitment and mutual gains—loyalty of
employees in return for employment security, good compensation, and
opportunities for growth and promotion. Obviously, these values were
easier to maintain *because* their firms were successful and growing
rapidly.

But it is too easy to dismiss their commitment as simply a convenient by-product of rapid and sustained growth. These firms attempted
to stay with their employment security pledges long after Wall Street
analysts and numerous executives within their own firms urged them,
or their successors, to abandon these policies. Eventually all needed
to accept layoffs or their equivalent; however, there is little doubt that
the organizational cultures that their leadership embedded in these
firms supported progressive human resource policies and standards

well beyond what would have occurred in the absence of their leadership. The central question we take up later, however, is, Why do so few entrepreneurs today espouse the same values? How can we instill these values more deeply in a large enough number of executives and enterprises to sustain the benefits of the employment systems they support through the more mature stages of their organizations and business life cycles?

Xerox stands out as a company that has maintained its support for mutual gains principles for more than a decade under the leadership of three different CEOs. Although, as we stress at various points in this book, there are a number of mutually reinforcing features to Xerox's human resource practices that helped it sustain this commitment, one feature that has been critical is that the company always has had various means for giving voice to employee and human resource interests in strategy formulation and organizational governance. William Asher, the former director of Corporate Industrial Relations, described one means by which this voice for mutual gains human resource strategies was passed in the transition from one CEO, Peter McCollough, to his successor, David Kearns.

In the late 1970s Kearns was recruited to a senior management position at Xerox after working his way up the corporate ladder at IBM. Once it was clear that Kearns would eventually be the CEO, Asher realized that he had a potential problem. In the United States IBM is a totally nonunion company, and Xerox blue-collar workers were organized by the Amalgamated Clothing and Textile Workers Union and had, at McCollough's urging, embarked on a joint labor-management effort to introduce employee participation. The question was, How could Kearns relate to a union-management setting? The solution was a series of "Friday afternoon seminars," informal chats in which Asher described the history of the union-management relationship, the vision he and McCollough had for moving it to a full-fledged partnership in innovation and cooperation, and the value that unions hold for a democratic society.

Slowly but surely, Kearns was brought into direct contact with local and international union leaders and not only became comfortable with this partnership but indeed became one of its most vocal champions. In addition, voice for labor and human resources was institutionalized at Xerox under his leadership through his quarterly meetings with other top executives and the leadership of the union at which the competitive situation of the company, decisions about future investments and plans, and their employment implications, including the sourcing of products and jobs worldwide, were discussed. This information sharing and informal consultation provided an umbrella of trust at the top of the organization needed to carry the partnership process through the crises that inevitably occur over time and threaten the continuity of mutual gains principles. Kearns's successor, Paul Allaire, who moved up through the managerial ranks at Xerox as these changes were taking place, has continued to support and lead them, and, indeed, has become a visible national champion for this approach to management.

There is no single way to integrate human resource policies with other strategic decisions. As the Xerox case suggests, in some instances the top human resource or industrial relations executive, in this instance in partnership at this strategic level with union representatives, has sufficient influence to ensure that these issues are adequately taken into account. But as we will see in later chapters, this is the exception rather than the rule in American corporations. In Germany, law requires that workers be represented on corporate boards of supervisors (directors) and, as we later discuss in more detail, establishment-level works councils must be consulted before major decisions affecting employees are made. In Japan, more than 80 percent of large firms have active labor-management consultative committees that receive information and discuss similar decisions with top management. All of these are alternative means of ensuring that human resource considerations and employee interests are taken into account in strategic decision making *prior to* formalizing such resolutions. This may be the Achilles heel in efforts to sustain mutual gains principles and policies in American corporations, since this is all too rare a feature of American business.

Obviously, the principles we have outlined are idealized organizational practices. No organization is expected to meet all of them perfectly or through the same practices. Nonetheless, we are suggesting that when these principles are properly operationalized they will come together in the form of an integrated system that, other things equal, will produce globally competitive business results as well as globally competitive standards of living for employees.

Evidence: Effects of Mutual Gains Practices

What are the effects of mutual gains practices on firm performance to date? We have at least three kinds of evidence: (1) self-reports of managers or union leaders of the results of their experiences, (2) case studies, and (3) quantitative assessments. As researchers, we would like to place the greatest reliance on the third kind, less on case studies, and relatively little weight on the parties' self-reports. Unfortunately, the bulk of the evidence to date comes in the opposite order: most of the evidence is self-reports; there are a limited number of in-depth case studies; and only a handful of quantitative evaluations have been conducted. Among all the studies, a small number of familiar leading examples are routinely reported, including such well-known companies as Xerox, Motorola, NUMMI, Saturn, Hewlett-Packard, Federal Express, Corning, Chaparral Steel, Lincoln Electric, Donnelly, and Steelcase. Exhibits 3-3 through 3-8 provide capsule summaries of some of these "best practice" cases put together by the Department of Labor.

Moreover, reviewing the quantitative evidence presents a real paradox. On the one hand, our theory argues that these practices reach their full potential when they are combined in a comprehensive system. Employee participation, for example, is unlikely to survive for long in an organization whose business strategies rely primarily on minimizing costs and there is little or no commitment to employment security. Although we do not necessarily believe that organizational decision makers fully comprehend this point when first considering innovations, they do come to understand it as they are forced to deal with inconsistencies among different organizational practices over time. For example, it became quite clear to Xerox executives that their 1982 fledgling employee involvement program could not be sustained unless they stopped laying off workers who took the risks of cooperating with their employee involvement experiment! Similarly, in the late 1970s the United Auto Workers made it clear to GM that the union's support for quality of working life efforts in current plants would not be sustained unless the company abandoned its "southern strategy," i.e., opening new nonunion plants in the South. Yet most existing organizations cannot and do not transform their practices completely all at once. Instead, they tend to experiment with incremental changes in one or more practices at a time and then, as was the case at Xerox, deal with demands for additional change as problems arise. Usually it is only when designing a greenfield site or making a major technological or physical change in an existing facility that the parties can easily introduce entirely new systems of work organization and related human resource practices.

So it is not surprising that most empirical studies of human resource practices tend to focus on single or small sets of innovations. Indeed, research that is generally judged by accepted standards of social science

Exhibit 3-3

Company: Magma Copper Company
Location: Tucson, Arizona
Industry: Copper mining and smelting
Union: United Steelworkers of America (USWA)
Size: 4,400 employees

Since facing severe competition and abysmal labor relations in the mid-1980s, the Magma Copper Company has transformed itself into a high-performance workplace. The cornerstone of this transformation was a unique fifteen-year contract signed in 1989, which created labor-management "work redesign" teams to improve productivity, joint "problem-solving" teams to resolve contract disputes, and a guarantee of eight years with no work stoppages.

Magma has introduced a number of workplace changes including the use of work teams and decentralization of decision making. It has undertaken an extensive education effort, opened its books to its employees, and provided seminars to teach employees how to understand financial information. The company also has a bonus program that rewards improvements in operating results. Magma's employee involvement efforts are based on a Joint Union-Management Cooperation Committee, which reviews corporate results, strategic plans, and breakdowns in labor relations. Ad hoc committees called breakthrough teams exist throughout the company to solve production problems.

Since 1988, productivity measured in pounds of ore has increased 43 percent while cash costs have fallen 24 percent. The company's smelter is operating at 107 percent of design capacity, and the company produced 524 million pounds of copper in 1991, compared with 402 million pounds in 1988.

Source: The summaries included in Exhibits 3-3 through 3-8 were prepared by the staff of the Office of the American Workplace, U.S. Department of Labor, Washington, D.C., June 1993.

to be the most rigorous and credible generally seeks to isolate the "independent" effects of specific practices, holding constant or controlling for all other potential determinants of the outcome of interest. Researchers want to know, controlling for everything else, just what does an employee participation process add to productivity or quality? Our theory suggests this is the wrong question and the wrong test. We argue that employee participation cannot and will not be divorced

Exhibit 3-4

Company:	Saturn Corporation
Location:	Springhill, Tennessee
Industry:	Automobiles
Union:	United Automobile Workers (UAW)
Size:	6,800 employees

Saturn has made an enormous investment—both financially and philo-sophically—in people. At each managerial level, from the president on down, and within each staff function, a UAW counterpart shares decision making equally with Saturn managers. All employees are part of at least one team. On the production floor, workers are formed into teams of five to fifteen people who manage themselves, from budgeting to scheduling to hiring and training. Decisions are made by consensus. There are no time clocks, no privileged parking spots, and no private dining rooms.

The whole system is undergirded by enormous amounts of training. Each new employee at Saturn goes through a week of orientation training before he or she hits the floor. Even then, workers work only part time for the first two or three months, as their time is split between classroom and on-the-job training. Production workers can expect to spend half their train-ing time learning "soft skills" such as conflict resolution, problem solving, presentation, and communication. While at Saturn, employees can expect to spend 5 percent of their time annually in training. The company guarantees 95 percent of their base wages and does not pay the remaining 5 percent unless everybody meets this training goal. The first-quarter goal was 155,687 hours; Saturn employees logged more than 300,000.

Saturn reduced work classifications and thereby increased the company's flexibility to deploy workers. The company has one classification for produc-tion workers and five for skilled trades. Everyone is on salary, and lifetime employment is guaranteed to 80 percent of its work force, barring "severe economic conditions" or "catastrophic events."

From 1986 to 1992, there were only seven formal grievances at Saturn. There have been improvements to quality, productivity, cost savings, reduc-tion of waste, communication, labor-management relations, and morale. From 1985 to 1990, Saturn reduced defects from 3.5 to 1.5 per vehicle. In 1991, Saturn sold more cars per dealer than any other manufacturer, including Honda—the first time in fifteen years that a U.S. car maker claimed the number one spot. In a survey by *Popular Mechanics,* it was reported that 83.4 percent of Saturn owners would buy another Saturn.

Exhibit 3-5

Company: Federal Express
Location: Memphis, Tennessee
Industry: Freight transportation
Size: 90,000 worldwide

In 1987 Federal Express instituted a pay-for-performance/pay-for-knowledge system, recognizing that programs rewarding outstanding performance and superior job knowledge translate into outstanding customer service. Federal Express rewards customer-contact employees with higher pay and promotions for superior job knowledge and performance. The system is built around job-knowledge testing, measuring how well an employee knows his or her job. The measuring system includes performance evaluations of how well the knowledge is applied.

Because of FedEx's far-flung locations, most training is provided through an interactive video disk (IVD) system. For example, FedEx developed an IVD course to teach its mechanics how to troubleshoot and repair electrical problems. The course allows mechanics to take readings, test components, replace equipment, and evaluate procedures. FedEx has more than 900 employees working officially in a training capacity. The company devotes 3 percent ($225 million) of its annual expenses to training.

Employees are grouped into teams as part of a performance-improvement and quality-enhancement program. One team analyzed and redesigned the minisort process, which re-sorts and redirects mail that arrives late or is misdirected by earlier operations. This redesign saved FedEx $1 million yearly and reduced the number of employees needed from 150 to 80. Federal Express established one cross-functional team for each component (12 in all) of its Service Quality Indicators program and a formal Quality Improvement Process (QIP) has been instituted throughout the company. The objective of the QIP is to achieve a 100 percent service level, increase profits, and make FedEx a better place to work.

In 1990 the company won the Malcolm Baldrige National Quality Award and in 1992 was awarded the RIT/USA Today Quality Cup for service. FedEx was also awarded *Distribution* magazine's number one quality ranking in the air express carrier category in 1991.

In addition, the company has invested in new technologies. At its Memphis hub, UNIX-based workstations equipped with expert systems software track and launch aircraft. A Ramp Management Advisory System synchronizes flight-processing times, ensuring that aircraft arrive at destinations on time.

Exhibit 3-6

Company: Chaparral Steel
Location: Midlothian, Texas
Industry: Steel
Size: 950 employees

Chaparral Steel is one of the most successful companies in the highly competitive minimill segment of the steel industry. In a recent study, company managers credited Chaparral's success to concentration in three distinct areas: (1) a marketing strategy sympathetic to customer needs, (2) an insatiable thirst for technological improvement, and (3) the application of participatory management techniques to encourage productivity.

To encourage employee participation, Chaparral was created in 1975 with only four layers of management. The company's emphasis on employee involvement is supported by its egalitarian work culture, which allows all employees to set their own lunch hours and does not require them to punch time cards. Pay is based on individual performance, company profits, and skills learned. Bonuses and profit sharing have accounted for as much as 20 percent of wages, depending on company profits and employee corporate responsibilities.

A Chaparral policy requires that at least 85 percent of its workers are enrolled in some type of training course at any one time. A compulsory annual educational sabbatical program requires employees to visit customers, companies, and universities worldwide to learn about new processes and technologies. In its zealous efforts to be at the cutting edge of technology, Chaparral spends 15 percent of its annual sales on modernizing plant and equipment, compared with the integrated steel industry average of 4 to 7 percent.

Chaparral practices extensive multiskilling and cross-utilization of employees. Production employees investigate customer complaints—all 935 employees are considered members of the sales department—and the traditional sales, billing, credit, and shipping departments have been consolidated into a customer service center where all employees are empowered to handle any request.

Chaparral Steel, the nation's tenth largest single-site steel company, was at the end of the 1980s the only American minimill as cost competitive as an overseas exporter. Chaparral produces steel at a record low 1.6 hours per ton, compared to an average 2.4 hours for other steel minimills and 4.9 hours for integrated producers. The company practices a no-layoff policy, which it maintained throughout the 1980s despite three consecutive years of net losses.

Exhibit 3-7

Company: Shenandoah Life Insurance Company
Location: Roanoke, Virginia
Industry: Insurance
Size: 220 employees

Insurance underwriting tasks at Shenandoah Life were redesigned around autonomous work groups of four to seven employees each. Work teams have responsibility for scheduling work and vacations, final selection of new members, designing office space, determining the basics of the compensation system, interacting with managers and other units, and discipline and training. With the advent of these self-directed teams, teams no longer have direct supervisors; instead they report to two managers who have responsibility for twenty-plus employees each. Instead of first-line supervisors, the company now has advisers who act as technical support for specific work teams.

Employees who work on teams receive training in group dynamics, brainstorming, conflict resolution, decision making, planning, and team functioning, in addition to task-related training. By moving to self-directed work teams, Shenandoah has benefited through higher efficiency and streamlined operations. The employees have benefited through gaining more responsibility and more interesting work lives.

With the move to self-directed teams, the company instituted a pay-for-knowledge compensation system, which rewards employees on the basis of their knowledge of a number of different tasks. The cross-training provided to the employees has resulted in more creativity and better utilization of manpower. From 1985 to 1987, the number of people employed in the teams declined by 15.6 percent while the volume of work increased by 28.5 percent. Complaints from customers have decreased, and the supervisor/employee ratio has declined from 1:7 to 1:37.

Shenandoah Life has been so successful in implementing its team-based structure that it has established a for-profit consulting subsidiary.

---

from other human resource practices and organizational strategies. The implication of this argument is that we need to look at the total set of organizational strategies and assess their effects on performance.

Since it is harder to measure empirically all these organizational practices, this approach encourages broader, more qualitative case studies and self-reports of the parties' experiences with these innovations, and their own assessments of the results. Because these approaches often

Exhibit 3-8

Company: Rohm & Haas Bayport, Inc.
Location: LaPorte, Texas
Industry: Specialty chemicals
Size: 81 employees

Rohm & Haas Bayport, Inc., has implemented a high-performance work system involving innovation in technology design, work organization, and employee evaluation and compensation.

Each of its eight autonomous work teams has four to seven process technicians and is in one of two operating units. Each operating unit also has an autonomous technical team of seven or eight professional chemists and engineers who provide support to the technicians, design new equipment, figure budgets, and manage outside contractors who occasionally work at the plant. The plant has no supervisors. Technicians train one another, read manuals, view videotapes, and are generally encouraged to learn all they can. They can also repair equipment without permission, whatever the cost of parts.

A pay-for-knowledge system gives technicians periodic pay raises as they demonstrate proficiency in each of six jobs; in less than three years workers can increase their salary by more than 50 percent. Technicians decide how often to rotate jobs with other team members, generally every four to twelve weeks.

Technicians also have input into decisions like performance evaluation that were traditionally centralized in personnel departments. Job applicants are initially interviewed and rated by administrators of technicians and must then meet their prospective team, which makes the final hiring decision. A task force of technicians, technical staff, and management tries to resolve major problems such as modifying the evaluation system.

Inspectors for one of Bayport's customers awarded the plant the highest quality rating ever given to a supplier. The plant also has a near-perfect record in recent years of producing to specifications, while volume has increased. When technicians were trained to take part in interviewing job applicants, the turnover rate fell from 50 percent to less than 10 percent.

---

involve descriptions of firms that have been judged to be successful, we are too often left with several serious questions. First, How many failures go unreported? Second, Which, if any, of the practices of these organizations accounts for the firm's success? And third, How do we know what is cause and what is effect? Put differently, would the same performance results be achieved if another organization in a similar product and labor-market environment copied exactly these practices? This kind of total organization research often cannot answer this question.

Our resolution of this dilemma, and the one we urge professionals and policy makers to follow, is to be open to considering all kinds of quantitative and case study research and testimonials of the parties involved, but at the same time to be skeptical of it, always asking the researcher to "show us" the results. With these caveats in mind, let's look at what the evidence to date has to say.

Workplace Innovations

Innovations at the workplace are a good place to start, since they served as the most frequent source of experimentation in the past decade. Some early, and to us rather convincing, evidence that traditional workplace systems, involving rigid and narrow job classifications, detailed written work rules, and little or no employee participation, produce inferior quality and productivity came from quantitative studies in the auto industry. In a series of cross-plant comparative studies covering the years 1970 through 1979 led by our Cornell colleague Harry Katz, we observed strong and negative correlations between quality and productivity and the number of grievances, number of local union demands and time spent on negotiating work rules, and a low-trust climate between supervisors and employees.[22]

This was strong confirmation that the traditional system of industrial relations in these plants was not producing the economic results needed to be competitive in the world auto industry, even in the early 1970s. As is now well known, auto industry executives shared this view and in the 1980s introduced a host of experiments first with employee involvement, later with work teams, and most recently with fundamentally different production, human resource, and organizational governance strategies in selected cases such as Saturn and various GM, Chrysler, and Ford plants. What did these efforts produce? We can summarize the evidence to date as follows:

1. Early efforts to introduce quality of work life (QWL) or related employee involvement on its own, or as stand-alone experiments, failed the rigorous social science test of producing measurable and

sustained improvements in quality and productivity, controlling for other factors that affect these performance outcomes.

2. But the majority of the employees, managers, and union representatives involved in these early experiments saw the value in breaking down traditional relationships and practices and supported broadening the experiments to modify work rules and introduce work teams. Again, the quantitative tests suggested that teams per se did not produce significant advances in productivity and quality, although they did contribute to lowering indirect (supervisory) labor costs.

3. Then along came the Japanese "transplants." Honda opened a plant in Ohio in 1982, Nissan followed with a plant in Tennessee in 1984, and Toyota negotiated its joint venture with GM (NUMMI) and reopened a GM facility in Fremont, California, that had been shut down for more than a year. The superior quality and productivity results of some of these transplants, particularly Honda and NUMMI, shook up the industry and led to the conclusion that the total new system of human resource management, labor relations, and production techniques introduced in these plants could achieve economic results unreachable under traditional systems or with minor or incremental modifications to traditional systems such as employee involvement and work team structures.

4. Subsequently, a quantitative set of studies comparing the performance of assembly plants around the world, performed by MIT students John Krafcik and John Paul MacDuffie, provided the empirical evidence to support this general view.[23] The results of their work were widely disseminated to the industry in a bestselling book, *The Machine That Changed the World.*[24] "Lean production" as the book labeled this system, is now widely accepted as the benchmark against which to measure "best practice" in auto assembly plants around the world.

In summary, the auto industry research presents the best and worst case for reaching conclusions on the basis of quantitative research. Studies that attempted to isolate the effects of individual practices showed little or no positive effect. Studies of the traditional system showed that it produced negative effects, although variations in performance of the system indicated that a wide diversity of results could be produced under traditional systems, depending on how much they deteriorated into a low-trust/high-conflict cycle. Yet plant-level cases and experience showed that significant positive results could be achieved, particularly when new plants adopted systemic new approaches to workplace relations and manufacturing practices. Then the general industry acceptance of the evidence from transplants and the codification and dissemination of this knowledge in a clear and concise way via the assembly plant studies and *The Machine That Changed the World* made the new model accepted wisdom in the industry.

The auto industry experience and research serve as the best and strongest evidence to date that a mutual gains model produces superior manufacturing performance compared with traditional or partially modified human resource systems. But even in the case of this industry, we cannot isolate the "independent" effects of the human resource innovations—they are tightly coupled with the effects of the production strategies and overall management and governance systems in place in these plants.

The steel industry. A recent study of the effects of workplace practices in the steel industry provides additional evidence on the effects of different models or "bundles" of human resource practices. Casey Ichniowski of Columbia University and Kathryn Shaw and Giovanna Prennushi of Carnegie-Mellon have collected an extremely detailed and rich body of data on human resource practices and productivity of finishing lines in steel mills located in the United States.[25] Some of these are union, some are nonunion; some are U.S. owned and some are joint U.S.-Japanese facilities; some are relatively new lines and plants while others are older facilities that have been in operation for many years. Their quantitative analysis showed strong positive effects on productivity for indices of various innovative human resource practices, most of which mirror those included in the mutual gains model presented in Exhibit 3-1. Moreover, consistent with the auto industry results reported above, they found that "systems of human resource management policies determine productivity. Marginal changes in individual policies have little or no effect on productivity. Improving productivity requires substantial changes in a set of human resource management policies."[26]

Along with the auto industry research, this is the most comprehensive and well-designed study of the effects of human resource practices across firms and plants within an industry. We hope to see more similar work in the future.

Other cases of workplace innovations. Xerox Corporation represents another favorite example of all who want to emphasize the success of the mutual gains model. We studied developments at Xerox over the course of its evolution from 1981 to the end of the decade, using a combination of case studies and quantitative analysis.[27] The quantitative tests conducted by Joel Cutcher-Gershenfeld sought to overcome the problems of looking only at single practices and instead examined the effects of combinations of workplace innovations in Xerox plants. He surveyed a number of separate worksites in Xerox and for each collected data on work organization and on output, quality, and scrap. He found that the bundle of innovative practices, which taken together constituted a transformed workplace system similar to the mutual gains model in Exhibit 3-1, outperformed traditional systems. But again, neither our empirical research nor the managers involved could pinpoint the specific or independent effects of a given innovation. The proof of the managers' commitment was in their behavior—plant managers and Xerox executives stated that they could not have achieved the turnaround in manufacturing performance and overall organizational renewal Xerox gained in the 1980s without these human resource management innovations. Again, the story is clear: human resource innovations do not stand alone but are essential components of a broader organizational transformation strategy.

The Xerox case history is matched by a large number of similar case studies and testimonials of managers about the positive results of workplace innovations. Exhibit 3-9 presents an excerpt from a recent exhaustive review of the range of workplace innovations introduced

Exhibit 3-9
Are "High-Performance Firms" High Performers?

Most of the evidence of improved performance currently available is self-reported by firm managers, though it should be noted that the Baldrige Award has stringent requirements with respect to measurement and record keeping on an array of performance measures, including meeting customers' needs.

These caveats must be kept in mind when reviewing the impressive performance gains reported by companies that have implemented a coherent set of innovations and appear to have transformed the production process. Gains are reported in quality—reductions in cycle time; reductions in defects, reductions in waste; improvements in customer satisfaction; sometimes in improvements in productivity; and sometimes in gains in market share or in return on investment. While the following list is not exhaustive, it does suggest the range of improvements transformed firms have obtained.

Exhibit 3-9
Continued

Among the Baldrige winners, Milliken reported a significant increase in on-time delivery and a 50 percent reduction in defects in goods over ten years; Motorola developed methods for measuring quality in white-collar settings and improved quality tenfold between 1981 and 1986; at Xerox, defects in component parts dropped from 10,000 parts per million in 1980 to 360 in 1989; at IBM's Rochester plant, write-off for scrap and excess inventory dropped 55 percent between 1984 and 1990; Solectron Corporation reported a 50 percent improvement in the average product rejection rate between 1987 and 1991; the Wallace Company increased sales 69 percent between 1987 and 1990 and raised market share from 10 to 18 percent; Zytec Corporation increased its on-time delivery rate and achieved double-digit annual growth in productivity between 1988 and 1991.

Corning reports that in its transformed plants, scrap is down 46 percent and productivity is up 30 percent. Return on investment, which had slipped in the 1980s, increased to 15 percent in 1991, putting Corning back in the top quartile of *Fortune* 500 companies. While it is too early to report on improvements in productivity and quality performance at Saturn, there is already evidence of accomplishment in terms of dealers' performance and customer satisfaction. J. D. Power and Associates ranks Saturn second in dealer satisfaction, just behind Lexus and ahead of Infiniti, and third in 1991 new-vehicle gross profit per dealership, behind Lexus and Infiniti. In terms of owners' overall satisfaction, Saturn ranks well ahead of the industry, in sixth place behind cars that compete in the luxury segment and in first place among the top five basic small cars.

Source: Eileen Appelbaum and Rosemary Batt, "Transforming the Production System in U.S. Firms," report to the Alfred P. Sloan Foundation (Washington, D.C.: The Economic Policy Institute, January 1993), pp. 155–157.

in the United States over the past two decades, which was conducted by Eileen Appelbaum of the Economic Policy Institute and Rose Batt of MIT.[28] The range of firms and performance outcomes discussed attests to the conviction of managers involved in these cases that such innovations are critical to their success, yet as in the cases cited above, they find it difficult, if not impossible, to sort out the "net" effects of any single innovative practice.

How do employees react to workplace innovations? The direct and indirect evidence is overwhelmingly positive—employees generally prefer to have some say in decisions involving their jobs and work environment and prefer jobs that have greater task variety and autonomy. These trends have strengthened over the years as the general educational level of the work force has increased. But the psychological benefits associated with more flexible and participative work systems are not likely to outweigh most employees' need of and interest in making a good wage and preserving job security.

For example, in a study carried out for the National Industry Labor Management Committee, Ellen Rosen found that women sewing machine operators were hesitant to accept "multiskilling and teamwork opportunities." The reason was that they did not trust their white male supervisors to "protect their rates." They preferred to remain specialized on the same line because they could control their own earnings.[29]

The lesson here is again one of linkage. The multiskilling initiative these firms were attempting to introduce would fail unless the supporting changes were introduced in an environment of trust and fair compensation practices. Thus, we should not expect these workers, or any others for that matter, to take an interest in workplace reforms that come at the expense of their individual or collective earning power or sense of control over their jobs and work environment.

Human Resource–level Practices

The evidence on the effects of innovations in compensation, employment security, and training on economic performance and worker welfare is also limited. Like the workplace innovations, the findings of the studies conducted on these issues seem to indicate that in isolation, single innovations have at best limited positive impacts. When combined with workplace innovations discussed in the previous section, their effects become stronger.

This point is best illustrated by the studies done on the effects of contingent, i.e., variable, compensation arrangements. Variable-pay systems range from individual bonus systems to group-based incentive plans, to organizationwide profit-, productivity-, or equity-based gain-sharing plans. Such plans as piece-work systems tend to be limited to production workers; annual bonuses tend to be largely limited to high-level executives; and merit-pay systems tend to be exist mostly among middle managers.

A number of studies have found, after holding constant occupation and technology, that piece-rate workers earn more than straight hourly wage earners do.[30] This higher pay presumably reflects higher productivity as well as a risk premium. The literature on executive pay is murkier, primarily because of difficult technical issues: how to measure performance (e.g., accounting versus stock market rates of return), how to hold constant general industry effects versus firm effects, and whether to examine short- or long-term bonus-pay systems. The bulk of the literature looks at short-term compensation-performance relationships (e.g., this year's pay and next year's performance) rather than such arrangements as long-term stock options.

The overall conclusion is that there is a modest relationship between executive-pay systems and firm performance. For example, Cornell's John Abowd finds that if a firm were to increase the bonus-to-pay ratio by one standard deviation, it would increase economic rates of return by between 5 and 16 percent of one standard deviation.[31] Other studies report even weaker results.[32] The best conclusion is that there is evidence that a properly designed executive-compensation system can improve firm performance, but the magnitude of the effect is most uncertain.

An additional, quite common form of individual pay incentive is merit pay. Whereas under the previously discussed incentive systems pay is directly related to an observable outcome, under merit-pay schemes a certain portion of a firm's annual pay pool is set aside for rewards distributed to employees on the basis of supervisors' judgments. The general conclusion about these systems is that they are not very effective. Firms rarely set aside a substantial fraction of compensation for merit awards (a typical firm might set aside 5 percent) and, perhaps more important, supervisors are rarely willing to make sharp distinctions among employees. As a result, most employees receive comparable ratings, hence comparable pay increases. While these kinds of individual incentive-pay practices have been used for many years, they do not mesh with efforts to promote greater teamwork and cooperation. Group or organizationwide incentive programs seem to be more supportive of these innovations. Yet most surveys find these practices adopted in fewer than 20 percent of U.S. firms. What has been the experience with these plans to date?

Under a typical gain-sharing plan, a base level of output and wages is determined, as is a method for valuing additional—or reduced—output.[33] All members of the group receive pay increases, or decreases, depending on whether output increases or decreases relative to the base. Although there is considerable variation in how plans are organized, surveys suggest that the typical plan pays benefits on a monthly basis, focuses on reducing labor costs, and shares more than 50 percent of gains with employees. Profit sharing is similar to gains sharing in that it links pay to firm performance, although in this case the outcome variable is profit rather than a more direct measure of productivity gain.

Much of the evaluation evidence on gain-sharing plans comes from case studies. However, a few statistical studies are available and these, along with the case studies, paint a positive picture. For example, in a study of more than a hundred firms that introduced a gain-sharing program known as Improshare, Roger Kaufman found that the average cumulative productivity improvement was 15 percent three years after initial implementation, compared with an average 6 percent increase in comparable manufacturing firms without gain-sharing programs. A substantial portion of the gains resulted from the reduction in defects and downtime.[34] Similarly, the U.S. General Accounting Office in its survey found that those firms with gain-sharing plans in place for more than five years averaged an annual 29 percent reduction in labor costs.[35] This seemingly precise estimate should be viewed with some caution, however, given the limitations of the survey on which it is based.[36] However, a more comprehensive study of a number of gain-sharing plans by Michael Schuster of Syracuse University also found positive effects on labor costs and productivity, although these gains tended to plateau after a period of time.[37]

An exhaustive review of profit-sharing and gain-sharing plans conducted by Harvard's Martin Weitzman and Rutger's Douglas Kruse uncovered six surveys of employees who participated in such plans and fifteen attitude surveys of employers.[38] One typical survey of 2,703 workers who were in twelve different profit-sharing plans found that 91 percent were positive about the plan in general, 51 percent said that it made people work more effectively, and 86 percent said that it was good for the company and the employees. The fact that people were more positive about the plan on dimensions other than work effort suggests that the plan improves the working conditions of the firm. The surveys of employers also produced positive responses with between 73 and 100 percent reporting that the plans were successful. Weitzman and Kruse also reviewed the evidence from their own and other econometric studies of profit sharing. They found that profit or gains sharing had positive impacts on productivity in the sixteen studies examined. Although some of these effects were small and failed to reach statistical significance, they found no studies in which profit or gains sharing had a negative effect on economic performance.

A common finding in both gain-sharing and profit-sharing studies was the importance of having a supportive, collaborative arrangement between labor and management. These plans seem to work only if the labor force is given sufficient access to information to be confident that the system is fair. More important, the plans can accomplish their goals only if workers have sufficient power in the production process or distribution system to make a contribution. Again we see the importance of achieving systemic rather than piecemeal changes in human resource practices, workplace innovations, and strategic-level information sharing and decision making. The paradox is that most firms still introduce innovations on a piecemeal, trial-and-error basis rather than in a comprehensive overhaul of their employment relations systems. This is why in later chapters we stress the importance of sustaining the innovative process over time to allow it to encompass a wider range of innovations and supporting human resource and strategic-level practices.

Training and skill. A central function of a firm is to train employees to be productive contributors to the organization. Although a considerable amount of skill training is delivered in schools, in most nations formal and informal training within firms is the major source of vocational-oriented learning. What is the payoff from training?[39] The evidence from a wide range of quantitative studies is rather consistent and convincing: (1) education and training are associated with significant productivity increases, and (2) training and associated flexible human resource systems are associated with higher levels of productivity and quality.[40] These results reinforce our view that adequate entry-level training and lifelong skills development and learning must be provided if mutual gains are to be achieved and sustained over time.

Strategic-level Innovations

If the evidence on the effects of innovations at the workplace and in supporting human resource practices is thin, the evidence on the effects of strategic-level innovations is nearly nonexistent. This is partly because we have little experience with labor-management consultation or worker representation in strategic managerial activities in this country. The little experience we have is discussed in more detail in Chapter 5. For now it is sufficient to note that we know of no studies that systematically analyze the effects of integrating human resource considerations and employee concerns into strategic managerial decision making. On this issue, the rhetoric and the aspirations of human resource executives and worker representatives continue to be far ahead of organizational reality.

There have, however, been a few relatively recent studies that attempt to test whether the full range of human resource practices employed by firms affect their financial performance. For example, Mark Huselid at Rutgers University has conducted the most comprehensive such study to date. He examined the relationship of a bundle of "progressive" human resource practices similar to those listed in Exhibit 3-1 to four different measures of firm profitability and shareholder returns in a sample 700 firms in different industries. He found that, compared with all the rest, the firms with the most progressive practices (those in the top 25 percent) experienced more than twice as high a return on capital, higher total shareholder returns (share price growth plus dividends), higher gross profit margins, and higher market values. The effects of these human resource practices remained significant after controlling for industry effects and other relevant variables.[41]

Similarly, Barry Macy and his colleagues at Texas Tech University recently completed a massive review of virtually every individual quantitative study since 1960 of the effects of the workplace, human resource, and strategic level principles shown in Exhibit 3-1. They found that the most significant positive effects of these practices on firm financial performance measures were reported in cases involving multiple or more systemic innovations containing more than one practice introduced in conjunction with changes in technology, human resources, and organizational strategies and structures.[42] Once again, the systemic effects seem more powerful than those of individual practices.

Summary and Conclusions

This chapter has provided a thumbnail sketch of the principles underlying the mutual gains enterprise and the evidence to date on the economic effects of these principles in action. As example after example has shown, there is no single set of best practices for implementing these broad principles. Instead, there appears to be a variety of ways in which American managers and, where they are present, union leaders are implementing these principles. Nor, outside the case of greenfield facilities, is there strong evidence that the parties are implementing the full range of principles all at once. Instead, what we have observed is piecemeal, experimental phasing in of these practices, even though the empirical evidence to date from managers' testimonials, case studies, and quantitative assessments all suggest that the cumulative and combined effects of integrating these principles with equivalent innovations in manufacturing and service delivery systems produce the biggest payoffs.

A recurring theme throughout this chapter is that these human resource innovations do not stand alone but are most effective and most often a part of a larger transformation of production and service delivery strategies that emphasize product quality and innovation. As we stress throughout this book, achieving these broader transformations in strategy and practice holds the key to going beyond benefits to individual firms and workers and having a noticeable and sustained impact on macroeconomic performance and social welfare.

We must issue a caveat before moving on. We do not see these principles as necessarily fitting *all* employment settings. They are not a universalistic "one best way" to structure employment relationships, any more than Frederick Taylor's scientific management system applied universally to all settings found in the earlier decades of this century. Craft production systems did, after all, continue to dominate in certain sectors like construction, printing, and even in important jobs within manufacturing. So we do not believe that *all* jobs, firms, or professions must adhere to these mutual gains principles or be doomed to be inefficient. Some settings—for example, the description of McDonald's in Exhibit 3-10—will undoubtedly continue to be organized efficiently with low-skill, routine, and narrowly defined jobs and the personnel policies and labor-management relations associated with a Tayloristic approach.

Our argument has two guiding principles. First, as we show in the next chapter, changes in markets and technologies have increased competitive pressures on firms to make a choice as to how to compete in today's markets, and one choice, i.e., the one that emphasizes productivity, product quality, and innovation, can best be achieved and sustained over time by investing in human resources and implementing appropriate variants on these mutual gains principles. Second, movement to these principles is the only way to achieve improvements in the social and economic conditions of employment for workers in a world where labor costs vary greatly and competitors can undercut the wages and benefit levels most people expect in an advanced economy and democratic society. In short, broad-scale adoption and diffusion of these principles and strategies are required if we are to achieve and sustain truly *mutual* gains for individual firms, shareholders, and employees, and the overall economy and society.

Exhibit 3-10
Mass Production Working at McDonald's

Some organizations have had spectacular success using the mechanistic [Tayloristic] model. . . . Take for example the McDonald's hamburger chain, which has established a solid reputation for excellent performance in the fast-food industry. The firm has mechanized the organization of all its franchise outlets all over the world so that each can produce a uniform product. The firm serves a carefully targeted mass market in a perfectly regular and consistent way, with all the precision that "hamburger science" can provide. (The firm actually has its own "hamburger U" for teaching this science to its managers, and has a detailed operating manual to guide franchises in the daily operations of McDonald's system.) The firm is exemplary in its adoption of Tayloristic principles and recruits a nonunionized labor force, often made up of high school and college students, that will be happy to fit the organization as designed. And the "machine" works perfectly most of the time. Of course, the company also has a dynamic and innovative character, but this is for the most part confined to its central staff who do the thinking, i.e., the policy development and design work, for the corporation as a whole.

Source: Gareth Morgan, *Images of Organization* (Newbury Park, Calif.: Sage, 1986), p. 34.

chapter four

CHOICE AND DIFFUSION OF MUTUAL GAINS STRATEGIES

How do American firms choose their employment strategies and practices? What determines why some firms adopt mutual gains principles
while others continue with traditional approaches? Why, once initiated,
do some innovations diffuse widely within firms while others remain
isolated among only a small subset of the firm's work force? How do
workplace innovations relate to the broader range of human resource
strategies embodied in the mutual gains model outlined in Chapter
3? These are the issues taken up in this chapter.

   Strategic choices are, by definition, decisions that have long-term
effects. Thus, once human resource policies are in place, they are not
likely to change fundamentally on a continuous basis. Historical studies
have shown, for example, that periods of significant innovation in human
resource practices tend to coincide with some combination of the following: tight labor markets, government intervention, and rapid union
growth or increased threats of union organizing.[1] In the absence of these
factors, firms appear to be, as our British colleagues put it (see Exhibit
4-1), muddling through by adapting individual practices in piecemeal
fashion as new pressures, ideas, or business needs emerge.[2] Regardless of
whether new practices evolve incrementally out of a muddling-through
process or emerge out of response to a crisis, we need to ask: What are
the underlying forces that shape these practices in American firms?

   A valid understanding of the forces affecting adoption and diffusion
of workplace innovations is relevant to public policy as well as private
practice. The central policy question is whether some market or technological forces will produce a natural evolutionary diffusion of the
innovations needed to transform American firms, or whether firms
retain significant choices over how to adjust to external market and

Exhibit 4-1
Diffusion of Innovations in Britain

It is interesting to note that a debate has been under way among research-ers in Great Britain over the extent to which a new human resource manage-ment model has taken hold or diffused broadly across firms in that country as well. As in the United States, there is no surfeit of case studies of individual companies to attest to the fact that companies recognize the need to introduce changes in their traditional practices. Yet national survey data, as in the United States, tend to show that the dominant overall pattern is one of modest amounts of innovation. John Storey of Loughborough University examined the state of innovation in fifteen of Britain's largest and best known firms, such as ICI, Austin Rover, Jaguar, Eaton Ltd., British Rail, and so on. As in the United States, the primary motivating factors in inducing new approaches to human resources seemed to be the need to meet more de-manding business environment and customer expectations. Also, as in the United States, the views about what managers believe needs to be done are similar. He concluded that, as in the United States, line managers seem to have taken on more responsibility for human resource matters. He reports that the values and mind-set of British managers seem to have shifted from a defensive or reactive posture characteristic of British management in the years prior to the election of Margaret Thatcher to a more proactive, change-oriented culture and mind-set. Unions have been marginal participants in these efforts to date. Storey concludes, however, that these changes appear to be rather haphazard and disjointed. Rather than linking together in some systematic way that could add up to some strategic vision or role in the business affairs of the company, new practices tend to merely emulate what colleagues in other firms have done recently.

Whether these efforts congeal into a sustainable pattern and produce tangible benefits for British firms or the overall economy appears to be an open question in the minds of academics and professionals in Britain as well as in the United States.

Source: John Storey, "HRM in Action: The Truth Is Out at Last," *Personnel Management,* April 1992, 31–38.

---

technical developments. If the former is true, patience is the best public policy; allow the market and technical forces to follow their natural diffusion path and take a laissez-faire approach to government policy. If the latter is true, the policy question turns on whether government can play a positive role in overcoming the obstacles that limit the ability or willingness of individual firms to transform their employment practices. Understanding these obstacles or internal firm variables is therefore a necessary step in developing a well-informed and workable diffusion policy.

As in the prior chapter we rely on a mixture of case study and survey evidence to address these issues. Specifically, we draw on two surveys of workplace practices that we are using in our own research. The first is a nationwide representative sample of 875 establishments (i.e., individual offices, plants, or worksites as opposed to overall firms or corporations) that we conducted in 1992 as part of a broader study of work and family issues and corporate policies.[3] We refer to this as the national establishment survey. The advantage of this survey over most others done to date is that it collects data directly from managers closest to the workplace. This approach is preferable to asking high-level corporate executives to estimate the percentage of their work forces that are involved in one practice or another. As we report these data, we compare them to the results obtained in other recent corporate-level surveys.

The second survey we draw on is international in scope and focuses on the adoption and diffusion of total quality management (TQM) practices. In 1991, the American Quality Foundation in concert with Ernst & Young conducted a survey of quality practices in business units of large firms in the computer, auto, health care, and banking industries in the United States, Canada, Japan, and Germany. These data provide some interesting insights into how TQM practices vary across countries and industries and how they relate to other human resource and labor-management practices.[4]

Although we believe survey data provide the best overall picture of the distribution of these practices across organizations, they are not perfect. It is difficult to tell from cross-sectional surveys whether practices in place today will be sustained over time or whether we are simply capturing where American management is at a given point in time on the curve of a particular managerial fad. It is also difficult to judge from survey responses the true nature or quality of the activities reported. For these reasons we intersperse our review of these data with case examples of these practices in action.

Extent of Diffusion of Workplace Innovations: Survey Results

The practices examined here focus on the dimensions of the workplace practices discussed in Chapter 3, namely, the use of employee participation in problem-solving processes (or quality circles), job rotation, team-based work systems, and TQM practices. We first ask how widespread these practices are and what aspects of a firm's environment and strategy seem correlated with adoption. We then examine the extent to which these innovations are accompanied by the other human resource practices discussed as part of a mutual gains enterprise, namely, investment in training and development, contingent compensation systems, commitment to employment security, and high standards for employee selection.

Respondents to the national establishment survey were asked whether these workplace practices were employed in their establishment. Because it is impossible to generalize about work organization for all occupations, we asked about what we termed "core" occupants, i.e., the largest group of nonmanagerial employees involved in producing the establishment's main products or services.[5] To further probe the depth of commitment, we also asked what percentage of core employees was involved in each practice (the rate of adoption of a given practice within an establishment). The precise definitions for each practice are shown in the appendix of this chapter.

The international TQM survey complements our national survey by providing a more detailed list of TQM practices adopted in the four industries studied. This survey asks business unit-level respondents for their estimates of the extent to which practices such as Pareto analysis and statistical process control are used throughout their operations. We use this survey to compare the standing of U.S. firms relative to their key competitors within their industry in Japan, Germany, and Canada on the workplace innovations that have gained the most attention of managers in recent years. Depending on to whom one listens, TQM is the most recent managerial fad to capture American industry, or a systemic agent of change and transformation.[6] We do not subscribe to either of these extreme views. We prefer to look at the data and let them speak for themselves before drawing conclusions on the current or potential importance and sustainability of TQM practices.

Table 4-1 shows the distribution of each of the workplace practices included in our national establishment survey, for all industries and core occupations together, for two levels of adoption: whether the practice is used at all and whether at least 50 percent of core employees are involved.

It is clear if we simply ask whether a given practice is in use among any fraction of core employees, we would conclude that the workplaceelements of the mutual gains model are quite widespread.

Table 4-1

Percentage at Any Percent Level of Penetration

	All	*Manufacturing*
Teams	54.5%	50.1%
Rotation	43.4	55.6
TQM	33.5	44.9
QC	40.8	45.6
Nothing	21.8	16.0

Percentage at 50 Percent Level of Penetration

	All	*Manufacturing*
Teams	40.5%	32.3%
Rotation	26.6	37.4
TQM	24.5	32.1
QC	27.4	29.7
Nothing	36.0	33.2

Source: The data in Tables 4-1 through 4-6 are drawn from our national establishment survey. See Paul Osterman, "How Common Is Workplace Transformation and How Can We Explain Who Adopts It?" *Industrial and Labor Relations Review,* January 1994, pp. 175–188.

For example, more than half the establishments use teams and 33.5 percent of the establishments employ TQM.

A somewhat different picture of the extent of adoption emerges when we look at the percentage of the work force actually involved. We explore this issue in more depth by examining the number of establishments in which 50 percent or more of employees in these core jobs are covered by these practices. Using this measure reduces the estimates of the amount of innovation quite sharply. Each practice falls by roughly 15 percentage points. For example, 40 percent of these establishments report that half or more core workers are organized into teams, 27 percent have job rotation plans or quality circles covering half or more of their workers, and 24 percent of these organizations use TQM techniques.

These data lead to the question of whether the practices form groups from which emerge identifiable patterns that might be thought of as the mutual gains systems discussed in Chapter 3. Table 4-2 shows how the practices cluster together when a 50 percent coverage threshold is set (no conclusions are changed when other thresholds are imposed).

Table 4-2
Clustering of Work Practices (50 percent or more penetration)

	Entire Sample	*Manufacturing/Blue-Collar*
Nothing	36.0%	33.2%
All	4.8	5.0
Teams Only	14.4	5.5
Rotation Only	7.0	11.7
QC Only	3.1	2.4
TQM Only	2.6	4.5
Team/Rotation	4.8	4.6
Team/QC	4.3	3.3
Team/TQM	4.6	4.2
Rotation/QC	3.0	3.3
Rotation/TQM	1.5	4.5
TQM/QC	4.4	4.9
Team/TQM/QC	3.6	4.2
Team/Rotation/TQM	1.2	1.6
Team/Rotation/QC	2.3	3.4
Rotation/TQM/QC	1.4	2.9

It appears that there is no single major dominant cluster of practices. There is some representation for each of the possible combinations and, in most cases, the distribution of clusters seems rather even. This is further confirmation of a point made in Chapter 3: although the literature (and our own model) suggests that these practices go together and that the maximum benefit is apt to be derived from their combination, firms tend to adopt them either singly or in diverse mixtures or patterns. No single combination is likely to fit all circumstances. Perhaps this reflects the diversity of the American economy, or the incremental nature of the organizational change processes followed in most firms.

It is also worthwhile to examine how the use of these work practices varies by core occupation and industry. The data are shown in Tables 4-3 and 4-4 for the five occupations and three clusters of industries. It is obvious that there is considerable variation. When one examines occupation first, it is not surprising to learn that clerical work lags behind the other groups in the use of these practices. There are,

Table 4-3
Distribution of Work Practices by Core Occupation
(50 percent or higher level of adoption)

	Professional/ Technical	*Sales*	*Clerical*	*Service*	*Blue- Collar*
Teams	46.9%	47.9%	33.2%	46.8%	31.1%
Rotation	15.1	18.2	13.7	35.2	32.3
TQM	52.3	11.7	4.8	26.2	22.9
QC	37.4	25.6	20.4	19.4	29.2
Nothing	27.8	43.2	39.5	32.9	36.5

Table 4-4
Distribution of Work Practices by Industry
(50 percent or higher level of adoption)

	Wholesale/ Retail Trade	*Manufacturing*	*Finance, Insurance, Real Estate*	*Business, Legal, Health, and Engineering Services*
Teams	40.6%	32.3%	42.6%	54.7%
Rotation	31.9	37.4	23.3	21.2
TQM	12.2	32.1	4.3	55.0
QC	20.5	29.7	16.7	41.6
Nothing	41.8	33.2	41.7	21.3

however, fewer expected patterns across the other groups. In particular, the use of teams is much more widespread among white-collar employees than among blue-collar workers. By contrast, job rotation is more of a blue-collar phenomenon. TQM practices are reported to be more widespread among white- than blue-collar occupations.

The industrial patterns mimic the occupational data, which is to be expected given that most core manufacturing employees are blue collar and most core nonmanufacturing employees are white collar. The only real surprise in these data is the very low adoption rates of these innovations in finance, insurance, and real estate. This is particularly true with respect to quality practices, a finding we see replicated in the international TQM survey.

A final question is whether it is possible to provide a summary figure regarding the use of these mutual gains workplace practices. The numerous definitions in the literature make this a difficult question to answer. As noted, there is no dominant pattern. One simple way to summarize these data, however, is to consider an organization as a significant user of mutual gains practices if at least two practices are in place with a 50 percent or higher involvement of core employees in each. This is a rather liberal definition since it does not impose any requirements on the amount of influence actually decentralized to these teams, problem-solving groups, or employees. Nor does it require that these workplace innovations be combined with other human resource practices that we believe are helpful (perhaps essential) to sustaining participation, teamwork, and related workplace innovations over time. By using this liberal definition we therefore give the benefit of the doubt to those who would argue that we might otherwise minimize the amount of progress made in industry to date.

By this definition, 36.6 percent of the entire sample, 43.0 percent of nonmanufacturing, and 35.9 percent of manufacturing establishments are significant users of workplace innovations. These estimates are considerably higher than those commonly cited.[7] Although our definition is a liberal one, we believe it is a closer approximation of current practice than other accounts that rely on either corporate-level estimates or samples that are not representative of the overall economy. Our estimates may also be higher than others because we chose to focus on the subset of an establishment's work force that is central to its operations and thereby exclude a variety of managerial, staff, and auxiliary service personnel for which these practices are likely to have less relevance. But such core jobs are those which need to be involved if these innovations are to produce the gains they promise for individual firms and the overall economy.

The international TQM survey data provide another snapshot of the extent of diffusion of these practices and put the U.S. experience to date in an international and cross-industry perspective. Figure 4-1 and Figure 4-2 present the results of this survey. Figure 4-1 reports the international comparisons of the average use of twenty-one TQM tools in the auto and computer industries in the United States, Canada, Germany, and Japan. Figure 4-2 looks more closely at the distribution across four industries in Canada and the United States: autos, computers, banking, and health care. Unfortunately, insufficient data were

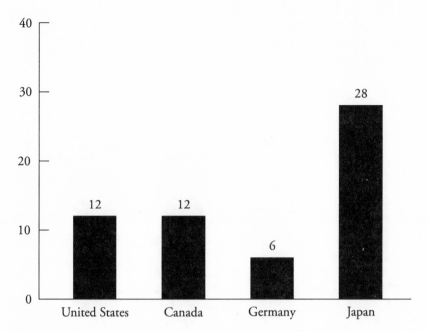

Figure 4-1
Percentage of Average Quality Tool Usage
Manufacturing

obtained from the banking and health care industries in Japan and Germany to warrant inclusion of these industries in the data base.

The measure of adoption used here is the percentage of the work force in specific business units (establishments) that reported using these practices.[8] The data in Figure 4-1 show that American firms lag Japan in the average use of most of these practices but are ahead of Germany and at about the same level of use as Canada. Specifically, 12 percent of the employees of these firms in the United States and Canada are using these practices, 6 percent in Germany, and 28 percent in Japan. Looking at the U.S. industry comparisons in Figure 4-2, one sees that the auto industry is ahead of the computer industry, and both these manufacturing industries are far greater users of TQM practices than are U.S. banking and health care firms. With one exception, the same pattern is true for Canada. The exception seems to be the Canadian banking industry, in which TQM practices are reported to cover 20 percent of the employees in the firms participating in this survey.

Because these numbers use the average rate of use of twenty-one different TQM techniques, one might argue that not all these

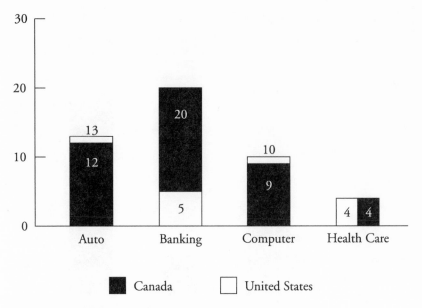

Figure 4-2
Percentage of Average Quality Tool Usage
North America

techniques are relevant to different settings. Indeed, the ones that receive the most attention in American industry are use of statistical process control methods and related charting and analysis procedures. A closer examination of the use of these techniques does show a higher rate of usage in the auto and computer industries. In autos, nearly all firms report using statistical quality control techniques and related charting and analysis tools somewhere in their firms. However, a majority of workers are reported to use these procedures in only about 30 percent of firms in this industry. The rate of adoption and diffusion across the work force is slightly lower in the computer industry and, as noted, almost no establishments report having a majority of employees using these basic tools in health care or banking. Moreover, once one goes beyond these basic TQM tools to more advanced techniques such as use of experiments, failure mode analysis, and quality function deployment, the proportion of firms involving a majority of employees falls to below 10 percent in virtually all industries in the United States and Canada.[9] In contrast, these are more widely used techniques in the Japanese auto and computer firms. These data suggest that TQM practices are still in the early experimental or trial stages of adoption in American industry.

It is worth comparing the results of the other study most like ours, the 1987 GAO-sponsored survey and its 1990 follow-up conducted by Edward Lawler, Susan Mohrman, and Gerald Ledford, Jr. This survey had a different sampling strategy: it was limited to the *Fortune* 1000 firms, and questions were directed to the corporate human resources department regarding practices in the entire organization. Nonetheless, the results are roughly consistent with ours. In 1990 they found that 56 percent in their sample had quality circles and that 47 percent had self-managed work teams. However, in both cases the percentage of employees covered by these practices averaged less than 20 percent for those firms which had the practice.[10]

Determinants of Workplace Innovations

Figure 4-3 is a schematic diagram of the factors that research to date suggests influence the adoption and sustainability of workplace

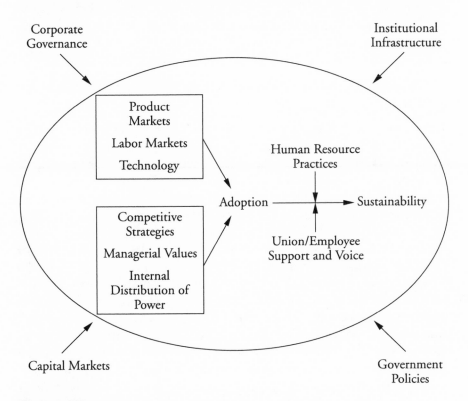

Figure 4-3
Adoption and Sustainability of Workplace Innovations

innovations in American firms. The first thing to note about this model are the factors outside the circle: capital markets and corporate governance structures, institutional infrastructure, and government policies. We discuss the role these factors play in later chapters because we see them as general features or constants in the American environment that affect the overall rate of diffusion of innovations across the economy. Here we focus on the specific forces affecting individual firms that help account for variation or differences in the adoption and sustainability of innovations.

Our examination of the model proceeds in three steps. We first lay out the arguments underlying each of the factors highlighted in the model. As we do so, we present case examples to illustrate the importance of each. We then draw on our survey data to measure and test more formally some of the propositions found in the model.

Before turning to the survey, however, we have to consider an alternative argument in some detail: technological determinism. This is the view that the choice of a human resource strategy and practices is really not up to individual firms or managers at all. Technological requirements of the production process determine the quantity, skill level, and price of labor required.

Technology and Production Strategies: Constraint or Option?

Just as some might argue that market forces are deterministic, others might argue that changes in technology will automatically require or lead to adoption of mutual gains workplace practices. Yet the available evidence neither supports this deterministic view of technology nor suggests that the process by which new technologies are designed and implemented necessarily promotes complementary workplace innovations.[11]

The technological determinism view dates back to the days of Frederick Taylor and scientific management. Taylor argued at the beginning of the century that there is one best way to organize production and work.[12] If properly left in the hands of the technically trained engineers, the appropriate technologies would be chosen and the work system and appropriate piecework compensation system would thereby be determined. Although the argument that technology or engineering science per se uniquely determines skill levels and other employment practices has been generally debunked and rejected,[13] alternative models have led to inconclusive predictions about the *direction* of the effect that modern technology has on skills. For a long time, industrial engineers and personnel specialists debated whether modern technology would produce a natural "up-skilling" or "de-skilling" in the demand for labor. It turns out, as so often is the case in the social sciences, that "it all depends." And it depends a great deal on *who* develops the technology, on the training and world views that designers and developers have of workers and production systems, and on the strategies to which the technology is put in place to pursue.

Consider the typical or traditional process by which new technology is developed and implemented in U.S. firms. The design of new process technology is normally housed in an industrial engineering department. As our colleague Robert Thomas has shown, the education, professional norms, world views, and personal interests of engineers, and the organization routines used to allocate resources to projects and design technologies, all influence how engineers choose technical solutions to workplace problems and how they approach the design process.[14] Engineers educated in American universities have been trained to design equipment that minimizes both the number of workers required (lowers labor costs) and eliminates potential variability in performance owing to "human error." If the goal is simply to "cut heads," i.e., reduce costs and gain greater control via increased investment in automated equipment, the result is often not only to reduce demand for labor but also to reduce the skills of the remaining workers.

This technical approach is not limited to manufacturing technologies or industrial engineers. We observed it in our work at Saturn. Although Saturn's philosophy and organizational design principles emphasize the centrality of self-managing work teams, the information systems developed to support the teams by Saturn's information systems specialists largely resembled traditional management and control systems. That is, they were designed to provide management with the information needed to monitor and control team performance. As a result, the information systems were not used by the teams to do their work. Data were entered as necessary to meet various reporting requirements, but they were not used to diagnose, track, or solve problems. Therefore, Benjamin Whipple, one of our Ph.D. students at Saturn, worked with a sample of team members to develop a "team tool kit," i.e., an information system that provides the team members what they told Whipple they would find helpful to solve problems and perform their various duties. This approach was well received by the teams but met with great resistance from Saturn's information systems specialists. Eventually, however, these specialists recognized the value of this alternative approach and sought to replicate it across the organization.[15]

What are the consequences of this world view of the engineer and information system designer? We return to the best evidence on this question so far—data collected by the MIT worldwide auto industry study.

In 1985, Haruo Shimada, our colleague at Keio University in Japan, took advantage of a year's sabbatical at MIT and teamed up with Ph.D. student John Paul MacDuffie to study Japanese and U.S. human resource practices in the auto industry. The most significant insight that emerged from their initial research and the studies that followed was that the demand for innovative workplace practices and their associated human resource policies is partly a function of the manufacturing strategy utilized in a plant. They first studied the Japanese "transplants" in the U.S. auto industry, i.e., Japanese-owned plants or U.S.-Japanese joint ventures operating in North America. These case studies found that the Japanese human resource management system arose not from unique features of the Japanese culture but from the manufacturing strategies of just-in-time inventory, small-lot production, and statistical quality control, all of which required high levels of worker commitment, skill, training, and participation in problem solving.[16]

Another MIT colleague, Michael Cusumano, reached similar conclusions in his detailed historical study of Nissan and Toyota in Japan.[17] He showed that the absence of natural advantages in raw materials or advanced technologies led these firms, and Toyota in particular, to develop manufacturing systems that relied heavily on human input. This put a premium on developing skills, attention to solving small problems in ways that made incremental improvements in the technologies and processes available to the resource-constrained Japanese, and over time led to a tighter integration of what Shimada and MacDuffie later called the "hardware" and "humanware" dimensions of the production system. As noted in Chapter 3, the follow-up quantitative tests of this model by MacDuffie and John Krafcik showed that world-class manufacturing results—simultaneous attainment of high productivity and high quality—were achieved in auto assembly plants that successfully integrated manufacturing practices such as just-in-time inventory techniques and statistical quality control with innovations in work systems and human resource practices.[18]

In recent years, recognition of the need to break down the engineering or information system specialists' monopoly on the design of new technology or work systems has led some organizations to try to better integrate the design of technologies with that of work systems. Reviving ideas from the sociotechnical school of thought,[19] firms such as Xerox, Boeing, Ford, and GM have formed teams of shop-floor workers, supervisors, human resource staff, and engineers to design the layout and choose the equipment of new plants or work units. These efforts have generally been positive when they were accompanied by strong leadership skills, high levels of trust, diverse technical and organizational expertise, and effective communications, negotiations, and conflict resolution.[20] But as the work of another colleague, Marcie Tyre, has shown, U.S. engineers and workers appear to be less efficient and effective when collaborating than comparable groups of engineers and workers in Germany and Italy.[21]

Unfortunately, these technology and manufacturing process variables were not addressed in either survey, so we are limited to these cases and related studies. But we include these variables in this discussion because the data convince us that both technology and manufacturing strategies have not only played important roles in helping or limiting adoption of workplace innovations in the past but, given the pace of technological innovation today and expected in the future, they offer tremendous opportunities for helping spread such innovations across the economy. But new technology will not automatically promote diffusion of workplace innovations. Technological change will do so only if decision makers consciously use it for this purpose and conceive of technological and organizational innovation as an integrated process.

Survey Results on Diffusion

We now turn to the other considerations in our model of diffusion and examine them with the aid of the national establishment survey. The survey results are reported in Exhibit 4-2, in summary form. The specific quantitative estimates of these variables (primarily derived from regression equations) are reported elsewhere for those interested in the technical underpinnings of the results discussed here.[22]

In addition to technology, the model starts with discussion of the influence of additional external environmental factors—product-market, labor-market, and demographic or occupational characteristics—that constrain the choices firms have in designing workplace practices.

Role of Market Forces

There is no question that product and labor-market forces set the upper and lower boundaries on the quantity and quality of labor an organization requires. Similarly, demonstrably superior ways of

Exhibit 4-2
Impact of Selected Variables on the Probability of Using at Least One Transformed Work Practice at the 50 Percent or Higher Diffusion Level

Age
   Establishments ten years older than average are 1.5 percent less likely.

Compete in International Markets
   If the establishment competes in international markets, it is 26.9 percent more likely.

Be Part of a Larger Organization
   If the establishment is part of a larger organization, it is 14.0 percent more likely.

Have a High-Skill Technology
   If the skill level of the technology is rated as high, it is 14.2 percent more likely.

Believe It Is Appropriate to Have Policies for Improving the Personal Life of Its Employees
   If the establishment believes it is appropriate to have policies to improve the personal and family life of its employees, it is 23.5 percent more likely.

Emphasize Quality and Service Relative to Cost in Its Competitive Strategy
   If the establishment is one standard deviation higher than the average on our strategy index, it is 10.7 percent more likely.

Note: The fraction of establishments that have at least one practice at the 50 percent level is .64. Hence, an establishment that is part of a larger firm (and is like other establishments in all other respects) has an average probability of .73 or, as the text indicates, it is 14 percent more likely. These estimates represent the significant coefficients in logistic regressions reported in Paul Osterman, "How Common Is Workplace Transformation and How Can We Explain Who Adopts It?" *Industrial and Labor Relations Review,* January 1994, pp. 175–188.

organizing work and managing employees should diffuse naturally by the pressure of market forces. Indeed, these "best practices" should be diffusing more rapidly or broadly in those environments most exposed to international or domestic competitive pressures.

Since much of the pressure to adopt new workplace systems has come from foreign competitors, it seems reasonable to expect that establishments which operate in international markets are more apt to be exposed to new ideas and practices. Indeed, there is both case study and survey evidence to suggest that international competition has played a significant role in inducing firms to adopt workplace innovations. The innovations in the auto industry and at Xerox discussed in Chapter 3 largely arose in the early 1980s when GM, Ford, Chrysler, and Xerox recognized that they were losing significant market share to Japanese competitors. In the case of Xerox, its Japanese partner, Fuji-Xerox, served as an important laboratory from which the American company learned about the value of TQM and related organizational innovations.[23] Moreover, nearly every case study we know of notes that an economic crisis of some magnitude provided the initial stimulus to consider changing workplace and human resource practices. Inertia and start-up costs are sufficient to deter organizations from engaging in continuous redesign of practices—they must feel sufficient pain before taking the risks associated with embarking on a new path.

Some firms go a step farther and use the threat of moving production overseas to convince plant managers, employees, and union leaders to introduce workplace innovations that improve quality and cost performance. Levi Strauss, for example, made this point explicit in its efforts to encourage diffusion of team-based production and human resource practices in its U.S. manufacturing plants. Levi's vice president of manufacturing, Peter Jacoby, made this point in a talk given to an international trade conference at MIT in 1992: either U.S. plants will improve their quality, customer service, and flexibility or more products will be sourced in low-wage countries.

The U.S. and the international TQM survey data provide considerable support for the proposition that international competition in particular has been a driving force leading firms to adopt workplace innovations. As noted earlier, the international quality survey data show that the two U.S. industries most exposed to international competition, autos and computers, are much more widespread adopters of TQM techniques than are firms in banking and health care. The national establishment survey provides even more direct evidence. The amount of international competition a firm experienced was significantly related to its rate of adoption of workplace innovations. The estimates shown in Exhibit 4-2 suggest that firms reporting significant international competition are approximately 27 percent more likely to report that 50 percent of their employees are engaged in some form of workplace innovation than firms that report little or no exposure to international competition. Interestingly, however, domestic competition was not significantly related to workplace innovation. Thus, there appears to be something different about international and domestic competition. Perhaps domestic competition is more mixed—coming from some firms that emphasize competition on quality and innovation grounds and others that emphasize cost and price competition. We now take a closer look at what our data say about this issue.

Competitive Strategies

Both the strategic human resource management and the competitive strategy literature argue that the type of competitive strategy followed by a firm is the critical determinant of its human resource practices. Those firms which respond to increased competition by emphasizing product and service quality, differentiation, technological innovation, and speed to market should have the most innovative practices.

Jeffrey Arthur's study of the competitive and industrial relations strategies in a sample of steel industry minimills tested this hypothesis.[24] He found a strong relationship between these two choices. Ninety percent of the minimills that followed a cost-minimization competitive strategy adopted traditional, cost reduction–oriented industrial relations strategies (low relative wages, narrow job classifications, tight supervision, little employee involvement in problem solving or decision making, and so forth). In contrast, 60 percent of the mills that followed a product differentiation strategy adopted mutual gains industrial relations practices. Interestingly, in this sector union status (about half the mills were unionized) was not a significant predictor of industrial relations strategy. (The national establishment survey also found union status not significant.)

Examples from other industries reinforce the findings of the mini-mill study. Recall the comparisons made in Chapter 3 of Continental Airline's efforts to be the low-cost carrier versus the service quality strategies of Delta Air Lines.

Our national establishment survey made a special effort to obtain a good measure of the relative importance of cost versus these other competitive strategies. Respondents were asked to estimate the importance of cost as a competitive strategy relative to the importance of quality, service, and product variety. The results of this analysis appear in Exhibit 4-2. Firms that place greater reliance on quality, service, and variety relative to costs are more active users of workplace innovations than those that rely more heavily on cost as a competitive strategy. Specifically, these estimates suggest that if a firm is one standard deviation above average with respect to its emphasis on quality, service, and variety, it is about 11 percent more likely to employ at least one innovative work practice at the 50 percent or better level. The international TQM survey found similar but weaker results with its competitive strategy variable. Thus, it is not just product-market competition per se that matters, but how firms choose to respond to increased competition. Market forces do not act with an invisible, deterministic hand to diffuse workplace innovations.

Management Values

Although market and technological factors play important roles in shaping firm-level work organization and human resource practices, they do not tell the whole story. Firms have a significant amount of choice over the type of employment system adopted. Indeed, this range of variation is central to our theory, since we argue that the lack of external—government, labor, or other institutional—forces and the political weakness of human resource professionals within American firms explain both the limited range of diffusion of workplace innovations and the limited prospects for diffusion in the future. Therefore we need to look at the key factors within the firm that influence the adoption and sustainability of innovations. The first organizational factor that we believe warrants consideration is the values espoused by the top management.

The values of the founder have been shown to matter significantly in leading firms such as Polaroid, Hewlett-Packard, IBM, DEC, and Xerox. In previous work we also found that values exert a significant effect on labor relations strategies adopted within a firm.[25] Moreover, the importance of top management commitment to organizational change is so well accepted that it is almost a cliché to repeat the fact. We would therefore expect managerial values to be just as important in this area as in others that require strategic direction and leadership.

In order to measure managerial values we asked respondents to our survey whether their organizations believe it is appropriate to take responsibility for the personal and family well-being of their employees. The reason for this question was that our survey was designed to explore broad work-family policy issues as well as work organization issues. We treated the answer to this question as an indicator of the extent to which humanistic values were important in these organizations. Slightly more than half the respondents (55 percent), reported that these humanistic values are considered important in their organizations.[26] Exhibit 4-2 shows how respondents' answers to this question differ between organizations with high and low rates of workplace innovation. Those reporting that their organization espouses these values are 24 percent more likely to adopt workplace innovations than firms reporting less support for work-family values. This finding reinforces the case study evidence that the values ingrained in the culture of an organization have an important effect on organizational practice.

The central conclusion from all these data seems to be that while market pressures provide the initial motivation to innovate, there are no deterministic market or technical forces that diffuse these innovations. Instead, firms have considerable discretion over whether to adopt workplace innovations. Moreover, as we will see in the next section, while external market pressures are an important stimulus to the initial adoption decision, it is internal organizational dynamics and relationships that determine whether, once adopted, these innovations are sustained over time.

Sustainability

So far we have stressed the forces that are leading some American companies to move toward mutual gains workplace practices. But what is to keep these innovations from becoming just another of the fads that have come and gone in American industry? This is a real concern because the few historical or longitudinal studies available show that there is a relatively high attrition rate for workplace innovations. Consider, for example, the evidence from employee representation plans established after World War I by companies partly to ward off union organizing. These plans spread quite rapidly between 1916 and the mid-1920s during the height of the "red scare"—the fear that the Bolshevik revolution in Russia might spread to the United States via trade union organizing efforts. At their peak, these programs covered just under 10 percent of the work force, mainly in the largest manufacturing, communication, and financial service firms in the country. But gradually over the course of the 1920s their growth tapered off as manufacturing employment levels declined, the 1921–1923 recession took its toll on plans in smaller firms, and the threat of union organizing declined. The Great Depression dealt another blow to these efforts. "Company unions" were then outlawed by the passage of the National Labor Relations Act in 1935, which served as the final nail in the coffin of the employee representation or American Plan movement.[27] Perhaps more than any other historical example, the employee representation movement of the 1916–1935 era serves as a historical parallel to the current wave of workplace innovations.

Paul Goodman looked back at the major cases of workplace innovation sponsored in the 1970s by the National Commission on Productivity and Quality of Work and found that none had survived.[28] Other studies reported a high attrition rate for quality circles started in the early 1980s.[29] A longitudinal study in Canada confirms this as well. Gordon Betcherman and Anil Verma found that one-third of the employee participation programs and pay-for-skill programs reported to be in place in establishments surveyed in 1986 were no longer present in 1992.[30] There is no guarantee that once started, these initiatives will be sustained. The question therefore becomes, What influences their staying power? We answer this question by considering the three forces outside the circle in Figure 4-3 in the next three chapters. Here we consider the role of two key forces within the control of decision makers in individual enterprises that our model suggests are critical to sustaining innovations: reinforcing personnel practices and employee and union participation in the innovation process.

In Chapter 3 we suggested that for a company to sustain workplace innovations it must embed them in supporting human resource practices and strategic decisions. Without this support the work practices cannot survive. Three clusters of personnel practices seem to be of special importance: employment security, training, and compensation. The involvement of the human resource staff in strategic decisions also appears to be important. We describe the argument for each of these factors along with case examples, then summarize our survey results.

Although we use our survey data to explore whether the human resource practices contribute to sustainability of workplace innovations, a word of caution is in order. We lack longitudinal data, so we cannot follow the course of workplace innovations and determine in which settings they are sustained and in which they are abandoned. What we can do, however, is ask whether the human resource practices discussed in Chapter 3 as important for reinforcing workplace innovations—commitment to employment security, investment in training and development, and use of some form of contingent compensation system—are present in those firms which have sustained workplace innovations for an extended period of time. This is a second-best strategy, but it provides suggestive evidence of the factors that influence sustainability.

To test propositions concerning sustainability, we turn again to the two surveys. The national establishment survey, as we have already seen, shows that a substantial proportion of American firms have two or more innovative work practices in place at the 50 percent or better adoption rate. The idea of sustainability, however, implies that these practices have been in place for some time. Specifically, we define an establishment as having sustained innovation if the practice has been in place for five or more years. Table 4-5 shows the fraction of establishments having zero through five practices (at the 50 percent level of adoption) that have been in place for five or more years.

It is apparent that the percentage of establishments that meet the sustainability criterion falls well below those which have the practice in place. Indeed, 63 percent of the sample have no innovative practices that meet this criterion! Twenty-four percent have one, and only 13 percent have two or more practices that cover at least 50 percent of their core workers in place for at least five years. This divergence does not necessarily imply that most innovations fail to last: some of the difference may simply be due to the fact that the spread of these policies is fairly new and some have not had the chance to meet the five-year test. Nonetheless, it is striking that the distribution of long-lasting innovations is so limited.

For each of the human resource practices, we tested whether there was a statistically significant relationship between the presence of that practice and whether the organization had sustained innovations in place. These tests controlled for other important factors.[31] The fraction of the establishments that have each of the human resource practices in place is shown in Table 4-6.

Table 4-5
Distribution of Sustained Practices

Number of Practices	Percentage of Organizations
0	63.0
1	23.8
2	9.9
3	2.1
4	1.0
5	0.0

Note: A practice is sustained if it involves 50 percent or better of core employees and has been in place for five or more years.

Table 4-6
Supporting HR Practices and Their Role in Sustainability

Percentage of Establishments That		
Have pay for skill	30.4%	**
Have gains sharing	13.7%	**
Have profit sharing/bonus	44.7%	**
Assign an important role to the HR Department in strategic decisions	54.1%	**
Have an explicit or implicit employment security policy	39.8%	
Percentage of core employees who receive formal off-the-job training	32.0%	
Percentage of core employees who receive cross-training	43.5%	**

Note: ** = statistically significant predictors of sustainability.

Employment Security

As noted in Chapter 3, employment security poses a paradox for both workers and employers. Although it is a well-accepted fact that workers are reluctant to contribute to making the enterprise competitive if they perceive the result to be that they work themselves out of a job, few, if any, individual firms can offer credible, iron-clad guarantees of lifetime job security to employees. Moreover, improved productivity reduces the number of workers required unless the productivity gains increase demand for the firm's products or are recycled into new job-producing investments within the firm.

What role, then, does employment security play in the innovation process? Several examples may illustrate the complexities involved here and reinforce the conclusion that employment security may be more important in sustaining support for innovations once begun than in the initial stages of the adoption and implementation process.

Consider the now familiar case of Xerox and its experience with the decision of whether to contract out the assembly of wiring harnesses for its copiers. About a year after starting its employee involvement process, Xerox announced a significant downsizing and employee severance program that reduced its blue-collar work force by nearly 15 percent. As part of efforts to reduce manufacturing costs, it also began seeking opportunities to outsource work that could be purchased more cheaply from outside vendors. One area targeted for outsourcing was the assembly of wiring harnesses. Management estimated that it could save more than $3 million by contracting out this work and thereby reduce its work force by approximately 300 people. But employees and the local union, already upset by the general work force reductions, were even more upset by this decision because there was an active employee involvement program in the wiring harness area. The employees and the local union made it clear to management that if it went ahead and outsourced this work, the employee involvement effort was doomed. As a result, company and union leaders agreed to let a cross-functional task force of workers, supervisors, engineers, and accountants study this operation to see if changes could be made to reduce the costs of doing the work in house enough to be competitive with outside vendors. The task force produced recommendations for reorganizing work, supervision, accounting systems, plant layout, work scheduling, and staffing that exceeded the $3 million target. Subsequently, the company and union agreed to use a similar procedure in all future contracting-out situations and in return negotiated a no-layoff pledge for the following three years.

Our own surveys and case study evidence showed that unless something had been done to deal with employment security concerns of the work force, the overall employee participation program would soon have lost the support of the work force.[32] Management, on the other hand, would never have agreed to a no-layoff pledge without some expectation that it had already gotten the overall numbers down to an appropriate level, given projections of future product demand, and that it had the flexibility to contract out high-cost operations or work with the employees and the union to introduce changes needed to make those operations productive.

Another vivid example of the importance of employment security is the experience of Analog Devices with its TQM program. Analog Devices is one of Massachussetts's prime high-technology success stories. Its founder and CEO, Ray Stata, has been a leading advocate of TQM, organizational learning, and other human resource innovations. The company started and, by all accounts, implemented a highly successful TQM program in the late 1980s. A systems dynamics study of the plan, conducted by our MIT colleagues Fred Kofman, Nelson Repenning, and John Sterman, documented how over the first several years of the effort the training of employees and managers in TQM methods paid off in significant improvements in product quality, on-time delivery, reduction in cycle time, and increases in productivity.

Unfortunately, these improvements coincided with a stagnating market for the company's products that paralleled the declining fortunes of other high-technology firms in New England. Because new products had not been developed to utilize the excess human and manufacturing capacity that was freed up, the firm began to appear overstaffed to outside analysts. The company's stock price plummeted and Analog was forced to lay off employees for the first time in its history. The layoff, however, led to a breakdown in the trust and commitment built up within the work force, and the effectiveness of the TQM efforts declined and atrophied.[33]

These cases illustrate that employment security, productivity, and workplace innovations are highly interdependent. But given the complex bargains, trade-offs, dynamics, and lagged effects involved, it is not surprising that cross-sectional surveys do not necessarily observe a positive correlation between employment security and workplace innovation. Indeed, this is exactly what we found in our establishment survey. Although 40 percent of the firms indicated that they followed policies to minimize or avoid layoffs, those which reported making these efforts had no higher rates of innovation or more sustained innovation over the five years examined than did firms that did not indicate a commitment to avoiding or minimizing layoffs. This suggests that if employment security is critical to workpace innovation, it either has to come from someplace other than the policies of individual firms or individual firms have to manage their resources in a significantly different way. The paradox is real and presents an important challenge to public policy makers, private decision makers, and individual employees alike.

Training

A second human resource practice believed to be important to sustaining workplace innovations is training and development. New work systems entail higher levels of employee skill, and to sustain these systems the employer must be willing to invest in the skills of the labor force. High levels of training investments do not come naturally to American employers, partly for the reasons just noted—firms' investments in training are lost when employees leave an organization, either voluntarily or involuntarily. One of the two training variables in our survey—cross-training of workers for different jobs—was significantly related to sustainability.[34]

Compensation and Reward Systems

Compensation and reward systems are often noted as additional human resource practices that can either reinforce or deter support for workplace innovations. Case study evidence suggests that many firms which have moved toward more flexible work organization have accompanied the shifts in work systems with comparable changes in compensation practices. This is on the theory that when employees are given more power to determine outcomes, they should have a financial stake in enterprise success. Indeed, David Levine and Laura Tyson's review of the evidence led them to conclude that employee participation and contingent compensation, taken together, produce stronger positive payoffs than each can achieve individually.[35]

Our survey asked about three different contingent pay practices: pay for skills, group incentives or gain-sharing plans, and profit-sharing or bonus plans. All pay practices proved to be significantly related to sustained innovation.

The Strategic Role of Human Resources

Throughout this book we have stressed our argument that in those firms in which there is a powerful constituency for human resource considerations, innovations are more likely to take root. We noted that although human resource departments have aspired to play a more strategic role in decision making, by and large this has proved difficult to achieve and sustain in American corporations. We explore the reasons for this in greater depth in the next chapter. Our national establishment survey provides some unique evidence on this point. In those establishments in which the human resource department is reported to be an important player in policy making regarding strategic issues, workplace innovations are more likely to be sustained.

The international TQM survey also contained measures of the use of a variety of reinforcing human resource practices, although they do not correspond exactly to those used in our national survey. The TQM list of human resource practices covered training, various group activities, suggestion systems, merit pay, group incentive pay, and employee involvement in strategic decision making. Unfortunately there was no measure pertaining to employment security in the survey. We examined sustainability of innovations in TQM in several ways similar to what we did with the U.S. establishment data, by looking at the extent to which firms sustained their commitment to these practices over a three-year period and increased the percentage of their employees covered by TQM. An index measuring the number of reinforcing human resource practices in place in these firms proved to be the strongest and most consistent predictor of persistence and growth in quality practices over time.

Taken together, the establishment and TQM survey results strongly support the view that workplace innovations are more likely to be sustained over time when reinforced by human resource practices governing training, compensation, at least some aspects of staffing, and where human resources have an important role in strategic decision making. Employment security, however, remains a more complicated matter.

Unions and Employee Voice

One of the more controversial issues in U.S. circles involves the question of the effects of unions on the innovation process in organizations. It may come as a surprise to some that, congruent with other surveys completed in recent years, neither the establishment survey nor the international TQM survey found a significant negative or positive relationship between the presence or absence of a union and the initial adoption of workplace innovations. But our own case study provides many examples of situations in which, if it weren't for the support and the insistence of union leaders, initial management commitment to the innovation process would have given way in the face of financial or other obstacles. Similarly, we have observed cases in which innovations have been held hostage to broader labor-management conflicts or slowed up because of internal union political conflicts or leadership challenges. Thus, we do not believe that there is a universal "union effect" on the innovation process. However, ever since the initial stages of research on employee participation, we have consistently found that where unions are present, the innovation process is unlikely to succeed unless the union leaders are involved as joint partners.[36] More recent work has led to a stronger hypothesis: the active involvement and support of unions increases the sustainability of the innovation process.

One case that brought home the power of this hypothesis is our study of Chrysler and the United Auto Workers' (UAW) joint efforts to introduce team production and labor-management systems in a number of it plants. The joint agreements covering these plants are known as modern operating agreements (MOAs). We studied the implementation of MOAs in six Chrysler/UAW plants between 1989 and 1991.[37] During this time Chrysler experienced severe financial losses and hovered near the edge of bankruptcy. Despite this, the company and the union continued their mutual support for the MOA process and made the more than $300 million investment in training needed to implement the massive shift from the traditional structure of jobs, compensation, labor relations rules, and management systems to full-fledged team production and labor-management systems in these plants.

Even more interesting was the fact that during this time a number of rather major conflicts erupted in the company-union relationship and among corporate executives. For example, at one point the company announced its intention to sell its parts business but changed its mind in the face of strong union opposition. At another point the company removed the UAW president from its board of directors (there's more about this in Chapter 6). Conflicts developed among several high-level company executives over whether the MOA process was paying off and over how to evaluate its long-run potential. Despite these difficulties and the enormous financial problems the company experienced, the parties continued to support the MOA process. Our sense is that the process would not have survived these countervailing pressures in the absence of a joint union-management commitment to and management of the innovation process.

A similar conclusion emerges from other cases. We have described the sustaining role that the union played in critical pivotal events in the Xerox case. At Saturn we saw the local union leaders reinforce the underlying principles of participation, commitment to quality, and support for training and teamwork. Indeed, at one point in 1992 the Saturn employees wore black armbands to protest what they perceived as a weakening of management's commitment to quality.

Our international quality survey data reinforce these case study findings. When we examined the relationships between sustainability and the presence and role of a union, we found that, on average, slightly fewer unionized firms lost ground in the percentage of employees covered over the three-year period and that, on average, coverage within unionized firms grew marginally greater than in nonunion firms. But more important than the simple union-nonunion difference was the *role* of unions where they existed. When unions played a consultative role with management in strategic decision making, TQM practices expanded more rapidly. In the few (less than 8 percent) cases in which unions were reported to be interfering with use of TQM techniques, they slowed the pace of adoption. More specifically, the presence of a supportive union that was consulted by management increased the use of TQM by 36 percent relative to the absence of a union. Where a union was present but uninvolved and unsupportive, the rate of adoption was slowed by approximately 32 percent compared with nonunion settings.

These results are consistent with those of an earlier study of quality circles by Robert Drago[38] and a recent follow-up survey of labor-management committees in metalworking plants by Mary Ellen Kelley.[39] Both studies found about a 30 percent attrition rate for these programs, but those in unionized firms were more likely to be sustained than those in nonunion firms. Thus, unions today no longer appear to be a significant obstacle to workplace innovation. On the contrary, if involved as a joint partner in managing an innovation and if consulted in strategic affairs of a company, unions can and do serve as an important positive force in sustaining commitment to these innovations. These results suggest the importance of having a mutual, joint commitment of two independent forces to workplace innovation.

Summary and Conclusions

The data presented in this chapter suggest that the majority of American workplaces have experimented with some form of workplace innovation. The same is true with respect to adoption of a variety of TQM techniques. The good news is that there is no lack of information about these practices and that a good deal of experimentation is under way in American industry. Indeed, our interpretation of these data suggests that there is more innovative activity in American industry than most previous estimates have suggested. Using the criteria of whether at least 50 percent of an establishment's core work force is covered by two or more workplace innovations, we conclude that innovations have spread to at least one-third of American workplaces. The TQM survey shows a similar, albeit slightly more pessimistic, picture. Using the same 50 percent criterion, it found that TQM practices cover, perhaps at most, 20 percent of American workplaces in the auto industry, 10 to 15 percent in the computer industry, and well below 10 percent in service industries such as banking or health care.

Firms that are more likely to adopt innovations are exposed to international competition, require above-average skills in their jobs, espouse humanistic values, follow competitive strategies that emphasize quality and product innovation more than costs, give much consideration to human resource issues in managerial decisions, and, among manufacturing firms, have adopted flexible production systems.

But not all firms that adopt these innovations are apt to sustain them over time. Those with a better chance of doing so are ones in which a union is present and involved as a co-partner in overseeing the innovation, employee interests are taken into account in strategic management decision making, and other human resource practices involving compensation and reward systems and training policies reinforce workplace innovations.

These are the factors over which individual enterprises have at least partial control. The one human resource practice that seems most difficult to control is commitment to employment security, although there is ample evidence that this issue looms heavy in the decisions of individual employees and their representative over whether to support and participate in workplace innovations. It follows that the parties can, to some extent, control their own destiny by attending to these issues. Yet there are formidable obstacles to further diffusion that we believe need to be overcome if the progress and the momentum unfolding in the workplace today are to continue so that the full potential of these innovations is realized. We now turn to a discussion of the broader obstacles and ways to address them.

Appendix

The interviewers used the following definitions when respondents requested clarification.

Self-directed work teams. Employees supervise their own work; workers make their own decisions about pace and flow and occasionally the best way to get work done.

Job rotation. Self-explanatory example: in some banking firms an employee spends six months in the real estate division, six months in pension plans, and so forth. Simply rotating jobs.

Problem-solving groups/quality circles. Quality programs in which employees are involved in problem solving.

Total quality management. Quality control approach that emphasizes the importance of communications, feedback, and teamwork.

chapter five

HUMAN RESOURCES AND ORGANIZATIONAL GOVERNANCE

Last month, when Eastman Kodak's chief executive, Kay Whitmore, announced "involuntary" layoffs—as opposed to the kinder and gentler strategies of early retirement and buyouts—Wall Street staged a little round of applause, bidding Kodak shares up 50 cents to $49.375. Shares had risen to $51.625 by Friday's close.

Layoffs are cheaper than buyouts, Mr. Whitmore said. They also had the appeal of sending a signal to Wall Street that the company was being tough, he added. Mr. Whitmore has caught on that nice guys can finish last in the Wall Street derby.[1] [Kay Whitmore was replaced as CEO of Kodak in 1993.]

"The essence of business leadership . . . is to be able to turn your back on the demands of the financial world." (Edwin H. Land, 1987)[2]

In the previous chapter we emphasized a variety of factors that influence the choice of human resource strategies and the degree to which firms invest in training and development. One of the central findings was that firms which invest heavily in human resources and sustain workplace innovations have elevated human resource policy issues to a high level of influence in corporate decision making and integrated them into their long-term strategies and ongoing operations. Yet why are human resource issues so seldom integrated or weighed heavily in corporate strategic decision making? Are capital markets and their Wall Street agents, as the above quotes seem to suggest, the archenemy of employees and those who argue for greater consideration of human resource issues in corporate policy? Are there ways to bring employee and shareholder interests into better alignment? We take up these issues in this chapter by exploring a controversial hypothesis: the root cause of the weakness of human resources in corporate governance and strategy lies in the basic legal foundations, financial institutions and capital markets, and governance structures of the American corporation.

The argument behind this hypothesis goes as follows. American corporate law establishes the principle that the objective of a firm is to maximize shareholder wealth. This makes obtaining finance capital and maintaining access to capital markets and the investment community the dominant consideration in managerial decision making and produces a governance structure and internal functional distribution of power that reflects the centrality of capital-market reactions to managerial actions and policies. In turn, American capital markets and financial institutions are structured in ways that place great emphasis on short-term profits, costs, and movements in stock prices and relatively less value on long-term investments. Human resource investments are visible for their short-term costs and produce only long-term and difficult-to-measure benefits. As a result, human resource considerations do not weigh heavily and human resource executives are generally among the weakest executives in the corporate hierarchy.

Therefore, achieving a sustainable increase in investment in training and human resource innovation requires changes in corporate governance or capital markets. But for employee and human resource interests to promote *mutual gains* rather than simply greater distribution of a fixed sum of benefits to employees, these new institutional structures and the people who fill them need to add value and be as committed to the goals of the enterprise as those who participate in strategic decision making and corporate governance.

This chapter explores the basis for these arguments and discusses several options that have been put forward for achieving the desired change in corporate governance and decision making. They include changing tax rules and capital-market regulations to lengthen the time horizons of investors, i.e., creating more patient capital markets; changing corporate governance structures to give greater voice to shareholders and to bring shareholder and managerial interests into closer alignment; and giving employees greater voice in corporate governance by encouraging their representation on corporate boards of directors or through European-style works councils.

We present this material as hypotheses rather than final conclusions because these are rather new and as yet rather untested arguments. The hypotheses are based upon two interrelated and expanding bodies of research: (1) debates among American economists over the sources of short time horizons of U.S. managers, and (2) comparative analyses of the financial markets, governance arrangements, and human resource practices of U.S., Japanese, and German firms. We start therefore with a review of these debates.

Time Horizons, Capital Markets, and Investment in Human Resources

One of the most recent arguments to be advanced for U.S. firms' underinvestment in human resources or organizational innovations stems from the broader argument that American managers suffer from short time horizons because they are under strong pressures to maximize the price of their firm's stock in the short run. The logic is as follows:[3]

Conventional finance theory argues that efficient capital markets value corporate investments and expenditures accurately for the long and short run because the price of the stock conveys an accurate estimate of all future cash flows to the company, discounted for the time value of money. But a growing number of economists are beginning to recognize that U.S. capital markets do not approximate this pure model. A compendium of studies sponsored by the Council on Competitiveness and coordinated by Michael Porter at the Harvard Business School explored this hypothesis.[4]

American capital markets, or more precisely the human agents who enact these markets (investors, stock market analysts, debt underwriters, and so forth) have little valid information about the market conditions, investment opportunities and risks, and technological possibilities open to most U.S. firms as they generally have an arm's-length relationship with top management and little effective influence on corporate boards. This produces "information asymmetries," a situation in which corporate managers or insiders have better or more information on market developments and long-term prospects or possibilities than is available to the investment community or the capital markets.[5] These differences in information may in turn lead capital markets to undervalue expenditures that reduce current earnings but promise long-term returns. Thus, managers are discouraged from making investments that promise long-term payoffs but depress current or short-term earnings.

This is especially likely to be the case when intangible investments such as R&D or human resources are concerned, since these are all charged as expenses at the time they are incurred rather than as a long-term debt amortized into the future, which would be the case if the company borrowed money to build a new plant or buy a piece of new equipment. Michael Jacobs provides a concise summary of this argument.

> This [information asymmetries and underinvestment] is a particular problem for intangible investments that fail to show up on the balance sheet. Research and development, employee training, and other expenditures that are not capitalized as assets according to today's accounting norms are important investments in the long-term health and competitiveness of a company, yet they are immediately charged to earnings. Absent a way to communicate the merits of these expenses to shareholders, corporations would tend to minimize the amount of funds allocated to intangibles. This becomes a greater concern as shareholders place increasing emphasis on reported earnings, and disproportionately penalizes companies that invest heavily in training and research.[6]

In a recent meeting, a CEO of a large company made this point vividly.

> When I brief Wall Street analysts on our current earnings, sale projections, downsizing program, and capital spending plans they busily punch all these numbers right into their laptops as I speak. When I then start telling them about our plans to invest in training and reform the workplace, they sit back in their chairs and their eyes glaze over.

Some of the clearest illustrations of the inability of Wall Street analysts to value investments in human resources can be seen in the impatience expressed with firms such as Delta Air Lines and Polaroid over their unwillingness to break with their traditions of employment security and related mutual gains policies. The quotation that opens this chapter is only one of many examples of the Wall Street reaction.

Indeed, these examples are not isolated phenomena. Econometric studies have shown that layoff or other downsizing announcements which reflect a decision to restructure a firm typically produce a small and otherwise unexpected increase in stock prices.[7]

The Case of Cummins Engine

Cummins Engine Company provides a vivid illustration of the links between capital markets, governance structures, and human resource practices in an American firm.[8] Cummins substantially transformed its work systems along the lines we propose and supported these reforms with substantial investments in training and related personnel policies. Yet it came under intense investor pressure for making too many "soft" investments that promised only long-term and largely unquantifiable payoffs. It was able to maintain its strategy only because it was shielded from the investor community partly because a large portion of its stock was in the hands of the founding family and partly because it found patient long-term investors to buy a large equity share. Other firms wanting to invest in human resources may not be so fortunate.

Founded in 1919 by William Irwin and his mechanic Clessie Cummins, who created the original Cummins diesel engine, the company has remained closely held throughout its history. J. Irwin Miller, the founder's nephew, was named general manager and later became CEO. Henry Schacht replaced Miller as CEO in 1977. Schacht visited Japanese plants in 1979 and was inspired to further modernize Cummins's plants and work processes.[9] In 1979, Cummins was the clear leader in its industry. In thirty years it had grown from $43 million to $1.7 billion in sales.

But in the 1980s Cummins faced rising research and engineering costs, competition, and changing customer expectations. The company needed to invest a billion dollars in current and new products at a time when its stock market value was less than $300 million.[10] At the same time, it had already begun to invest heavily in employee training and to introduce teamwork, statistical quality controls, and flexible production techniques in some of its nonunion plants; it was in the midst of extending these practices to its union plants and did not want to abandon its efforts.

In the mid-1980s, Hanson PLC bought large shares of Cummins stock, and a hostile takeover was feared. Edwin Miller, the last representative of the founding family and a substantial shareholder, paid Hanson 7.5 percent above market value to keep the company from outside control.[11]

While fighting immediate threats to its market share and independence, Cummins continued to take the long view—investing in employee training and introducing workplace reforms to both its union and nonunion plants and seeking investors who would share the company's long-term perspective. In response to growing product-market competition in the mid-1980s, the company had increased its efforts to improve product quality.

The company formed the Quality Investigation Trainers, a group of unionized employees with business cards, in the Columbus engine plant. The program was costly because it covered the salaries of seventeen full-time workers and sacrificed their experience from the immediate production process. By 1989, however, there was evidence that the program was paying off. Costs were staying constant or declining in the six months subsequent to introduction of new products rather than, as previously, rising and remaining high for up to eighteen months. Also, there was a general decline in failures per hundred engines as the program progressed.[12] A major personnel journal applauded their efforts, stating that "the Cummins example shows what a real commitment [to training] looks like, and how it can lower costs and improve quality."[13]

Outside investors, however, were getting impatient with the absence of earnings. In late 1988 the business press expressed the opinion that "with his reputation and the company's independence on the line, [Schacht] has to prove his long-term view will finally pay off."[14]

In 1990, Cummins's search for patient capital was rewarded. To secure the capital it needed and to provide the stability it felt its customers and other stakeholders deserved, Cummins sold 27 percent of the company to three of its largest customers, Ford, Tenneco, and Kubota. In a unique and controversial move, Cummins invited its new shareholders to sit on the board, asked them not to sell their shares for six years, and requested that they support the nominating committee's choices for the board during that time.[15]

At the same time, Cummins bought back from the Millers, at a loss to the family, the preferred stock the family had purchased to thwart the takeover attempts. Some debt was also retired at this time, resulting in net stock dilution. But the stock market was pleased and the book value went up. An analyst predicted that "investors like Ford, Tenneco, and Kubota won't let [Schacht] get away with disappointing returns."[16] Another analyst referred to Cummins stock, though "hated by investors," as a good value.[17] There was some evidence too that the company's extensive investments in research and development, as well as its investments in human resources, were beginning to pay off. Owing in part to research and development throughout the 1980s, 64 percent of its sales in 1990 came from products that did not exist in 1981.[18]

Through 1991, however, the losses continued, and by mid-1991 share value was at $35, a new low. Market share also hit a low of just over 35 percent. Analysts were still troubled by the company's debt load, at 40 percent of total capital, and predicted in late 1991 that if business did not improve soon, Cummins would need a cash infusion from equity investors.

The year 1992 was a turning point for Cummins. In the spring, Ford and Chrysler pledged to buy 60,000 Cummins engines over the following two years, and Cummins's stock price rose substantially. The *New York Times* reported that "analysts say the Cummins Engine Company is humming on all cylinders."[19] By 1993 the business press was applauding its growing market share and the profits Cummins was experiencing and heralded Cummins management for having the foresight and fortitude to ignore the criticisms of market analysts in prior years.

Like other examples described in this book, we do not present Cummins as an unqualified success story. Of course it has had financial ups and downs over the years. Indeed the verdict is still out over whether its long-term investment and human resource strategy will pay off for shareholders, customers, and employers. But clearly, the closely held nature of the company, and the patient and knowledgeable capital provided by potential customers, allowed the long-term commitment to an aggressive human resource development and utilization strategy in the face of considerable criticism. As such, the nexus among the capital markets, corporate governance arrangements, and human resource strategies and policies at Cummins nicely illustrate the power of our theoretical arguments regarding the effects of these factors on human resource practices and innovations in American industry.

Human Resource Management and Corporate Governance

If human resource investments and strategies come under pressures from financial markets, what determines the relative priority or influence these issues and concerns receive? Obviously, the personal views and values of a CEO matter, as illustrated by Schacht at Cummins. But to go beyond individual cases we need to look more deeply at a structural issue, namely, Where do human resource considerations and employee interests stand in the overall governance structures and processes of a firm? The best way to explore this issue is to take both a historical and a comparative-international perspective, since there have been wide swings over time and considerable variation across firms in different countries in the influence accorded these issues. At least some of this cross-national variation is attributable to differences in the nature of a corporation and its governance structures.

Human Resources and the American Corporation

The American firm has historically been governed by a legal doctrine that sees its sole purpose and the responsibilities of its officers as maximizing shareholder wealth. Moreover, American labor law draws a clear line of demarcation between workers' and union representatives' rights to bargain or file a grievance over wages, hours, and working conditions and management's right to make the strategic decisions of the firm without worker or labor union participation or representation. Thus, in the United States, the influence accorded to employee interests and human resource considerations comes down to the relative power or influence of the top managers responsible for this functional domain. We saw in Chapter 4 that the influence of human resource professionals in strategic decision making varies across firms. About half the respondents reported that human resource units participate in strategic decision making in their organizations. Moreover, the degree of their involvement was shown to matter. Workplace innovations and related human resource policies are more likely to be adopted and sustained over time in organizations where the human resource group plays this strategic role. As we will see, however, its ability to reach this level of influence varies not only across firms but also over time as the external environment changes.

One of the best understood principles of organizational theory is that the power of a functional unit, e.g., finance, marketing, human resources, and so forth, is directly related to the importance of the external resources that unit is charged with managing. The greater the costs an external resource can impose on the firm, or the greater the uncertainty associated with the resource, the more firms allocate decision-making power to specialists or professional units responsible for managing this aspect of the business. This proposition has been widely tested in organizational theory.[20] One area close to our concerns showed that as laws provided rights to public employees to organize and militant unions arrived, city governments created and delegated power to professional labor relations departments to manage these affairs.[21]

In general, the history of the rise and fall of labor relations professionals within the private sector follows the rise and fall of unionization in the economy from the 1930s to the 1990s. Industrial relations managers appeared to peak in their influence in the 1960s, just after unionism peaked, and these professionals had demonstrated their ability to manage union relations effectively and protect the "core" of the organization from unpredictable or unwanted strikes. More generally, historical studies have shown that the power or influence of human resource and industrial relations professionals within management rises and falls in direct response to (1) the tightness of labor markets, (2) the threat or actual presence of unions, and (3) the passage of new government regulations, e.g., safety and health, pension, or equal employment opportunity laws or rules.[22]

With the gradual decline in unionization has come a reshuffling of the distribution of power within the professional unit charged with managing employee relations. Over the past two decades, labor relations professionals were supplanted by human resource executives responsible for all employees, from entry-level production workers to top executives. Management development, improving productivity and quality, executive compensation and succession planning, and attraction and retention of key technical and professional talent became the top substantive priorities of human resource executives.[23]

But with this shift in substantive focus also came a change in mind-set and orientation. Labor relations professionals had tended to be externally oriented, i.e., they sought to develop good working relations with union leaders, arbitrators, mediators, and government officials. In contrast, human resource executives tend to be more inward oriented, for good reason. Given the declining ability to use the threat or presence of unions or government regulations as a source of power and influence in corporate decision making, human resource executives recognized the need to view line managers and top executives as their key customers. They too recognized that to have significant influence in corporate decision making required that they be part of the inner circle of top executives who set long-term corporate strategy and make the difficult trade-offs among competing priorities for scarce resources.

So, in the 1980s in particular, the rhetoric of the human resource management profession stressed the need to become partners with line management. This shift in orientation was expected to elevate the influence of human resource professionals within the firm, gain them entrée into the inner circle of top management, and support a more "strategic" model of human resource management.[24]

Although leading human resource management professionals generally endorse this hope for their function, their own survey data demonstrate that on average they have yet to achieve it. Figure 5-1 reports data from a 1991 survey of leading human resource executives, consultants, and academics conducted by Towers Perrin, a leading human resource consulting firm. When asked about their vision for the human resource function in the year 2000, a majority of the respondents described it as "strategic," "proactive," and a "partner with line management." But when asked to describe the current state of the human resource function within American corporations, the major-

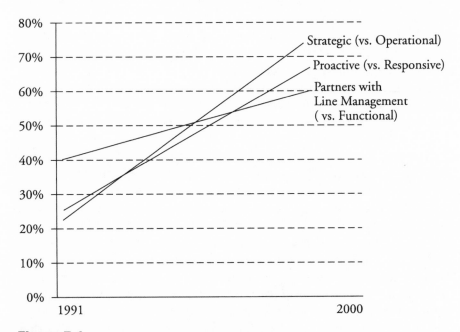

Figure 5-1
A New Role Model for HR Management
Source: *Priorities for Competitive Advantage: A Worldwide Human Resource Study.* (New York: Towers Perrin, 1992), Exhibit 7, p. 21.

ity of these professionals described it as "operational," "responsive," and "functional."[25] Thus, there appear to be formidable obstacles that limit the ability of human resource professionals to take on proactive and powerful roles within American corporations.

Those executives who achieved a significant degree of influence in management did so largely by serving as agents, carrying out the expressed priorities of top management without exerting a significant independent voice or by challenging management policies. Frank Doyle, the senior vice president of human resources and external relations at GE, and one of the most influential and respected professionals in this field, described human resource executives of the 1980s as "perfect agents." That is, they were excellent at carrying out the wishes of top management for downsizing, attempting to control health care and other labor costs, and so forth. Doyle wondered, however, whether human resource executives were able to challenge or question their senior executive partners on issues for which the instincts and preferences of top executives may not be in the long-term best interests of the company, let alone its work force.[26]

Internal survey data from a large firm illustrate the inherent dilemma of human resource professionals. This corporation surveyed its managerial, supervisory, and professional employees to get their views of the human resource function. The data it received were quite sobering. On average, the human resource function received approval ratings of between 25 and 40 percent, depending on the specific questions asked. But of equal concern was the fact that 80 percent of the respondents regarded the human resource function to be an advocate of management's interests while only 33 percent regarded it as advocating salaried employees' concerns and 31 percent saw the function as advocating hourly employee concerns.

At the same time, although seen as an agent of management, the human resource function was also rated poorly for its contribution to the objectives of the corporation. Human resources received favorable ratings for its contributions to increasing efficiency from only 23 percent of the respondents; 27 percent rated it favorably for its contribution to improving product quality, and only 29 percent rated it favorably for its contribution to reducing overhead costs. On the one hand, the human resource professionals feel they must respond to employees as important customers of their services. On the other hand, they have to better serve the needs of their business units. But they lack the resources or the influence to provide better training, more opportunities for career development and growth, and more communications and input into decisions affecting employees' jobs and work environment.

These tensions are not unique to this company and do not simply reflect a lack of professionalism on the part of the human resource staff. They mirror the structural weakness of the human resource function in American firms, which is unlikely to be overcome by improved capabilities and managerial skills. Human resource professionals lack the power, independence, and perspective needed to promote the mutual interests of their business, unit, their corporation, and their employees.

Perhaps the most striking evidence of the difference in the role that human resource executives play in U.S. corporations is found in their pay relative to that of finance executives in U.S. and Japanese firms (see Table 5-1). The data show that in the United States the top finance executive typically earns 58 percent more than the top human resource executive. In contrast, in Japanese firms of comparable size the pay is almost identical, with the human resource executive earning 2 percent *more* than his or her finance counterpart.

Given the supremacy of shareholder interests and the impact that acquisition and use of capital has on American firms, it is not surprising that finance tends to be the most powerful group in most U.S. firms. Indeed, Michael Useem reports that the 1980s corporate restructuring

Table 5-1

Relative Compensation of Top Executives across Functional Areas: Large U.S. and Japanese Companies

Function*	Country	
	Japan	United States
Manufacturing	1.00	1.00
Sales/Marketing	0.93	0.91
R&D	0.87	0.90
Finance	1.00	1.32
Human Resources	1.02	0.83

*For indexing purposes, compensation (salary plus bonus) received by the top manufacturing executives in each country is set at 1.00.

Source: A. T. Kearney, Inc., 1991. Based on manufacturing companies with sales in excess of $2 billion. Index values were computed by Professor James Baron of the Stanford Business School.

which occurred in response to increased shareholder and institutional investor activism increased the emphasis given to finance and shareholders at the expense of other corporate stakeholders.[27] Therefore, it is not surprising that human resources tends to rank significantly lower, often at the bottom of the managerial influence ladder, and that it is unable to deliver policies and practices which serve the interests of employees. To further understand why this is the case we must look at alternative models of the role of human resources in corporate governance.

Although the shareholder-maximizing model of the corporation has been taken for granted, it has come under closer scrutiny recently, in large part because of research in the nature of corporate ownership, financial markets, and governance arrangements of Japanese and German firms. These comparisons reveal that human resources and employee interests are accorded more importance in Japanese and German firms. To see why, we need to examine the differences in the financial markets and corporate governance arrangements in these nations.

Human Resources and Corporate Governance in Japan

The best analysis of the relationship among financial markets, corporate governance, and human resources of Japanese firms is found in the work of Japanese economist Masahiko Aoki.[28] He describes the Japanese firm as a coalition of shareholders and employees, with managers acting as mediating agents. Individual shareholders receive more of their investment returns through long-term capital gains than through dividends or rapid turnover of stocks. Institutional investors—banks, other firms, insurance companies, and so forth—which own nearly 75 percent of the shares of large Japanese companies, also receive income from long-term capital gains, but they receive significant income from the interest paid on debt they hold and from income derived from goods and services sold to the firm. The dense networks of cross-shareholdings, customer relationships, and creditors are strongest in the sixteen or so keiretsu—large company networks tied together by a lead bank—like Mitsubishi, Hitachi, or Matsushita.[29]

Employees, in turn, receive their most significant rewards in the form of long tenure and meritorious service—lifetime employment within what Aoki calls a rank hierarchy, in which promotion to top-paying and high-status jobs depends on a combination of length of service and demonstrated individual performance. Other human resource practices are designed to make this coalitional model work by delivering long-tenure, loyal, and motivated employees who share a deep interest in the performance and growth of the firm. These practices include internal promotion, an informal training and development system that relies on job rotation and lateral transfers, steep age earnings profiles (the average retirement wage in Japan is 257 percent of the entry wage compared with 107 percent in the United States), large retirement bonuses, enterprise unions, frequent and broad-based labor-management consultation, and annual bonuses. So it is easy to understand why human resource executives are influential in Japanese firms. The policies they develop and administer must reinforce this long-term orientation and commitment or the mutual gains to employees and shareholders will not be realized.

The governance structure of Japanese corporations reflects these differences. The boards of directors of large corporations are composed of several outsiders, usually a representative of the company's main bank, and a group of internal senior managers, normally the heads of the key departments of personnel, finance, R&D, and the main factories or business units. The chairman of the board serves as the chief executive of the company. Retiring chairmen normally pick their successors. The board also appoints a "full-time board," essentially a subgroup of the board composed mainly of the heads of the departments and the CEO. Therefore, the board is not a pure representative of the shareholders but a coalition of insiders and outsiders, with the insiders holding the most important positions.

The company's main bank, which normally holds up to the legal limit of 5 percent of the shares of the company, is the key monitoring agent for other shareholders. Not only does it have equity and creditor stakes in the company, it has a reputational stake as well. This helps explain why, if a firm gets into financial trouble, the main bank often works closely with management to help solve the problem. In so doing it protects its reputation—as well as its investment.

These financial and governance structures of the Japanese corporation make it difficult for a hostile takeover threat to surface or serve as a source of discipline on management. The intricate intercorporate shareholding simply makes it almost impossible for an outside investor to accumulate a large portion of shares.

The form of the Japanese corporation illustrates an important point often overlooked by those who are deeply wedded to an American notion of the corporation. That is, the underlying goals and behavior of management are not shaped by the invisible hand of the market, as neoclassical economics suggests, but by a combination of the financial markets, governance structure, and distribution of power within the management hierarchy. Japanese firms do not maximize short-run shareholder value but pursue long-term joint gains for shareholders and employees.

We should not glorify these Japanese financial and governance arrangements because, like their U.S. counterparts, they have been under increased scrutiny and criticism in recent years, owing partly to several highly publicized scandals involving business executives and high-level government officials. But beyond this, deeper questions are producing pressure for changes in financial practices that may lead Japanese capital markets to move closer to the American institutional arrangements we are criticizing! But regardless of the direction of change in Japanese financial markets and corporate governance arrangements, the lesson here is that the close interdependence of these markets, governance structures, and human resources increases the probability that mutual gains strategies and practices will be adopted and sustained over time.

Human Resources and Corporate Governance in Germany

Germany presents yet another approach to encouraging a longer-term time horizon and a higher level of investment in human resources.[30] Like Japanese banks, German banks hold equity stakes in the companies to which they loan money; moreover, they normally hold the proxy rights to the shares of other stockholders who deposit their securities in the bank. Banks thereby control appointments to supervisory boards. The supervisory board, the functional equivalent of a U.S. board of directors, is made up of a majority of outside directors plus one or more representatives of the firm's *employees*. Normally the lead bank has a representative on this board.

As in Japan, internal governance and human resource practices reinforce the long-term time horizons and the importance of human resources in corporate decision making. As noted, by law an employee representative sits on the supervisory board of all companies with more than 2,000 employees. In the iron and steel industry a special law gives employees one less than a majority of seats on the supervisory boards. In addition, German companies have what is often referred to as a dual board structure. A management board consisting of employee- and management-nominated representatives serves as an internal board. One member of this board, the *Arbeitsdirecktor,* is the equivalent of the head of the human resource department in a U.S.

firm and can be *removed* by employees if they lose confidence in his or her behavior.

The effects of codetermination.   Although there have been few empirical studies of the effects of codetermination in Germany or in other European countries where workers have representatives on corporate boards, the conclusions of recent studies mirror those of the German government's Biedenkopf Commission, which examined this issue in 1970:

> Worker participation . . . has led to a greater emphasis on the social aspects . . . of company activities, but has not called into question the validity of the profit motive as the guiding principle of company initiative and planning. Thus, for example, rationalization measures aimed at reducing [production] costs never encountered labor resistance so long as adequate provisions were taken to maintain the social [standard] of the workers in the firm.[31]

For example, using recent data, Katherine Abraham and Susan Houseman examined the process of employment adjustment in response to changing demand conditions in industries in Germany and the United States and found that although German industries laid off fewer workers in response to short-run changes in demand, they made equal, and in some cases greater, adjustments over time in response to more long-term structural declines or shifts in consumer demand.[32] This approach requires German firms to develop a plan for cushioning the income losses of displaced workers and helping them make the transition to jobs in other industries.[33]

Representation on corporate boards of directors cannot stand alone or apart from other institutional arrangements, as we will see later in this chapter when we discuss the limited experience with employee representatives on U.S. boards. Board representation is reinforced by works councils that are required by law in every German facility with five or more employees. Representatives are elected by the full range of blue- and white-collar employees and managers in the facility. The councils have rights to consultation and negotiation over a wide range of human resource issues, from safety and health to training to strategies for adjusting to technological change.

The evidence on works councils.   For reasons we explore in more depth in later chapters, interest in works councils has increased remarkably in the United States in recent years. Therefore, the evidence on how they work in Germany and elsewhere warrants a brief review here. We can draw on three different types of research on works councils: theoretical treatises by economists or political scientists,[34] a few case studies of councils in action,[35] and interviews with employer and labor representatives as well as study tour reports.[36] The general consensus of this research can be summarized as follows:

Although they opposed works council legislation when it was first enacted in 1952, German managers (and unions) accepted the councils and now view them as a positive forum for communications and for integrating employee and management interests. In her interviews with a sample of thirty-seven German managers, Kirsten Wever of Northeastern University found near unanimous support for the positive roles played by works councils (see Exhibit 5-1). No manager expressed a desire to be rid of them. Nor, given the option, did any favor either the American union or the nonunion model over the German system. Specifically, the managers offered five reasons for preferring to continue with works councils:

1. Works councils were more pragmatic and involved people closer to workplace problems than unions. Moreover, council representatives had more technical or job-specific expertise and more commitment to the objectives of the enterprise than union representatives.
2. Councils served as a conduit for employee views and interests.
3. Councils provided a means of implementing solutions. Strong councils in particular spoke for workers and, once committed to policies, sold them to the work force.
4. Works councils were a more humane and cooperative system for employee participation than American-style collective bargaining and union representation within the enterprise.
5. Works councils were helpful in managing change, particularly in introducing new technologies and upgrading skills to meet the requirements of new methods and equipment.[37]

Richard Freeman of Harvard and Joel Rogers of the University of Wisconsin interviewed a number of human resource executives in large German and American multinational firms and reached similar results.

Exhibit 5-1 contains excerpts from some of these interviews. Overall, they concluded,

> What we heard [in the interviews], overwhelmingly, was that while councils have costs (slowing management decision making, taking employee and manager time away from other work, etc.), and can malfunction, they have important positive effects which in general make them a net benefit to firms.[38]

Lowell Turner's comparative study of the extent of cooperation of German and American unions with management in the auto, telecommunications, and apparel industries provides another body of data on works councils.[39] His key conclusion is that the works councils have helped diffuse new production concepts and flexible work systems more quickly and more broadly in Germany than in the United States because they level out differences in managerial ideologies, union politics, and other factors that limit diffusion in America. He attributes the greater success of works councils to two factors: (1) required by law, they are therefore present in all comparable and competing firms, and (2) they require managers to take worker concerns into account *before* making a decision or, in this case, before designing a new manufacturing system or practice. Moreover, unlike their American counterpart, the German union representing auto workers (IG Metall) has developed its own concept and principles governing teamwork and related forms of workplace reform (it is called group work). Thus, the stronger role of law and the institutional requirement for consultation, along with a well-articulated union strategy from which works councils can negotiate workplace reforms, together have supported broad innovation in this sector of the German economy.

It should be noted that these generally favorable evaluations of works councils do not necessarily translate into an acceptance on the part of European managers that councils be required. Indeed, the European Economic Community's Parliament has been split on this issue for more than a decade. The strongest opposition to requiring works councils or information sharing in European companies has come from the British government and employers and from American multinationals operating in Europe. The European Employers Federation has also vigorously opposed extension of the works council model to all firms operating within the European Community. European employers, like their American and British counterparts, tend to oppose legislation that limits their autonomy and potentially increases labor's

Exhibit 5-1
Excerpts from Interviews with German Managers about
Works Councils

"On a day-to-day basis the councils play an important role in the implementation of technology and training. They know the needs of the company and are closer to the problems of the employees and how the jobs actually get done than managers are. For that reason, it wouldn't necessarily be such a good idea for managers to work entirely without the councils. But the main point is that because of this connection to the work, it's better to deal with the works council than the union." (Consultant, Printing Industry Employers' Association)

"When [management] cannot know the woman on the line . . . in the interest of a good workplace climate of relations . . . the employees need interest representation that can serve as a conduit, which can also from time to time competently tell management where to get off. My personal experience . . . with our council chair is that often my solutions to problems were changed when she was consulted so that both sides [labor and management] could endorse the solution." (Acting chief operating officer, Betrix Cosmetics)

"One of the reasons why we have this [social] peace is that we have the works councils. Though at the same time there are daily lots of problems which we wouldn't have if we didn't have to deal with the works councils. But [as a whole] it's a sensible system. . . . In any case, better our system than the American." (Central Works Council Liaison, Commerzbank)

Source: Kirsten R. Wever, "What German Employers Think about Employee Representation and Competitiveness," Northeastern University, 1993. Used with permission of the author.

"There are three major advantages of councils. First you're forced to consider in your decision-making process the effect on the employees in advance. . . . This avoids costly mistakes. Second, works councils will in the final run support the company. They will take into account the pressing needs of the company more than a trade union can, on the outside. And third, works councils explain and defend decisions of the company toward the employees. Once decisions are made, they are easier to implement." (Manager of a U.S. multinational auto firm located in Germany)

Source: Richard B. Freeman and Joel Rogers, "Who Speaks for Us? Employee Representation in a Non-Union Labor Market," National Bureau of Economic Research, 1992. Used with permission of the authors.

power in enterprise decision making. But once the councils are in place, managers not only learn to live with them, but a majority appear to derive significant benefits from them for their firms. The lesson here, however, is that it takes a law to defuse the initial resistance of employers to this type of institution.

The result of the financial-governance–human resource system in Germany is that German managers not only have learned to manage in a fashion that accepts workers' rights to participate and be consulted in decision making, but more important, consider it only natural and appropriate to make decisions that take into account the long-term social and economic impacts of their strategies on their workers.

We must be careful not to view works councils in isolation from other industrial relations and labor market institutions in Germany. For example, these internal human resource and governance arrangements are supported by well-developed apprenticeship and training institutions that are jointly overseen by business and labor representatives. (We discuss the German apprenticeship system more fully in Chapter 7.) There are also industrywide collective-bargaining structures that equalize wages among competitors within an industry and therefore keep these wage issues from hindering efforts to find mutually acceptable solutions to human resource problems within individual enterprises. Finally, the labor movement in Germany is more integrated into national economic and political policies and, in general, is more widely accepted as a legitimate actor and "social partner" by both business and government than in the United States.[40] These intertwined features of the German system suggest that we need to be cautious about importing any one feature such as works councils or board representation into the American environment. As we will see below, the absence of some of these supporting institutional features has made it difficult for the limited experiments with these institutions in the United States to achieve anything near the acceptance or perceived effectiveness they have achieved in Germany.

Efforts at Joint Governance in the United States

The fact that neither U.S. labor nor corporate law sanctions formal institutions for employee participation or representation in corporate governance makes it difficult to assess how formal board representation or works councils as found in Europe or informal labor-management consultation as found in Japan would work in this country *if* sanctioned and encouraged by law. There are isolated examples of efforts to introduce versions of these institutional arrangements in U.S. companies voluntarily. We summarize the lessons that can be learned from these experiments with the obvious caution that they are, in some ways, not representative cases. The U.S. experience might be quite different if these practices were sanctioned by law and supported by mutual gains practices at other levels of the firm, labor movement, and economy.

Board Representation

There is a small and highly unusual history of employee representatives sitting on boards of directors in American corporations. This situation is not typical for at least three reasons. First, normally these firms are nearly bankrupt *before* employees are given a role in governance, usually a quid pro quo for wage concessions to keep the firms alive. Second, neither American labor law nor corporate law mandates a role for employees on corporate boards.[41] Third, both American managers and union leaders have historically disdained a role for workers on company boards.

One legal constraint of the American corporation as an instrument designed to maximize shareholder wealth proves to be particularly problematic for employee representatives on corporate boards. They must function not as agents for worker-owners as *employees* but as *shareholders.* That is, except in those states which have amended their corporate chartering laws recently, employee representatives are held to the same fiduciary responsibility to consider only the long-term interest of shareholders in making decisions as are the other directors. (Twenty-nine states amended incorporation laws in the 1980s to aid local firms threatened by hostile takeovers to allow board members to consider such other criteria as the impact on the community and job loss; however, most firms remain incorporated under state laws that have not made this change.) As we will see, this corporate doctrine has implications for who might sit on boards without having a conflict of interest, and it can pose difficult choices in situations where a strategic decision involves a choice between jobs and the short-term value of the company's stock.

Chrysler and the UAW. Chrysler's experience with two presidents of the UAW on its board is perhaps the best-known example of union leaders in this role in the United States. Douglas Fraser, the president of the UAW, was nominated to the Chrysler board in 1980 as a quid pro quo for the union's support of the government loan guarantee that kept the company from bankruptcy at the time. He resigned from the board when he retired as UAW president in 1983, and Chrysler replaced him with his successor, Owen Bieber. This arrangement continued until 1991, when Chrysler announced a reduction of the number of board members, including the seat held by Bieber. Fraser evaluated his role on the board positively (in fact, he now sits on the board of another company as an employee-director). He noted that his greatest accomplishment was to persuade the board to change the way it decided on whether to close a plant by first preparing an analysis of the alternatives to closing and the impact of the decision on the community.

Despite Fraser's positive evaluation of his experiences, the UAW did not protest when Chrysler announced its elimination of Bieber's seat. Apparently the union saw little value in board participation. This case is instructive because it demonstrates the historic ambivalence of American union leaders toward board membership. It also illustrates a point that we make again later; for board membership to add value to workers and the firm, unions must have a conscious strategy for using this forum to represent worker interests in ways that are not possible under collective bargaining and do so in a manner consistent with the norms of boardroom decision making. If board representation is viewed as a simple extension of bargaining, one vote provides little leverage; however, if seen as an opportunity to bring new employee- or community-centered criteria into board decision making, it offers an opportunity to influence decisions before they are made—something difficult to do in traditional bargaining relationships.

Several other firms brought employee representatives onto their boards in the 1980s as part of wage concessions and employee stock ownership plans (ESOPs) designed to save the company. Of these, Rath Meatpacking, Western Airlines, and Eastern Airlines were the most visible. Each experiment ended when the company either failed (Eastern and Rath) or merged with another firm (Western was purchased by Delta).

The lessons of these cases are that board representation cannot succeed or add significant value to a firm or to employees unless it occurs in firms that have a viable and supportive business strategy for the long run, one that supports mutual gains. At Eastern the low-wage strategy and decision to sell the airline to Frank Lorenzo was the final nail in the coffin of an airline that was already failing because of strong personality conflicts and cost-cutting pressures it experienced in late 1985. At Rath, a viable business strategy could not be developed or sustained, and the workers and other directors never developed an effective workable relationship. At Western, worker directors took different views of their roles, employees, other than the pilots, had little interest in this role, and in the end the experiment ended because the company was purchased by a larger carrier, most of whose employees were nonunion. Thus, because the collective-bargaining contract did not transfer to the merged organization, neither did rights to board representation.

Another chapter in the history of worker representation on corporate boards was written in the 1980s by the United Brotherhood of Teamsters and its policy with respect to demands for wage concessions from medium-size over-the-road trucking companies. Medium-size "less than truckload" carriers were especially hard hit by deregulation of the trucking industry. They were too big and had too many assets to follow a differentiation, regional, or niche market strategy, and they were too small relative to the three giants in the industry to benefit from economies of scale. Yet they represented a significant number of employees—perhaps as many as 20,000 or 30 percent of the prederegulated industry employment—to be allowed simply to fail in the expectation that their workers would be absorbed by the survivors.

The strategy adopted by the Teamsters was to agree to significant wage concessions only in return for an ESOP with the right to nominate candidates to the company boards. In all, twenty companies had agreed to this arrangement by October 1986.[42] Most of them, however, eventually either merged with another carrier or went out of business. As with Western Airlines, some valuable lessons were learned about the role of an employee director in firms that need to reorganize or merge to save jobs. The most important lesson was that it is critical for employee interests to be considered in merger negotiations *before* the fact, since the choice of the merger partner may involve trade-offs between short-term or one-time shareholder profits and long-term prospects for jobs and operations. Moreover, these rather small cases illustrate a point made on a much larger scale in books on deal making and merger negotiations of the 1980s, namely, the multiple lawyers, financial advisers, and potential investors typically involved in mergers are driven by a variety of short- and long-term self-interests, none of which tend to give significant weight to employee or human resource considerations.[43] Unless employees are represented directly, their interests continue to be dealt with only as a footnote in the merger discussions concerning the liabilities and contractual obligations a potential buyer will inherit.

There are other, perhaps less dramatic, examples of the conflicts experienced in merger negotiations. For example, interviews with other employee directors documented the fact that they were often instructed by legal counsel that they had to be careful to consider only the employees' interests as shareholders equal to all other shareholders' interests, and that they would violate their fiduciary responsibilities if they favored employees' job-related interests at the expense of shareholder value.[44] These examples are presented not because they are typical but to emphasize the point that current law makes it difficult for employee representatives to do their job in a straightforward and sensible fashion. Living within the law eventually pits employees' interest in job security against shareholders' interests in short-term profit maximization. Any effort to sanction or encourage further experimentation with board representation will have to resolve this dilemma.

Quantitative Evidence on ESOPs

ESOP firms are not limited to large, special examples that are driven by crisis. There are also a large number of medium-size and smaller ESOP firms that have existed for some time, including companies as diverse as the *Milwaukee Journal,* the Bureau of National Affairs (a publishing firm located in Washington, D.C.), and Lincoln Electric. Indeed, various estimates put the number of firms that have implemented some form of ESOP between 4,000 and 7,000, depending on how liberal a definition one uses. Collectively, perhaps as many as 11 percent of the labor force is employed in firms that have some form of ESOP. The vast majority of these have nonvoting and nonparticipatory arrangements; that is, no significant control or formal representation in governance or participation in decision making goes with employee ownership of company shares.

The available quantitative evidence on the effects of ESOP and board representation suffers from the same self-selection bias as the case studies do. One cannot be sure that these firms are representative of other firms in their industries that do not have an ESOP. Given this caveat, long-time students of these plans, Michael Conte, Jan Svenjar, and Joseph Blasi summarized the results of studies performed prior to 1990 as follows:

1. No studies show that ESOPs reduce productivity or profitability.
2. Most studies show that ESOPs are associated with increased (or higher in comparison to comparable non-ESOP companies) performance; these estimates, however, are not often significant and are sensitive to changes in the specification of the model used to estimate these effects.
3. There is considerable evidence to suggest that ESOPs are more likely to be associated with higher or increased firm performance when combined or supplemented with participation of employees in decision making than in cases where there is either no employee participation or where participation is limited to employee representation on the company's board of directors.[45]

Once again we are left with a familiar message—it is the combination of different forms or levels of participation and organizational strategies that produces mutual gains to shareholders and employees.

General Principles on What Makes Board Membership Work

We appear to be entering an era of renewed interest in employee ownership and employee representation on corporate boards. Again the airline industry is leading the way. In 1993, TWA and Northwest and their unions negotiated wage concessions in return for 35 and 40 percent employee ownership stakes, respectively, and employee representation on their corporate boards. As of this writing, United's unions and the company's board have approved a buyout in which the employees would become the majority shareholders and be represented on the new board of the company. Delta employees also own approximately 15 percent of that firm through an ESOP, but lack formal voice in corporate governance (only the pilots at Delta are unionized and the ESOP was established by the company in the 1980s, in part to ward off hostile suitors). But there appears to be growing interest by unions and employee groups in other industries as well.

The Steelworkers union recently negotiated for board representation as part of a comprehensive new partnership strategy with companies in its industry (more about this in Chapter 6). Some advocates of ESOPs recommend that the tax advantages ESOPs enjoy should be available only to those firms which provide employees with a voice in their governance. The issue for these new experiments in joint governance is whether they have learned from the previous experiences with board representation. We now summarize the lessons we have learned from these experiences.

As noted at the outset of this section, generalizing from these experiences is rather dangerous. However, with this warning in mind, we offer several hypotheses about the conditions needed for board representation to add value to both employees and shareholders, derived from our personal experiences, other case studies, and the limited quantitative evidence available to date. For board membership to pay off in mutual gains to employees and shareholders, we believe the following:

1. The board must function as a team—there cannot be a division among directors between those who are trusted representatives of shareholders and those who represent employees. If this happens, real decisions will be made by the dominant coalition and the formal board meetings and other interactions with the employee-directors will become a sham. Decision making in boards must be integrative in nature. This does not mean there is no room for vigorous debate and disagreement, which is natural, healthy, and, in the long run, essential. But in the end, decisions must be accepted and the board must function as a team.

2. Employee directors must add something of value. Board representatives are valuable to the extent that they bring connections and communications with resources needed for corporate survival. Bank representatives are in contact with the financial community and serve to monitor the bank's investments. Employee-directors presumably bring connections and communication links to employees and the unions that represent them. From time to time, this avenue of communication must be important and the representatives need to be able to facilitate them for the benefit of both parties.

3. Board representation cannot stand alone. Unless it is integrated into a business strategy, management culture, and workplace practices that emphasize the value of employee participation, commitment, trust, and motivation to the success of the business, and unless human resource policies of the firm reinforce this with compensation, training, and participation systems that produce these benefits, board representation will add little if any value. At best, board representatives can then serve only as watchdogs against unscrupulous or opportunistic behavior that would harm employee interests. Thus, board representation makes sense only in those organizations which want to compete in this way

and are ready to make the management and organizational commitments to this approach in their business.

4. Perhaps most important, employees must have a financial stake in the firm either through an ESOP or another deferred or contingent compensation arrangement. This requirement both focuses employee interest and attention on overall firm performance and provides workers with a legitimate claim to board representation, equivalent to that of other external owners and financial stakeholders.

"Works Councils" in America: The Case of Polaroid

If we are forced to rely on unrepresentative cases for board representation, American versions of works councils are even more rare and special. American labor law makes it difficult, if not impossible, to have an employee council outside of a union-management setting. The case of Polaroid illustrates this point.

Polaroid is a unique case for several reasons that can best be understood by reviewing its corporate history. Since its founding by Edwin Land in 1937, Polaroid has been guided by values that emphasize mutual gains. Land made this clear in a booklet he wrote:

> We have two basic aims here at Polaroid. One is to make products which are genuinely new and useful to the public, products of the highest quality, at reasonable cost. In this way each of us can have the satisfaction of helping to make a creative contribution to the world. The other is to give everyone working for Polaroid personal opportunity within the Company for full exercise of his talents; to express his opinions, to share in the progress of the Company as far as his capacities permit, to earn enough money so that the need for earning more will not always be the first thing on his mind—opportunity, in short to make his work here a fully rewarding, important part of his life. These goals can make Polaroid a great company—great not merely in size, but great in the esteem of all of the people for whom it makes new good things, and great in its fulfillment of the individual ideals of its employees.[46]

Although the company has never been organized by a trade union, in 1947 Land established an Employee Committee that functioned very much like an American equivalent of a German works council.

Representatives were elected by employees, and the committee discussed the full range of the company's personnel policies, although it had no formal authority to make decisions. In 1988 the company established an ESOP and added an employee—a manager in the company's marketing department—to the corporate board of directors. The ESOP came at the same time that Polaroid was under threat of a hostile takeover. The company successfully argued in court that its decision to establish the ESOP reflected a longer-term judgment consistent with the company's long-standing culture and business strategy and compensation policies. (The company had a profit-sharing plan for all employees in place for nearly a decade prior to the ESOP.)

The role of the Employee Committee and related governance arrangements can be seen in Polaroid's handling of an interesting problem it faced in 1992. The company won a patent infringement lawsuit from Eastman Kodak in 1991 for $928 million. Given its practices, culture, and business strategy, it seemed natural that some of this windfall settlement should be shared with employees. Employees had, after all, shared in the loss of profits to Kodak. This logic ran into one problem: Polaroid's corporate lawyers informed management that it might very well run afoul of corporate law and risk losing a shareholder's lawsuit if it shared these funds with employees, because these were the *shareholders'* returns and could not be given away to employees as a gift for past loyalty or service. If the settlement were to be shared at all, management would have to make a convincing case that implementing it would benefit shareholders in the future by increasing *future* productivity and profitability, presumably through higher employee motivation and job performance.

The Employee Committee representatives and the employee representative on the board made it quite clear, however, that employees expected a share of the award and communicated this to management. Indeed, MacAllister Booth, Polaroid's CEO, strongly agreed with employees and had gone on record as favoring dividing the award among shareholders, employees, and reinvestment in the company. In the end the company took this approach and divided the award equitably between employees and shareholders.

Polaroid did this in part because of its long-standing value system and in part because its employees in the governance structure could articulate the "costs" to employee morale and loyalty of *not* doing it. But not all companies have these mechanisms. Indeed, in reviewing cases of similar windfalls from lawsuits, Polaroid's staff could find no examples of such an award being shared with the entire work force of a company. In prior cases boards either distributed the proceeds to shareholders or shared the proceeds only with *top executives.*

This case again illustrates how the existence of governance structures and human resource policies that rely on mutual gains produce results different from the normal decisions made in U.S. firms.

An interesting footnote to the Polaroid case is that about a year after the award was distributed, the Employee Committee was found to be illegal under current labor law and was disbanded. The company then put in place a new, less influential "focus group" of employees, which its lawyers believe meets the constraints of contemporary labor law. The ultimate lesson here, therefore, is that we are unlikely to see this form of employee participation in corporate governance on a meaningful scale in the United States unless it is sanctioned by changes in labor law. We return to this issue in Chapter 8.

Summary and Conclusions

A number of proposals have been put forward to reform corporate governance structures largely in response to the increased activism of shareholders and their institutional investors. Will increased influence of institutional investor and other shareholder representatives lead to more or less consideration of human resource and employee interests in corporate decision making? Our hypothesis, based on the evidence presented in this chapter, is that in the absence of additional reforms which encourage large investors to hold their shares for a longer period of time so that their interests and time horizons are more closely aligned with those of long-term employees, increased shareholder influence is likely to exacerbate the conflicts between the interests of employees and shareholders.

Similarly, finance experts have proposed modifications in tax laws, capital-market institutions, and regulatory rules set by the Securities and Exchange Commission that would help lengthen time horizons by encouraging more patient capital investment. How would these reforms influence investments in human resources and workplace innovations? We feel that they would help and may be a necessary condition for increasing corporate investments in human resources and innovations. But they are not a sufficient solution. Rather, the lessons from comparisons with Japanese and German capital markets and governance arrangements suggest that such reform is only one component of a systemic solution. Capital-market reforms must be accompanied

by changes in corporate governance that bring human resource considerations directly into strategic decision making and governance processes.

But the evidence to date from board representation in the United
States suggests that simply bringing employees or human resource
managers into corporate governance—in the absence of a closer alignment of their interests with shareholders—would simply result in more
distributive conflicts. Instead, employee representation seems to work
best in cases where employees have a direct financial stake in the
enterprise and the management culture and human resource practices
reinforce the treatment of employees as stakeholders. Thus, the combination of changes in capital markets that encourage patient capital,
more active involvement of shareholders who have longer time horizons, and participation of employee representatives in corporate
governance together would increase the probability that sustained innovations in human resources would produce mutual gains for all
stakeholders in contemporary corporations. These suggestions mean
nothing less than a new conception of the American corporation that
seeks to align shareholder and employee interests more closely and
create the institutions needed to bring consideration of human resource
policies directly into the corporate governance process.

chapter six

THE ROLE OF LABOR AND WORKER REPRESENTATION

Historically, democratic societies have relied on free labor movements to represent worker interests at the workplace and in political and social affairs. It is ironic, therefore, that just as the need for a strong and consistent voice for employees and human resources in enterprise strategy and in national economic policy is being recognized, the American labor movement has shrunk to its lowest level of membership and political influence since prior to the Great Depression and the passage of the New Deal labor legislation in the 1930s. Currently, fewer than 12 percent of all private sector workers and 16 percent of all workers are represented by trade unions, compared with approximately 24 percent of the work force in 1980 and 35 percent of the work force at its peak in the mid-1950s.

What accounts for this long-term and more recent precipitous decline? Many studies have been devoted to this issue, so we need not explore it in depth here.[1] For our purposes it is sufficient to note that most of these studies conclude that no single factor can account for the decline of union membership in the United States. Instead it is the combined, and interacting, effects of (1) changes in the occupational and geographic structure of the labor force, (2) increased employer opposition to union organizing, (3) improvements in personnel management that have reduced the incentive for some workers to join unions, (4) weaknesses in labor law that make it expensive and risky for workers to organize, (5) slowness of the labor movement to adapt new strategies for organizing and representing the work force, and (6) the fact that the *form* of worker representation built into our traditional industrial relations system is no longer well suited to the needs of workers, companies, and the broader economy. In this chapter we focus on the last factor, that is, the efforts by individual unions and the labor movement as a whole to experiment with new forms of worker representation that overcome the weaknesses in traditional collective bargaining.

Why Worry about Union Decline?

Before we review experiments with new approaches to worker representation, a threshold question has to be addressed. Should we worry about the decline in unions and worker representation? Certainly many within the American management community applaud this development. Some argue that unions have outlived their usefulness because management is enlightened enough to take care of workers' needs, market forces require employers to meet worker expectations, or individual workers are independent enough to assert their own interests. More than any other management community, U.S. managers have always felt that labor is important in the abstract, but that unions were not necessary in their shops or offices. Douglas Brown and Charles Myers probably captured the essence of American managers' views best in what is now a classic quote from a paper they wrote in 1957: "It may well be true that if American management, upon retiring one night, were assured that by the next morning the union . . . would have disappeared, more management people than not would experience the happiest sleep of their lives."[2] Indeed, it is usually viewed as a major black mark on a manager's record if a successful union-organizing drive occurs. In some companies managers can expect to be fired should their operations be organized.

Although it is easy to understand why individual managers prefer that their operations remain unorganized, we suggest four important reasons why American society cannot afford another decade of declining worker representation.

The first is the value unions and other institutions for worker representation bring to a democratic society. The majority of Americans, including a majority of managers, recognize the value of a free trade union movement in a democratic society and therefore do not wish to see labor representation decline to a level where workers are completely disenfranchised. Table 6-1 summarizes the most recent national poll about unions. In general, 69 percent of the sample agrees that unions are good for the nation as a whole. For our purposes, it is perhaps even more significant that 90 percent of the respondents

Table 6-1
Gallup Survey of Attitudes Toward Union Participation

	Total Sample	Approve (%)	Disapprove (%)
Overall Approval of Unions	100	61	25
Percentage who agree that:*			
Labor unions are good for the nation.	69	87	31
Without union efforts, most laws that benefit workers would be seriously weakened or repealed.	68	80	49
Corporations sometimes harass or fire employees who support unions.	69	71	67
Employees should have an organization for discussing and resolving concerns with their employer.	90	94	82
Existing American laws should be strengthened to prevent corporations from denying workers the right to organize.	66	76	47
It's not fair for employers to resist employees' union-organizing.	78	86	62
Workers' rights and abilities to organize unions have faced a strong challenge from corporations in the past few years.	73	81	68

*The second and third columns report the percentage agreeing separately for those who approve and those who disapprove of unions in general.

Source: Synopsis of the 1988 Gallup Survey of Public Knowledge and Opinion Concerning the Labor Movement. Adapted from Richard B. Freeman and Joel Rogers, "Who Speaks for Us? Employee Representation in a Non-Union Labor Market," in *Employee Representation: Alternatives and Future Directions,* Bruce E. Kaufman and Morris M. Kleiner, eds. (Madison, Wis.: Industrial Relations Research Association, 1993), pp. 13–80.

agree that employees should have some type of organization for discussing and resolving concerns with their employers. This suggests that the vast majority of Americans recognize the need for effective employee voice at the workplace, even if some question the effectiveness of traditional unions as the instrument of this voice. Data such as these, as well as comparable results from prior national surveys,[3] lead us to agree with Joel Rogers and Richard Freeman, who conclude that America currently suffers from a "representation gap" in the labor force and in American workplaces.[4]

No less a respected and experienced elder statesman than George P. Shultz, former secretary of Labor, Treasury, and State, former CEO of Bechtel Corporation, and former dean of the University of Chicago Business School, made this very point in a 1991 speech to other CEOs and labor leaders at the National Planning Association. He noted that he understood why an individual manager preferred not to have to deal with unions, but as a member of society he worried about the political and representative vacuum left by the continued decline of labor union membership and influence.[5]

In private conversations as well as public forums, other high-level executives echo Shultz's concern. For example, one can go as far back in American history as the turn of the century to find business leaders such as John D. Rockefeller and Andrew Carnegie participating in national committees like the National Civic Federation, endorsing public statements about the need for trade unions in a democratic society.[6] Or one can find similar statements in current national policy groups like the Collective Bargaining Forum or the various productivity or competitiveness commissions. The opening paragraph of the forum's first report in 1988 began by reaffirming the need for a strong labor movement in a democratic society. The forum went on to outline the principles that should guide the future of labor-management relations, again affirming the legitimacy of unions. These executives see the need for a more cooperative and innovative role for unions in their specific enterprises if they are to be competitive.

Nonetheless, endorsement of the general principle of the need for unions has not historically or currently been translated into acceptance of unions by American executives in individual enterprises. This fact is probably best shown in worker responses to other questions in the Gallup survey summarized in Table 6-1. When asked how employers respond to union organizing efforts, 69 percent agreed that corporations sometimes harass or fire employees who support unions and 73 percent agreed that workers' rights and abilities to join unions have faced strong challenges from corporations in the past few years. Therefore, we need to worry about the costs to society of the decline in worker representation and the long-standing tendency of American managers not to translate their general support for worker representation into implementation of this right in their workplaces.

The second reason why further decline in worker representation is not in America's interests is the distributive economic role that union representation plays, especially for workers at the lower end of the wage scale. Indeed, this is one of the reasons why individual managers resist unions in their operations; unions do have an effect on the distribution of economic returns to the enterprise. The weight of the evidence from econometric studies shows that traditional American unions and collective bargaining increase wages of union workers relative to nonunion workers and lead to reduction of wage differentials across organizational levels, occupations, workers with different levels of education, and among establishments within industries.[7] This has the desirable effect of leading some employers to take compensating actions to increase productivity that offset higher labor costs and to invest more in training those employees whose wages have been pushed up above what their innate human capital would otherwise warrant. Long ago this result was labeled the "shock effect" by Sumner Slichter and his colleagues at Harvard.[8]

Some employers respond to unions by keeping them at arm's-length and limiting their access to information and influence, creating a low-trust/high-conflict relationship within their enterprises. This type of management response reinforces adversarial relations, reduces productivity and quality, and makes it impossible for the parties to recoup the union wage effects through offsetting productivity improvements.[9] Unfortunately, this response is all too common. On average, the weight of the evidence to date shows that unions reduce firm profits, stock prices, and lead some managers to shift capital investment from union to nonunion operations.[10] So we should be as concerned with the ways managers respond to unionization as we are with unions per se.

A third reason for concern over continued union decline reflects the evidence presented earlier in this book on determinants of diffusion and institutionalization of workplace innovations. The active partnership of union representatives can be a powerful force for sustaining commitment to workplace innovations. We have already presented evidence that when unions and firms work together to foster workplace change, they can increase productivity, quality, and help sustain managerial commitment and institutionalize these innovations to the point that they produce significant economic benefits to the enterprise.

It is not worker representation and unionism per se that should be the target of managerial opposition; it is the form of representation and the quality of the relationship that should concern managers. This is a subtle and somewhat risky proposition, since there is no guarantee that worker representation will take on a specific form. Our national labor policy is structured to support only the traditional style of union-management interaction and relationship. It is not surprising, therefore, that the type of unionism in the minds of most managers, indeed, most American citizens, is the New Deal style of unionism, or even worse, the stereotype of "Big Labor," whose leaders exert political control through backroom deals and constrain employers in bargaining and contract administration.

The fourth reason why it is in the interests of American society to reverse the decline in worker representation is that further union decline will impose a high cost on those organizations which are currently organized. One might be tempted to dismiss this concern by arguing that this affects only a small proportion—less than 12 percent—of the labor force. But this statistic understates the true impact of union coverage. Unions are, and will continue to be, a significant force in many of our largest firms and key industries, such as autos, telecommunications, paper, steel, airlines, aerospace, and health care. These firms must have effective union-management relations to be competitive. Neither they nor the industries and communities dependent on them can afford another decade of deteriorating union-management relations.

Over time it will become increasingly difficult to sustain cooperative or innovative activity in existing unionized establishments as labor representatives get backed farther into a corner. This sets in motion a self-fulfilling cycle of conflict that not only imposes economic costs on the parties involved but also may escalate into a more serious social and economic crisis. Indeed, in a previous study we predicted this would happen.

> Under this scenario American society appears to be destined to relive its past history. That is, as unions decline to the point that their survival as a viable economic and social force is threatened, intensified labor-management conflicts will occur and eventually, when or if the political pendulum swings back to favor labor, a new set of legal and private institutions will emerge to govern employment relationships. This scenario suggests that events ultimately will overtake the ability of the parties to control their future. However, the pressures must intensify significantly before a crisis develops and new institutional forms emerge.[11]

American managers, policy makers, and labor representatives face a major strategic choice over which scenario will dominate the future of labor-management relations. The business community in particular must confront a difficult paradox. For ideological, economic, and political reasons, the majority of American managers and the trade associations that represent them in political affairs continue adamantly to oppose policies that might strengthen unions and lead to a return of New Deal–style collective bargaining.

But the longer managers resist efforts to address the decline of worker representation, the more likely that the type of unionism they fear most will reemerge. The question, therefore, becomes: Are there alternative models of worker representation that can adequately represent workers while contributing to the competitiveness of individual enterprises and the economy as a whole? Are such models feasible in America where adversarialism is so deeply rooted in our legal institutions, culture, and labor-management relations? The remainder of this chapter reviews the efforts of labor to develop such new models over the past decade. Some new models are in place, some are in the very early stages of development and experimentation, and others are available for import if we are willing to look abroad at alternative institutions for worker participation and representation.

Inching Toward a New Model: Union Efforts, 1973 to the Present

The first efforts to breathe a new approach into labor-management relations were stillborn. In 1972 the U.S. Department of Health, Education, and Welfare and the Department of Labor produced a report titled *Work in America.* It called for new and bold solutions to what was then referred to as the "blue-collar blues," the ailment that was causing disgruntled workers to strike at plants like GM's giant facility in Lordstown, Ohio. Subsequently, the term "quality of work life" (QWL) was coined for the new approach at a conference held in the early 1970s. With the support of the Ford Foundation and the newly created National Commission on Productivity and Quality of Work, experiments were launched in companies as diverse as a coal mine and an auto parts company.

But these top-down, government- and foundation-led efforts failed to build a grassroots constituency among business and labor leaders. The strongest opponents, unfortunately but consistently, were the industrial relations managers in large companies. They saw these efforts as infringing on their turf and disrupting the orderly collective-bargaining relationships they had so carefully constructed over the years. The lesson in this experience is that the government or other outside advocates are unlikely to be effective agents of change for ideas that lack strong grassroots supporters. We will need to remember this lesson in Chapter 8, when we discuss the appropriate role for government policy in this area.

The United Auto Workers

A few bright spots did emerge in the 1970s. In 1973, largely at the insistence of Irving Bluestone, the vice president of the UAW assigned to GM, the UAW and GM (later Ford and Chrysler) signed a letter of understanding to create a corporate-level committee to explore ways to experiment with QWL. Two provisions were key to making this agreement work. First, the efforts would be voluntary on the part of individual workers, local union leaders, and individual plant managers. Neither the company nor the national union would require QWL experiments or processes in all plants or local unions. Second, a provision stated what came to be boilerplate in all subsequent experiments: nothing done in QWL experiments would in any way infringe on or modify the rights of workers or management contained in the collective-bargaining agreement. That is, QWL would be a supplement to, not a replacement for, the contract rules and the collective-bargaining process. This proved to be both a brilliant enabler—it helped the parties get started in what was otherwise a political minefield—and an eventual constraint on how far the process could go, since it limited the range of problems and solutions that could be considered.

An important part of the trade-off that Bluestone eventually forced on GM was the end to its "southern strategy" of opening greenfield, nonunion plants. In 1987 negotiations, Bluestone and his UAW colleagues essentially put it to GM this way—one that other union leaders would like to have imitated but lacked the power: you can't have it both ways. You can't expect us to cooperate in your union plants and take the political risks associated with QWL and then tell us to go to hell in your new plants. Make a choice—either work with us cooperatively in existing as well as new plants or be prepared to do battle everywhere. GM chose the cooperative strategy and first agreed to a pledge to be neutral in organizing drives in their new facilities and later agreed to an "accretion" clause that extended recognition automatically to its new plants.[12]

By the time Bluestone retired from the UAW in 1980, QWL had been introduced into approximately 20 percent of GM's assembly plants. But our quantitative analysis of plants in two different divisions showed that while the high-conflict/low-trust pattern associated with traditional plants imposed significant productivity and quality costs, the QWL process was not powerful or large enough to produce quantum improvements in either measure of economic performance.[13] But QWL did provide a starting point which convinced enough managers and union leaders that improved trust and employee participation was in their long-run mutual interest and could, if expanded, open up their organizations to broader, more far-reaching changes. Thus the legacy of QWL in the 1970s and early 1980s was one of great promise, promise that opened the door to more fundamental change at the workplace but was slow to diffuse and, on its own, limited in economic impact.

The 1980s ushered in both new UAW leaders and more difficult economic problems for the industry and the union. Douglas Fraser took over as president and appointed Donald Ephlin to head the Ford Department of the UAW and Owen Bieber to head the larger GM Department. Ephlin had worked closely with Bluestone and shared many of his views. As a result, during Ephlin's tenure (1980–1983) Ford's version of QWL, called employee involvement or EI, gained considerable momentum. The negotiation of a new national contract in 1982 was a pivotal event because the industry was attempting to weather its deepest economic crisis since the 1930s. In these negotiations Ephlin and his management counterpart at Ford, Peter Pestillo, negotiated a comprehensive package covering new employment security and adjustment provisions, new joint training programs and funding mechanisms, and a commitment to move on to broader and more experimental forms of employee participation and union-management consultation.

In 1983 the momentum again shifted back to GM when Bieber was elected president of the UAW and Ephlin was assigned to head the union's larger GM Department. At GM he teamed up with his management counterpart, Alfred Warren, Jr., who, like Ephlin, shared a deep commitment to using employee participation and workplace innovations to improve the company's long-term competitiveness. In the six years of the Ephlin-Warren joint tenure at UAW-GM, the union and the company gradually broadened the concept of QWL to encompass the use of work teams and pay for knowledge and broader involvement of local and national union representatives in management and corporate governance. Adoption of these enlarged approaches continued to be at the discretion of local plant managers and local union leaders, but Ephlin and Warren actively promoted them and sought top GM management support and resources for their continuation.

But several setbacks during the Ephlin-Warren years slowed the diffusion of these concepts considerably. Perhaps the most visible and symbolic was GM's decision to close its Pontiac Fiero plant. Fiero had been heralded by the company and union as one of GM's best examples of a team plant—one that embodied high levels of employee involvement, teamwork, labor-management consultation, and decentralization of decision making. It ranked near the top of GM's plants in productivity and quality. Unfortunately the car was a failure, at least as GM measured it, and in 1988 GM decided to discontinue the model. Since much of the tooling of this plant was designed specifically for the Fiero, GM's finance staff judged the costs of bringing another product into the plant as too high. The decision to close Fiero, however, sent shock waves through the union leadership in plants across the country. It sent the message that GM management did not sufficiently value the new organizational model, exemplified by the union-management relationship, at Fiero to support it in the face of a product failure.

Despite this setback, two highly visible innovations of the Ephlin-Warren years stand out: (1) the agreement at NUMMI, GM's joint venture with Toyota, and (2) Saturn, GM's new division to build a small car in the United States.

NUMMI. As noted in Chapters 2 and 3, NUMMI served as America's most important learning laboratory for human resources, labor-management relations, and manufacturing processes of the 1980s. Opened in 1983 and managed by Toyota, the former GM plant was transformed from having one of the worst labor relations and economic performance records in the GM system (as measured by grievance and discipline rates, productivity, and product quality) to the best in the United States and within range of the best in the world. It did so with largely the same blue-collar work force, the same union, and only modest technological upgrades. NUMMI quickly became and continues to be a major success story, one that both data and work force reaction have validated.[14] Part of the reason for the success is that the UAW and Toyota agreed to a completely new contract and relationship that called for use of the team concept and the Toyota production system to organize work and structure the labor-management relationship.

NUMMI's economic success served as a potentially valuable public relations platform for the UAW because it showed that the same American workers and union leaders who, under traditional GM management and collective-bargaining relationships and contracts had such poor labor relations and productivity records, could, under Japanese management, production concepts, and a transformed labor-management relationship, meet world-class standards for quality and productivity. But internal controversies within the UAW limited the ability of the union to fully exploit the public relations or the learning opportunities from NUMMI.

Some union people criticized the NUMMI approach as high-stress management. Others saw it as importing a Japanese style of weak-enterprise unionism. Still others felt that the tight work standards and focus on continuous improvements in productivity at NUMMI gave insufficient attention to the goals of worker democracy, work-team autonomy, and union participation in organization governance.[15] These criticisms to some extent miss the main point of both the NUMMI case and this book. NUMMI is not designed to be an improvement in industrial democracy, but an economically successful operation that produces mutual gains for its owners and employees. On this basis it remains one of the most successful unionized sites in the country.

Saturn. If NUMMI was the most visible learning laboratory of the 1980s, Saturn is emerging as the most visible model in the 1990s. Saturn was conceived in a joint-planning process involving a "Committee of 99" union and management representatives assigned the task of designing an organization and labor-management system that could build a small car in the United States capable of competing with Japanese imports. This joint-planning process was the first stage in what was to become a joint partnership between the UAW and Saturn management at each stage of the organization's evolution—from initial conception and design to the management of the plant, from the teams and work units on the shop floor to the strategic advisory committee that serves as the liaison between Saturn and GM headquarters. The co-management role played by UAW representatives at Saturn represents a fundamental break from U.S. labor-management law, custom, and practice.

Saturn is a fascinating organization for many reasons, but for the purposes of this chapter the main point to note is that the UAW's role is creating a new American style of enterprise union. We have been studying and working with union and management partnership at Saturn for the past several years.[16] Let's look at some of the specific roles that the UAW is playing at Saturn.

The key organizational building blocks at Saturn are the work units, essentially self-directed teams of ten to fifteen employees. These work units are organized into modules that in turn are managed jointly by a UAW and a management partner called work unit module advisers. This type of union-management partnering extends both up the hierarchy to the plant managers and into such staff functions as marketing, finance, maintenance, engineering, quality assurance, communications, and human resources.

Why has the local union taken on this partnership role at Saturn? According to Michael Bennett, the union president at Saturn, the union sees itself as responsible for both the economic and social performance of Saturn. The economic results must demonstrate Saturn's ability to meet the performance levels of its toughest competitors, and the social outcomes must meet the interests of the work force as well as the expectations the broader community holds for a modern corporation. Bennett and his leadership team view these outcomes as highly interdependent. Their model of worker representation is based on the premise that long-term employment and income security cannot be negotiated independently of the economic performance of the firm, nor solely through collective bargaining after all strategic decisions have been made by management. Rather, employment security and other worker objectives can be realized only over the long run by the union's contributing to the economic performance of the firm and participating directly in business planning and decision-making processes to ensure that worker interests are given appropriate consideration. Indeed, workers and managers at Saturn recognize that they still have major challenges to overcome to provide an adequate return on GM's investment. Saturn must expand capacity and output, design and bring to market a second-generation model, bring down production costs without sacrificing quality, and help other GM divisions and UAW locals learn from its new governance model.

Saturn in some ways represents the return on the UAW and GM's decade of investment in trial-and-error efforts to reform their traditional management and labor relations practices. The UAW could not have agreed to the fundamental changes in its role and in its labor contracts at NUMMI or Saturn in the absence of the company's 1976 agreement with Irving Bluestone to abandon its southern strategy. Moreover, the big changes in practices at Saturn would not have gained corporate approval had the UAW not already demonstrated its ability to work with the company and produce mutual benefits. Nor would GM have had the confidence to go ahead without the trust the company placed in Ephlin.

But questions remain. Ephlin retired in 1989, partly because his influence with the union's top leadership was waning. The union has not chosen to use its experience at NUMMI, Saturn, or various other plants where innovative practices have been implemented to articulate a long-run strategy for how it wants to represent workers in the future, how it views teams, or how much of a role it wants in the management and governance of individual plants or the corporations it deals with. While the union's top leaders generally allow local unions to pursue innovations with local management, they have not chosen to capitalize on or take credit for these initiatives. Thus, at the present time, the UAW, like most other unions, maintains a pragmatic posture but fails to build on its contributions to the industry. It continues to demonstrate its willingness to work with management on innovations and changes where these make sense, but it shies away from a visible and public attachment to or championing of this new role.

The Communications Workers of America

The UAW and the auto industry were not alone in agreeing to experiment. In 1980, AT&T and its largest union, the Communications Workers of America (CWA), signed a similar national agreement to introduce QWL into its facilities. Led by president Glen Watts, the CWA became another visible champion for reform in American labor-management relations. Watts later became one of the co-founders and first co-chairs of the Collective Bargaining Forum, a top-level group of CEOs and union presidents committed to, as their first publication put it, "New Patterns of Labor-Management Relations."[17]

In a 1980 National Memorandum of Understanding, AT&T and the CWA described their joint vision for the future as follows:

> Recognizing the desirability of mutual efforts to improve the work life of employees and enhance the effectiveness of the organization, the Company and the Union express their mutual belief that activities and experiments initiated and sponsored jointly by Management and the Union can prove beneficial to all employee participation, work can be made more satisfying and organizational performance and service quality can be improved.[18]

Unfortunately, despite the support of Watts and top AT&T executives, QWL sputtered and faltered during and after the breakup of AT&T. The lesson here is clear—the breakup led to changes in the distribution of power and the decentralization of responsibility to business units at AT&T and in the regional companies. The newly empowered managers placed a low priority on labor-management cooperation as they had to deal with short-term pressures to reduce employment, and compete with newly emerging nonunion firms such as Sprint and MCI and companies in other parts of the rapidly changing telecommunications industry. As a result, by 1992 CWA, then led by Mortimer Bahr, who came out of the rough-and-tumble politics of New York Telephone, and AT&T were at loggerheads over questions involving the rise of nonunion operations, e.g., AT&T's new Universal credit card business, the nonunion operations of NCR—a major new acquisition that was accepted by NCR only after AT&T's CEO promised not to interfere with NCR's basic human resource strategies and practices—and the demand from business unit managers that they be given more flexibility in labor and human resource strategies. All this came in the context of a reduction of union employment levels at AT&T from 260,000 at the time of divestiture to 130,000 a decade later. No wonder the union had a hard time staying the course on QWL, participation, and "cooperation"!

But this is not to say that Bahr and his CWA colleagues are not committed to innovation and participation. He shares the basic views of his predecessor—a better way than traditional collective bargaining is certainly needed. His problem is the same one his management counterpart, CEO Robert Allen of AT&T, faces—the commitment to innovation is not shared at middle levels of the business and union hierarchies, where the intense and traditional oppositional values continue to dominate.

Thus, no less than thirteen years after the signing of the original national agreement to embark on joint QWL efforts, AT&T and the CWA found themselves starting over again with a renewed commitment to finding a better model. And again the parties succeeded in negotiating language to break the stalemate and move forward. The agreement commits the company and the union to work together to develop the "Workplace of the Future" (see Exhibit 6-1). Like the Saturn agreement, it provides for employee participation in individual workplaces, supplemented by consultation between labor and company representatives at various levels of the company. A national-level Human Resources Board is established to examine the full range of

Exhibit 6-1
The Workplace of the Future

AT&T, CWA and IBEW agree to institute this innovative model, the WORK-PLACE OF THE FUTURE, to facilitate greater participation by the Unions in human resource and business planning, benefit AT&T's market position and transform our traditional work systems to customer responsive work systems.

AT&T and the Unions agree to develop the four components listed below in order to implement the WORKPLACE OF THE FUTURE:
1) WORKPLACE MODELS . . . would include, but not be limited to

(1) employee participation initiatives, (2) self-managed/self-directed team environments, (3) continuous quality improvement efforts, (4) flexible, highly skilled work environments, (5) information sharing, and (6) Union involvement in the development of new systems of work organization.

2) BUSINESS UNIT/DIVISION PLANNING COUNCILS will . . . facilitate participation by the Unions in business decisions regarding . . . business unit market conditions, planned technological changes, and future work force management requirements.

3) The CONSTRUCTIVE RELATIONSHIP COUNCIL (CRC) . . . will continue to function to facilitate the leveraging of Workplace Models and Business Unit/Division Planning Councils. Any question or issue which may arise in the Planning Councils may be brought to the CRC for resolution.

4) A HUMAN RESOURCES BOARD will be formed to review key human resource issues worldwide and provide input to the Executive Committee of AT&T.

Source: Looking Ahead, vol. 14, no. 4, 23–24.

"strategic, global human resources and business issues with the context of the external environment over long range time frames."[19]

A key outcome of the negotiations that made it possible to agree on this joint approach to the workplace of the future, however, was that, like the UAW-GM agreement of 1976, the parties agreed on a process for avoiding protracted conflicts over whether new units at AT&T will be organized. This major obstacle to continued innovation between the company and the union, had to be overcome if their joint efforts were to continue to evolve. The finding of a compromise solution to this problem could move the process of innovation forward, just as it did in the auto industry in general, at NUMMI, and at Saturn.

United Steelworkers: The Case of a Canadian Leader

In 1983 a remarkable historical event in American labor history occurred. The first Canadian was elected to the presidency of the United Steelworkers of America (USW). Lynn Williams, the union's secretary-treasurer under Lloyd McBride, had experienced the tumultuous decline of the steel industry that occurred as the value of the U.S. dollar rose relative to the Japanese yen in the early 1980s and produced a flood of imported Japanese steel—steel that very quickly became the benchmark for quality that the American producers had difficulty matching.

Williams is widely recognized as one of the most articulate and effective union leaders of his generation. But even given his personal qualities, Williams faced enormous odds in an industry that had over-capacity, high labor and energy costs, outmoded technologies, highly centralized and autocratic management traditions, and a union structure that made change difficult. (Regional directors of the Steelworkers union are highly autonomous and have their own political base, making them relatively independent of the national union president.)

Despite these odds, the USW produced significant innovation in the past decade. Not only did the union's form of employee involvement at the workplace, called Labor Management Participation Teams, grow, but the union negotiated its way, through concessions and quid pro quos, into seats on the board of directors of companies like Wheeling Pittsburgh and negotiated with companies like Inland, LTV, and Kaiser and their joint Japanese partners to introduce teams and other mutual gains principles into several new greenfield plants and several newly revamped facilities in the industry.

But the largest firm in the American industry, USX, chose to take another course. It rejected the joint partnership strategy and insisted on restructuring through adversarial means—contracting out as much work as possible to lower-cost, often nonunion contractors, negotiating hard (it sustained a 184-day lockout in 1986) to pare labor costs. In the end, USX had reduced its costs per ton to a level that was lower than those of many of its competitors. *But* it also discovered that it could not foster *continuous improvements* without bringing the workers back into the problem-solving process and building their commitment.

This in turn required bringing the union into the process. So in 1992, after a change in the corporate leadership, the union and the company began joint discussions on how to improve relationships at the local level again! And the national union proposed that the union and the steel companies negotiate long-term agreements embodying the principles of flexibility and teamwork at the workplace and participation in strategic decision making at the corporate level.[20]

The union successfully used this strategy in 1993 to negotiate new partnership agreements providing, among other things, representation on the board of directors of all the large steel companies, including USX. In this way the Steelworkers have used their successes and failures over the past decade of experimentation to construct their own model of the union of the future and of labor-management relations.

What do we make of this story? One lesson is that a visionary leader on the union side can make a tremendous difference, even when the economic odds are stacked against him or her. But alone in a sea of adversarial relationships and declining employment and membership, threatened institutional survival, and mixed employer response, the union cannot transform itself in a way that embraces a whole new model. Change is slow and incremental in political institutions such as a union. Top union leaders can make a difference, but they must convince their colleagues at all levels of the organization of the need for a new approach and then invest heavily in training and leadership development to embed these skills in the union. The managers they deal with must be prepared to work with and negotiate within this transformed approach if the new model embodied by the Steelworkers and their colleagues in other unions is to survive and add value to the American work force and economy.

The Amalgamated Clothing and Textile Workers Union

Perhaps the most unlikely candidate for a leadership role in championing innovation would be a union of clothing and textile workers. This industry, like steel, has been declining for years and employs many relatively low-paid women and immigrants. Yet for several reasons, the Amalgamated Clothing and Textile Workers Union (ACTWU) has been a visible contributor to innovative activities at both the individual firm and the industry level.

Its role owes a great deal to historical happenstance. ACTWU represents all the blue-collar workers at Xerox Corporation, mostly because it was the dominant union in Rochester, New York, where

Xerox started, and has its largest manufacturing complex. As noted in previous chapters, in 1981 Xerox and ACTWU began an experimental QWL program that, over the next decade, became recognized as one of the most successful examples of labor-management innovation in the United States. In large part its visibility and reputation are the result of the company's success in reversing its declining market share and its demonstrated achievements in quality, product development, and innovation. ACTWU was a joint partner throughout the process of transforming Xerox.[21]

The experience at Xerox served as a learning opportunity for ACTWU's leaders. Both past president Murray Finley and current president Jack Sheinkman have been strong and enthusiastic supporters of the union's role at Xerox and have tried, often in vain, to introduce similar changes in the union's core industry, clothing. But the conditions in clothing are quite different—firms tend to be smaller, have less access to sources of long-term capital, are less professionally managed, and are less profitable than Xerox. Moreover, clothing manufacturers' competitive strategies and workplace systems are partially determined by the purchasing patterns and marketing strategies of retailers. Unless the retailers shift to a "quick response, or rapid replenishment of supply" strategy, the traditional mass-production piecework system is likely to remain in place.[22] Most significant, few clothing firms are willing to accept the union as a full joint partner in existing establishments, let alone in any new plants. As a result, there has been little diffusion of the lessons the union has learned at Xerox to the union's clothing markets.

But largely at the insistence of Jack Sheinkman, the union and one important segment of the clothing industry—the men's and boys' suit and sportcoat—has explored the new model. The union has done so in the same way it has traditionally contributed to innovation in the clothing industry—by seeking to promote change at the industry level: (1) encouraging industry- or regionwide bargaining and wage setting and (2) working with individual firms to improve their engineering, manufacturing methods, and technology.

In 1989, in an effort to resolve an impasse over the industry's demand for greater flexibility to import garments and the union's demand that the industry maintain its investment in and commitment to U.S. manufacturing, the union and the industry established a joint committee. The National Clothing Labor-Management Committee (NCLMC) subsequently negotiated a new policy allowing the industry to import garments, provided it continued to invest in American manufacturing and met some rather stringent employment and earnings guarantees. The committee also, largely at the urging of Sheinkman, argued for an industry strategy for promoting exports. In an early NCLMC meeting devoted to discussion of this export development strategy and program, industry consultants stressed that, to be successful, companies would need to make a long-term commitment of resources and personal managerial support to gain access to European markets. Unfortunately, only a small number of U.S. firms were willing or able to commit to such a long-term strategy, so progress has been rather slow. But without the union leadership and the joint committee's program, no industry effort would have been forthcoming at all. This example demonstrates again how labor representatives can often take a longer-run view that offsets the short-term focus of managers.

The NCLMC also encouraged adoption and diffusion of innovations in individual workplaces that are designed to help modernize the industry and move it away from its focus on repetitive piecework and low-wage-cost competition. The committee conducted a series of studies that culminated in a report that outlined a "Strategy for Innovation" for restructuring work in its industry.

The union then assigned a staff professional to work with companies in implementing the new strategy and, more generally, to help develop a long-range "industry strategy" for the union. Early in 1993, the Amalgamated broke new ground for the American labor movement by being the first union to commit itself publicly to promoting "new partnerships" with employers as a stated union strategy for representing its members and contributing to the competitiveness of the firms in which its members are employed. Exhibit 6-2 provides excerpts from this document. As of this writing, a number of individual company and union partnerships are in the developmental stage. Progress continues to be limited by the fact that too many clothing firms continue to see low labor costs, high turnover, and piecework systems as viable in the United States because of the continued availability of new generations of immigrants willing to work at low wages and under poor working conditions. Until stronger market or other forces produce a shift in managerial strategies for how to compete, these workplace and union-led innovations will continue to diffuse at a snail's pace. Yet, as was the case in the 1920s, the union in this industry has once again demonstrated that it can engage in a "dress rehearsal" for a new model of labor-management relations. Its act could come front stage and be the centerpiece for industry restructuring.

Exhibit 6-2
Creating New Partnerships

The Amalgamated Clothing and Textile Workers Union

Today, worker participation programs are spreading throughout our manufacturing base, including shop-floor problem-solving teams, autonomous work teams, and the use of continuous quality improvement. It is our belief that only workers who are members of a recognized union can be full partners in the employee involvement process. Only with the protection of a union contract are workers free to express their views.

But, workplace participation does far more than make companies more competitive. *It also provides the way of achieving many of our long-delayed labor goals.* True worker participation can be a way for our people to demand and get more control over the work they do. It can help bring greater job security. It can provide a higher standard of living. The truth is that real participation through a New Partnership can increase our strength and broaden our ability to improve the working conditions of our members.

The Amalgamated Clothing and Textile Workers Union believes in and is committed to . . . a new approach. That approach underscores *the power, creativity and talent of our people . . . and their dedication in helping their companies prosper* when they are treated as important and vital to the organization.

We both must move from traditional, often adversarial roles, to what can best be called a *New Partnership.* Clearly, this can and will only happen where companies are willing to join with us in a *true partnership based on mutual trust, respect and shared goals.* But, our policy is not just to hope for such partnerships, but to *actively work to create them* where realistically possible.

There are four strategies for creating the kind of New Partnership to which we are committed. All are essential to create both the kind of workplace our people deserve and the success the companies have to be world-class global competitors:

1. Strong Locals Actively Involved with Management
2. Employee Involvement
3. New Technology and Training
4. Work System Redesign

Source: "Creating New Partnerships," a policy statement of the Amalgamated Clothing and Textile Workers Union, January 1993.

This union and its leadership illustrate that currently, as historically, a union with the right vision and drive can contribute to industry policy and strategy by taking a long-run view of how to compete in ways that can promote higher labor standards. But the limited success of the effort also indicates that it cannot do this in isolation. It needs corresponding business leadership with a long-term view and a similar commitment to mutual gains strategies. (See Exhibit 6-3 for ACTWU's efforts to work with one such company, Levi Strauss.) This requires breaking out of a traditional mind-set that focuses on labor costs as the critical factor influencing success.

The Harvard Union of Clerical and Technical Workers

If American unions are to experience a resurgence they will need to find a way of appealing to the large number and diverse nature of employees in the service sector. These workers are not likely to respond to traditional organizing campaigns that rely on deep dissatisfaction with their employer. One innovative example of a union that organized around an alternative concept is the Harvard Union of Clerical and Technical Workers (HUCTW).[23]

In its organizing drive, HUCTW used the campaign slogan that epitomized its emphasis on the positive features of union representation: "You don't have to be anti-Harvard to be pro-union." But it still experienced strong resistance from the university. After a long—fifteen-year!—organizing drive, the union won a representation election in 1988 by a slim majority—1,530 to 1,486. But only after losing several unfair labor-practice appeals to the National Labor Relations Board (NLRB) did Harvard president Derek Bok finally agree to recognize the union and negotiate a first contract.

Once the recognition battle was over, the parties developed a highly innovative, broad-based participative approach to negotiating their initial contract. John Dunlop, long-term Harvard faculty member, former secretary of Labor, and the undisputed "dean" of U.S. industrial relations experts, advised the university in its negotiations. Together with Kris Roundeau, the innovative union president, he created a series of problem-solving committees that devised options on issues ranging from work and family issues, child care, health benefits, career progression, and health and safety. This problem-solving approach to negotiation produced a first contract without a strike or need for further government mediation or NLRB litigation.

Exhibit 6-3
Designing a Union Partnership Strategy: ACTWU and Levi's

In February 1993 the local and national leaders of the Amalgamated Clothing and Textile Workers Union who deal with the Levi Strauss Company held a historic two-day planning meeting to discuss how to build an effective partnership for innovation with Levi's. Never before had all the local and national union officers and staff who deal with a single company come together to share ideas and develop this type of union and corporatewide strategy.

The union also invited Levi's vice president of Industrial Relations to address the group along with two academics who had worked with the union on various workplace innovation and labor-management projects in the past. The Levi's representative reported on parallel management meetings under way designed to develop the company's approach to building a strategic partnership with the union.

In the 1850s Levi Strauss went to San Francisco to make tents to sell to gold rush miners. Finding the market already saturated, Strauss turned the canvas he had bought into pants. The company remained largely family owned and by 1981 was selling 5.6 million pairs of jeans. But the 1980s proved to be a rough period. Competition increased, market share declined, and a failed diversification effort led to a major downsizing. In 1984 Robert Haas, a descendant of the founder, became CEO and, to avoid a hostile takeover, took the company private and implemented a highly leveraged ESOP.

Production built up again and in 1991 the company and union (about half the company's plants are unionized and half are unorganized) agreed to develop a "New Management/Manufacturing System" based on team production.

The union's challenge in this case was to develop a consensus strategy to work with the company in implementing this new system in its plants and to work out an understanding about how its efforts to organize the nonunion plants would be managed. The company's challenge was to build support for the new system within its ranks and to reach internal consensus over how to relate to the union's role and long-run objectives for the nonunion plants.

Following these separate meetings, the company and union formed a joint task force. This joint effort is now overseeing the various joint projects under way in Levi's plants around the country.

The preamble to the Harvard-HUCTW contract reads:

[Harvard] has come to be governed, in the broadest sense of the term, through a cooperative process among governing boards and administrators, faculty, students, and alumni, in which each plays a role. This Understanding welcomes the support staff in libraries, in laboratories, and in academic and administrative offices and centers, represented by HUCTW, as a valued and essential participant in this process.

True to the preamble, the initial contract contained essential principles for joint committees to govern the relationship throughout the life of the contract. In addition, substantial improvements in wages, a new salary progression plan, and improvements in pensions and other benefits were negotiated, showing that traditional issues remain central and critical to the role of a union.

The second contract, negotiated in 1992 and 1993, proved to be almost as difficult as the original organizing drive. Harvard negotiators took a somewhat more traditional approach to the process and the union negotiations had to respond in kind. Although the union never threatened to strike, it did use innovative pressure tactics to communicate its determination to achieve a successful contract, including at one point greeting the new Harvard University president at Boston's Logan Airport on his return from an overseas trip by playing "Hail to the Chief" on kazoos! This union, which has a sense of humor and a deep sense of mission and militancy, has channeled that militancy and mission in a way that fits both the culture of its work force and employer.

It is also a highly decentralized and autonomous union, but one that is affiliated with and has benefited greatly at crucial times from the financial and political support of its national office, the American Federation of State County and Municipal Employees (AFSCME). It chose to affiliate with AFSCME after a bitter split with the UAW, which originally had tried to organize Harvard's clerical employees but failed after the UAW fired Roundeau and her colleagues as the result of a dispute with national union officers over how to conduct the organizing campaign. This case has another lesson for the labor movement—unions of the future may need to be highly autonomous and decentralized in order to be close to their members. But affiliation with a national organization that can provide the right type of resources and leadership support is critical to the union's long-run success.

Toward a New AFL-CIO Strategy?

Throughout the 1980s, the AFL-CIO also made efforts to forge new directions through an internal study group called the Evolution of Work Committee. This committee was formed in 1982 to examine the state of the labor movement and explore alternatives for its future. Chaired by Thomas Donahue, secretary-treasurer of the AFL-CIO, the committee undertook considerable internal analysis, commissioned a survey of attitudes of workers and union members, then issued a report, "The State of Workers and Their Unions," which laid the basis for a number of experiments in new forms of associate membership, member services, and communications and public relations programs. But its most important achievement was the internal self-appraisal and debates the committee fostered among the twenty or so international union presidents and AFL-CIO officers and staff that continued to meet during the 1980s. In its second phase of activity, the committee took part in a series of seminars with a wide variety of academic, management, and international experts over alternatives as far ranging as ESOPs, works councils, codetermination, employee participation, and nonexclusive forms of representation. Although in 1990 the committee reached a tentative, internal consensus on a new statement supporting broad experimentation with a number of these initiatives, the consensus dissolved among the top leadership of the federation before a final report was issued.

With the election of President Bill Clinton in 1992, a potential new era of strategic choice arrived for the labor movement. Should it attempt to capitalize on a more friendly Democratic administration by arguing for changes in a variety of labor laws and administrative practices that had either been set back or neglected under twelve years of conservative Republican rule? In other words, was it now time to make up for lost ground by promoting such things as the passage of a bill banning use of striker replacements, reform of union representation election certification procedures and rules, and strengthening of a variety of labor standards in need of repair? Or should it take a broad approach to the future of labor policy and capitalize on its experimental experiences and propose opening labor law and policy to more fundamental changes that would encourage and support new forms of employee participation and union representation in workplace problem solving, management decision making, and corporate governance? Should the labor movement serve as the champion for those changes?

In our own work, we have urged the labor movement to take a bold and comprehensive approach to its political and enterprise strategies and become the most visible national champion for new models of worker representation.[24] We have suggested that unions become "full-service agents" for representing workers in a variety of forums, ranging from employee empowerment at the workplace, to providing technical support and advice to employees and union leaders serving on joint committees dealing with topics such as health and safety, new technology, training and skill development, and business planning and strategy, to representation on corporate boards of directors in ESOP companies or in other firms where employees have a significant financial stake.

For this approach to be successful, however, corresponding changes in labor law and national economic policy will be needed. Just as the model that ushered in industrial unionism in the 1930s could not have been successful without fundamental reforms in national labor policy, so too will this new approach by labor require equally fundamental changes in national labor, human resource, and economic policy. There is also a chicken-and-the-egg problem. Should or can labor lead the reform process? Or will leadership by the president and other national policy makers be required to change the climate and policies governing labor-management relations? We return to this question in our final chapter.

In 1994 the AFL-CIO signaled its interest in leading this process by issuing a statement from the Evolution of Work Committee endorsing Labor Management Partnerships for introducing new models of work organization and employee participation (see Exhibit 6-4). This is the first time the federation has gone on record in support of workplace innovations. Whether it can translate this into significant change at the workplace and into a new image for the labor movement as a champion and catalyst of change remains to be seen. But it is a major first step in this direction.

Beyond Unions: Alternative Forms of Worker Representation

So far we have examined efforts by unions to develop new models within the confines of the existing framework of labor law and worker representation. But, as noted in Chapter 5, other countries, particularly in Europe, have at least two other options for worker representation: works councils and codetermination. Could either or both of these European institutions be adapted to the American context, culture, and organizational settings?

Exhibit 6-4

The AFL-CIO's Statement on Workplace Innovation and Labor-Management Partnerships

It is incumbent on unions to take the initiative in stimulating, sustaining, and institutionalizing a new system of work organization based upon full and equal labor-management partnerships. Such a system presupposes, of course, partners prepared to deal with each other as equals in an atmosphere of mutual recognition and respect.

Some general guidelines can be articulated to define the kind of partnership which the labor movement must seek to make the new model of work organization a reality.

First, we seek partnerships based on mutual recognition and respect. . . . A partnership requires management to accept and respect the union's right to represent the workers in units already organized and equally to accept and respect the right of workers in unorganized units to join a union.

Second, . . . the partnerships we seek must be based on the collective bargaining relationship. Changes in work organizations must be mutually agreed to—and not unilaterally imposed—and must be structured so as to assure the union's ability to bargain collectively on behalf of the workers it represents on an ongoing basis.

Third, the partnerships must be founded on the principle of equality. In concrete terms, this means that unions and management must have an equal role in the development and implementation of new work systems. . . .

Fourth, the partnership must be dedicated to advancing certain agreed-upon goals reflecting the parties' mutual interests.

Source: "The New American Workplace: A Labor Perspective." Report of the AFL-CIO Evolution of Work Committee, February 1994.

Until very recently such a question would have been answered by both labor and management experts with a resounding *no.* But recently, more interest has been expressed and more academics have either been studying or advocating works councils.[25] One reason for this new interest is the recognition that the void in worker representation in American society is not likely to be filled in a way that contributes to the competitiveness of the economy by a resurgence of traditional-style unions. Nor are the innovations in existing union-management relationships powerful enough on their own to attract workers to organize a union. Indeed, the same Gallup survey of worker views of unions found even stronger support for less adversarial associations of workers. Although 60 percent approved of unions, fully 90 percent approved of employee associations (see Table 6-1).

Taken together, the data from this poll as well as others suggest that there is strong pent-up demand for new forms of employee organizations that provide input at the workplace but avoid the conflicts, tensions, risks, and adverse management reactions of traditional unions. Indeed, if we extrapolate the expressed support for this type of organization in the Gallup poll to the unorganized work force, we estimate that there are more than 40 million workers in the labor force who would support this type of workplace representation. This is almost double the number of unorganized workers who would be interested in joining a traditional union if the opportunity were available. This suggests the need to find ways to provide these opportunities to the workers interested in participating in them.

In summary, the argument for some innovative forms of representation comes down to the fact that institutions can be crafted that will (1) increase the need for management to weigh the human resource consequences of strategic decisions more heavily before decisions are made; (2) increase the upward and downward flow of information and improve problem solving and provide feedback; and (3) enfranchise the full diversity of the labor force without building in an adversarial contest.

The advantages of works councils over the union-management partnership models discussed earlier are obvious. First, opening up to the possibility of works councils provides an opportunity for the 85 percent of the labor force that is not organized to gain access to employee representation without having to engage in union organizing for the purpose of collective bargaining. Second, it provides a form of representation that enfranchises the full diversity of an enterprise's work force. Third, it builds representation for workers that seeks integrative, joint gains solutions without limiting the opportunity to organize for collective-bargaining purposes if the latter, more distributive-oriented process seems preferable. We believe works councils, appropriately adapted to the American setting, would help to diffuse and institutionalize workplace innovations in the United States. In Chapter 8 we discuss ways to change national labor policy to allow this to happen.

Summary and Conclusions

For more than two decades American unions have been experimenting with new approaches to supporting employee participation and labor-management consultation while under siege from declining membership and working under a restrictive labor-law environment. Some progress has been made and new models have been developed and fitted to different environments. Several unions, such as the Steelworkers, Clothing and Textile Workers, and Communications Workers, having learned from these experiences, have endorsed new models of participation and representation and laid out clear guidelines for employers interested in and willing to work with them in pursuit of mutual gains. But the most far-reaching models in union and nonunion settings have had to go outside the law, arguably to break the law. Yet joint commitment and participation have been shown to be important factors in sustaining workplace innovations and reforms needed for mutual gains enterprises to realize their full economic potential.

Therefore, as in the 1930s, it may be time to recognize that the dress rehearsal is over and it is time to raise the curtain and let the real performance begin. That is, the time has come to open American labor law to an era of experimentation that can remove these obstacles to the diffusion and institutionalization of mutual gains principles.

chapter seven

INSTITUTIONS AND POLICIES FOR HUMAN RESOURCE DEVELOPMENT

Considerable innovation is under way in individual enterprises and unions. If more widely diffused and sustained over time, they would help the economy be competitive at high wages and living standards. But as long as these innovations remain isolated individual efforts, they are fragile, difficult to sustain over time, and unlikely to diffuse widely enough to achieve their full potential.

Left to their own devices, neither the invisible hand of the market nor the initiatives of individual firms will produce the changes and outcomes needed to achieve an economy that can compete in international markets at high standards of living. Instead, we have a classic case of a market failure. A more active government policy is needed to serve as a catalyst for change. The purpose of this chapter and the next is to outline the elements of employment, human resource, and labor relations policies that facilitate adoption and diffusion of mutual gains practices across the economy.

We begin discussion of the role of government by focusing on the need for an active training and human resource development policy for both new entrants and current members of the work force. The evidence presented in the previous chapters showed that investment in training and human resource development is essential to workplace reform. An adequate supply of workers with the necessary cognitive, behavioral, and technical skills is needed to make investments in workplace innovations cost effective for employers. These skills are also necessary for workers to command improvements in wages and long-run employment security in today's labor markets. Finally, a well-educated and trained labor force is critical to productivity growth and improved living standards for the overall economy and society. Training serves as a linchpin in the pursuit of mutual gains from workplace innovations.

Yet we have also shown that there is inadequate investment in training in the American economy both for new entrants and for the current work force. One reason is that the traditional work systems did not require the level or types of skills demanded by the new systems. A second reason is that individual firms compete in labor, product, and capital markets where the costs of investing in the required skills are high, visible, and immediate, while the benefits are uncertain, long term, and not likely to be fully captured by the firm that bears the costs. Therefore, the case for government policy to overcome these failures is quite strong.

The first step in laying out a framework for training policy is to investigate the nature of the market failures which that policy is intended to address. We do so by describing what we consider a most successful program.

Mary Rose Hennesey runs a training network—initially based in an employer association and now based at Northern Illinois University—for small and medium-size firms. These firms, typically suppliers, are pressured by their customers to adopt quality techniques such as statistical process control (SPC) and total quality management (TQM). Frequently having little idea how to accomplish this, they call Hennesey for assistance. In some instances the firms pay for the assistance; for employers that demonstrate a need and show that assistance will pay off, but cannot afford the cost, an Illinois state training program, Prairie State 2000, helps fund the intervention.

Hennesey's trainers not only provide skill training but also methods of changing work organization. Often employees also need basic skills (i.e., literacy) training. In short, a firm seeks training, the training is provided by a public authority, costs are shared, and that training is linked to changes in work organization.

This case illustrates several reasons why policy intervention is appropriate. The first is informational: many firms simply do not know how to introduce new quality systems and new work systems. Smaller firms particularly need help.

The second rationale concerns the constraints under which firms, again smaller firms particularly, operate. These companies often lack access to financial resources and operate on a very tight margin. They lack the organizational resources, and managerial time, to invest in the very changes necessary to keep them competitive. They are in what might be termed a low-level equilibrium trap and need help in ratcheting up to a higher level.

Third, these firms face the classic market failure associated with training. They fear that if they invest in upskilling their work force, their employees will leave, causing the firm to lose its investment. Again, this is especially a problem for smaller enterprises, which lack job ladders that can keep employees attached to the firm. One might think that the solution is to provide the training in schools to share the costs, yet much of the training is best done on the job site. So another form of a public solution to this problem is necessary.

Finally, these firms often operate in isolation. This is what might be termed an institutional failure, i.e., the lack of effective private or public-private networks, groups, associations, and other institutions that coordinate the efforts of individual actors and pool resources to generate public goods and distribute their benefits to individual participants. The United States has been known for its weak institutional infrastructure for supporting innovations. Richard Walton documented this point in an international comparative study of innovations in the maritime industry.[1] He showed that its innovations failed to diffuse in the United States as they did in other countries precisely because U.S. shipping companies guarded their independence, kept their trade association weak and without adequate professional resources, and kept their bargaining relationships with maritime unions decentralized.

Robert Cole reached the same conclusion in his comparison of the use of small-group problem-solving techniques in Japan, Sweden, and the United States.[2] He showed that quality circles and related problem-solving methods spread across Japan largely through the efforts of the Japanese Union of Scientists and Engineers. In Sweden, the strong and highly centralized Swedish Employers Federation embraced, then modified the sociotechnical work systems theories developed by academics at the Tavistock Institute in Britain and then used its centralized bargaining relationships with unions to implement these ideas across Swedish industry. Cole contrasts these approaches with the slow and uneven path of acceptance of group problem-solving processes in the United States, even though the fundamental ideas of both quality circles and employee team problem solving were developed by U.S. behavioral scientists.

We agree with Walton and Cole's thesis and therefore stress the need to build institutions that can aid in the diffusion of human resource developments and related workplace institutions. But it must be done in ways that take into account American traditions and managerial skepticism about collective associations and networks. Later in this chapter we discuss three types of institutional arrangements to promote investment in training: (1) state government–private sector partnerships, (2) labor-management joint training programs, and (3) employer networks and consortia. We realize that in making a case for active public policy, we must overcome years of well-grounded wariness about whether the government can actually play a positive role in the labor market. For this reason, we draw on examples of private-public institutions already at work and gain lessons from these examples.

Training for Adults

The case for an active government role in training adults who are already in the labor force rests on four propositions that we have documented throughout this book: (1) transformed work organizations require higher skill and more training, and, in turn, the availability of highly skilled workers increases the incentives for firms to adopt mutual gains systems; (2) American firms provide too little training, both in absolute terms and relative to comparable foreign competitors; (3) more than 70 percent of those who will make up the labor force in the first decade of the next century are already in the labor force; and (4) improved training for adults will help alleviate the adverse consequences of economic change that some workers will inevitably experience.

This last point deserves elaboration. Not only is it fair to say that the "winners" compensate the "losers," but by providing a measure of security, firms will have to deal with fewer obstacles in the path of innovation and change. The industrial relations and human resource management literatures are replete with examples in which groups of employees have delayed or obstructed workplace transformations. At a political level, opposition to economic policies which threaten the status quo are also fed by fears that workers lack the skills or opportunities to adjust to economic change. A strong adult training policy is one way to address these concerns.

The Shape of Public Policy

The foregoing illustrates several characteristics that should be part of any new programs. They should be broadly based and able to serve a wide range of clients. In addition they should be "employer-centered"—working directly with employers and worker representatives. This approach might take the form of assisting businesses to train new hires or to retrain their incumbent workers in a range of areas including new technology, techniques such as statistical process control, TQM, and literacy. Additionally, the employer-centered approach may also extend to provide support to firms that want to reorganize their production systems into autonomous work teams and other higher productivity arrangements.

An employment and training policy that views the employer community as a significant customer would be a considerable departure from current federal efforts. So isolated from employers is the current federal training program, the Job Training Partnership Act (JTPA), that a Bureau of National Affairs Survey of large employers found that only 9 percent had any contact with it.[3] Furthermore, virtually all federal job-training programs are income targeted, although some have long viewed this aspect as a major weakness of the system.[4]

If one were to rely on national experience alone, it would be difficult to assess the potential for building the type of public-private institutions needed to implement this employer-centered approach. In general, the only experience the federal employment and training program has had in working with employers is in subsidized on-the-job training efforts, which are typically aimed at a small subset (low-wage/low-skill) of the employer population.

There is, however, another source of experience. In the past decade state and local agencies experimented widely with employment and training programs. We believe that these can provide the basis for thinking about restructuring federal policy. Although recent state and local efforts are generally small and deal with only a piece of the problem, they tend to share characteristics necessary for a new federal policy: they are not income targeted and they work directly with firms as well as with individuals. Our recommendations in this section are based in large part on field studies of several state programs.[5]

State-level Training Institutions

At the state level, the typical program is administered either through a state agency expressly created for the purpose (e.g., the California Employment and Training Panel or the Illinois Prairie State 2000 program) or through community colleges. The programs accept requests from firms and determine whether a company can benefit from assistance and whether it is likely to undertake the training on its own without public help. The training can be centered around broad concerns such as changes in work systems (e.g., introduction of high-performance work systems) or more narrow issues such as the introduction of new machinery or adult literacy.

If the firm is eligible, the program provides funds for bringing in outside trainers or supporting in-house training. If there is a union, some states require that it be jointly involved in planning the training. The state programs are also proactive, for example, seeking out firms that need help or helping to pull together business associations.

To provide a more concrete "feel" for what these programs can accomplish, we describe in Exhibit 7-1 through Exhibit 7-3 "best practice" programs in California, Illinois, North Carolina, and South Carolina.

Constructing Federal Policy for Adult Training

Under what conditions is it feasible to use federal resources to expand and systematize the kinds of training programs we have described?[6] The problem facing federal planners is twofold. First, the interests of the federal government diverge at some point from those of the states. For example, states might prefer to use training funds to attract employers to move from other states (in fact, the evidence suggests that this does not work very well). But such a policy is obviously not in the federal interest. Clearly, program guidelines have to be developed to

Exhibit 7-1
California

California's Employment Training Panel (ETP) began in 1983 as a statewide effort to train unemployed workers and retrain potentially displaced workers in "at-risk" firms and industries. An unemployment insurance surtax of 0.1 percent of taxable wages generates a multimillion-dollar fund that was capped at $55 million annually until 1989, when the cap was removed. The 1991 ETP budget totaled more than $150 million. Between 1983 and 1991 the panel enrolled 160,000 trainees in more than 1,000 training contracts worth $300 million.

The unique features of the system are its employer-driven quality, its strong support and involvement of unions, its heavy reliance on private training providers, and its strict performance-based contracts, which link reimbursement to ninety-day job placements of trainees.

A concrete example of a successful panel program is the Los Angeles chapter of the National Machining and Tooling Association, a regional association of employers working in the machining industry. Drawing on an estimated 3,500 job shops in the region, the organization has 250 members and serves close to 500 employers through pre-employment training of new hires and retraining of skilled machinists.

In addition to ETP, the center currently operates JTPA programs for entry-level machinists, which cover 5 percent of the center's trainees, and administers a state-approved apprenticeship program serving 125 participants annually. Approximately three-quarters of the center's new-hire participants are minorities of Hispanic, black, or Asian descent. Two percent are women.

The center boasts a 98 percent placement rate for ETP-funded new-hire trainees who have completed 560 hours of training in a four-month program. The pre-employment program, which costs ETP $4,000 per trainee, covers the basics of precision machining from milling to blueprint reading; it readies graduates to work and continue their training at companies with in-house or state-approved apprenticeship programs. The latter require four years of classes one night per week plus on-the-job training to reach the grade of journeyman machinist. ETP thus serves as a bridge for unemployed workers to gain the basic skills for entry-level positions in precision machining and the opportunity for further training toward highly skilled tool and die making.

Source: Rosemary Batt and Paul Osterman, "Workplace Training Policy: Case Studies of State and Local Experiments," Case Studies for *A National Policy for Workplace Training: Lessons from State and Local Experiments* (Washington, D.C.: Economic Policy Institute, 1993), pp. 3–19.

Exhibit 7-2
Illinois

Illinois has funded two complementary employment training programs: the Industrial Training Program (ITP), established in 1979 to attract capital investment in the state, and Prairie State 2000, begun in 1983 to provide training to at-risk workers and firms. Between 1979 and 1990 ITP spent $106 million on training programs for 130,000 workers in 700 firms. The smaller Prairie State program funded $6 million in training for 330 firms involving 33,000 workers.

ITP has primarily provided training for large firms that invest in new plant and equipment within the state; grants not associated with new capital investment have funded training in small and medium-size firms in recent years. By contrast, Prairie State 2000 uses a combination of grants and loans to support training in small firms in financial difficulty. Through 1991, costs per trainee averaged $729 for ITP and $177 for Prairie State. Both programs cover 50

Exhibit 7-2
Continued

---

percent of the costs of training, thereby serving as an incentive for employer investments in training.

Prairie State field staff work with companies to develop training proposals, which are submitted and approved on a first-come, first-served basis. Employers determine the content and format of the training according to their particular production needs. They may choose among a variety of providers: private sector trainers, community colleges, in-house company trainers, employer associations, community-based organizations, or unions. In fact, private sector providers and in-house staff make up the bulk of trainers. In unionized facilities, employers must have the union's agreement for the proposed training.

Grants have commonly supported retraining in new manufacturing technologies and work processes for productivity and quality improvements. These include computer software training, computer-assisted design and manufacturing, CNC machine training, just-in-time inventory control, material resource planning, and statistical process control. The majority of employers that participate in this program have been parts suppliers whose customers are demanding improvements in quality and productivity as a condition for future contracts.

The Lawrence Box and Basket Co., Inc., is a typical example of a company saved by this program.* A firm of thirteen employees, in operation since 1903, Lawrence Box and Basket received a grant from Prairie State 2000 in 1988 to train workers to run new equipment designed to produce customized baskets. The company qualified for assistance because it had been operating at a loss. The formal training for mechanics and machine operators resulted in a reduction in scrap from 1 percent of stock to less than 0.1 percent. Setup time for the new machine was half an hour, in comparison with the half day needed for the old one. The new machine increased the volume and the quality of baskets produced.

---

*These examples draw on case studies conducted by Robert Sheets for the National Governors Association evaluation study of state-financed, workplace-based training. See Sheets, "Building a World-Class Workforce in the United States: The Need for a National-State System of Industry Skill Standards for State Workforce Preparation Programs," paper prepared for the National Center for the Educational Quality of the Workforce, University of Pennsylvania, July 1991.

Source: Rosemary Batt and Paul Osterman, "Workplace Training Policy: Case Studies of State and Local Experiments," Case Studies for *A National Policy for Workplace Training: Lessons from State and Local Experiments* (Washington, D.C.: Economic Policy Institute, 1993), pp. 19–27.

Exhibit 7-3
North Carolina and South Carolina

North Carolina and South Carolina's programs are examples of integrated technical training systems operated through the community college system. Begun in the late 1950s and early 1960s as industrial training programs to attract northern manufacturers south, and supported by the federal Manpower Development and Training Act, these systems are unique in their reliance on the public sector to administer and operate programs; their use of employers to define the content of customized training, which frequently "spills over" into the basic college curriculum; their labor-market orientation; their comprehensiveness in meeting the needs of diverse employers, industries, and workers; and their integration of an array of state and federal programs.

North Carolina has a more massive system with a decentralized structure, which gives local colleges more decision-making power. South Carolina has a more centralized structure and, in the last decade, has distinguished itself by establishing specialized regional centers offering state-of-the-art technology and training in particular occupational fields.

The North Carolina system served more than 660,000 students in fifty-eight colleges in 1989 with a budget of $450 million. The system provides entry-level training through associate degree and nondegree programs, further training for adults through continuing occupational education, and customized training to meet the needs of employers. The last category covers, among others, the New and Expanding Industries Program for firms that are locating in the state or expanding existing operations, and the Focused Industry Training Program, which targets training to small, in-state firms to make them more competitive.

The South Carolina system, with a budget of $150 million and a 1990 enrollment of 185,000 in sixteen community colleges, also takes a comprehensive approach to training. Like North Carolina, South Carolina provides three categories of training: curriculum, occupational extension, and "Special Schools," the South Carolina equivalent of North Carolina's program for new and expanding industries.

The state's technical training strategy over the past decade has centered around the development of state-of-the-art technology resource centers at various colleges across the state. Each center serves as a magnet for specialized technical fields: the eight centers currently in operation include robotics, applied microelectronics, electromechanical maintenance, computer applications, advanced machine tool technology, and plastics.

Source: Rosemary Batt and Paul Osterman, "Workplace Training Policy: Case Studies of State and Local Experiments," Case Studies for *A National Policy for Workplace Training: Lessons from State and Local Experiments* (Washington, D.C.: Economic Policy Institute, 1993), pp. 29–42.

prevent such actions. Another important risk is that public funds will be used to support firm-based training, which would be done in any event. This substitution leads to a waste of scarce public resources.

Targeting small and at-risk firms is a strategy for dealing with the problems of substitution. It is difficult for a public agency to collect the kind of firm-level data necessary to demonstrate that publicly funded training programs represent an effort beyond what would otherwise be provided by firms. Instead of attempting to collect such data, an alternative approach is to support training in firms that by their very nature would be unlikely to provide adequate training.

In our fieldwork we observed a number of programs that were successful in reaching small firms, including North Carolina's Focused Industry Training Program (described in Exhibit 7-3) and the use of employer consortia as brokers, which we discuss below. Another example is the Illinois Prairie State 2000 program, which targets small firms that are either losing money or reinvesting all their profits in the enterprise. The rationale is that these firms are on the margin and that any public assistance is a genuine addition to what they would do on their own. Prairie State appears to be successful in implementing this targeting scheme, but it places enormous demands on the analytical skills of the public agency. Not only must the agency be able to assess the current condition of the enterprise, it must also be able to make an accurate prediction concerning the survival of the firm.

Establishing General Training Standards

General training standards also provide a partial solution to the substitution problem. First, it is noteworthy that the problem is most troubling when firms use public funds to provide firm-specific training, because workers cannot move elsewhere to gain a benefit from the training. A solution therefore is to ensure that public funds are spent on training that has a substantial general component. One way to do this is to develop uniform occupational training standards that are employed by a range of training providers.[7]

In this model, support would be provided only for training that meets those standards, which would incorporate general skills. The state of Illinois, for example, is experimenting with the design of training standards along these lines,[8] and federal policy makers are also considering adoption of such standards.

An additional value of standards is that they establish a benchmark for measuring the content of the training that individuals receive and the skills they actually acquire. This is the first step toward measuring whether training dollars do what they are intended to do. Few evaluations exist with respect to the quality or effectiveness of employer-centered training or its link to productivity improvement.

A third advantage of standards is that they help avoid the bureaucratic fragmentation of the training system. Realistically, it is difficult to integrate high school vocational education, community colleges, JTPA programs, and private providers. However, if they were all required to train to a given standard, many of the benefits of integration could be gained.

Union-Management Training Programs

Just as innovative state programs have emerged in the past decade, so have creative union-management training programs. There are now important examples in auto, telecommunications, aerospace, apparel, and other industries. The case below describes in detail one of the most interesting examples: Alliance, which was created by AT&T, the Communications Workers of America (CWA), and the International Brotherhood of Electrical Workers (IBEW).

The CWA/IBEW/AT&T Alliance provides an example of how a labor-management training program can improve employment security and labor productivity.[9] The unique features of Alliance—its independent nonprofit status, its heavy reliance on joint worksite committees, its employee-driven character, and its flexibility to meet a wide and changing array of training needs—provide a useful model for other unionized firms interested in increasing job security and productivity. (See Exhibit 7-4.)

Exhibit 7-4
The Alliance

The CWA/IBEW/AT&T Alliance for Employee Growth and Development is a labor-management training fund established under contract in 1986 to fund a wide variety of opportunities for members, both to upgrade skills for jobs within the corporation and to pursue new occupations on the outside. The fund serves workers displaced by corporate restructuring and downsizing as well as those who continue in the active work force. While members gain from increased employment security, the firm benefits from improved employee morale and commitment to corporate productivity.

The Alliance funds training over and above that provided by AT&T as a normal part of doing business. The company, for example, routinely trains employees in the jobs for which they were hired and provides

Exhibit 7-4
Continued

---

retraining in relation to technology change. The Alliance, by contrast, provides training to meet entry-level requirements for employees who wish to change jobs within AT&T or find new jobs outside the firm. It also finances educational programs for personal growth and skill development.

The fund generates resources through a formula, initially set at $3.75 per employee per month and gradually raised to $9.50 in 1991. In its first four and a half years of operation, Alliance allocated $80 million, including $6 million generated from external sources, to training programs. With a union membership of approximately 108,000, the program had 122,000 enrollments in programs for 59,500 workers in a wide variety of training programs. Approximately 60 percent of the trainees have been part of the active AT&T work force; the remainder have been displaced workers.

The Alliance serves as a model of how joint training efforts can develop into longer-term union-management strategies that link training to broader human resource policies, as in the establishment of local Employee Resource Centers. Moreover, the significance of the Alliance's structural features are evident in its ability to command the support of both union and management, despite conflicts in other areas of the collective-bargaining relationship.

The Alliance, then, serves as a bridge between jobs—either inside or outside AT&T—for displaced and at-risk employees. Given the intense and ongoing reorganization at AT&T, however, most employees cannot dismiss the possibility of job loss or of new skill demands to remain employed. For displaced workers, the Alliance provides tuition assistance for up to one year following layoff, plus additional time based on seniority. For displaced or at-risk workers who wish to stay at AT&T, the Alliance fills an important training gap: it funds courses in basic skills and preparation for qualifying exams that AT&T administers to all new hires. This is training that AT&T has not provided and would not undertake on its own. Because many older employees have never taken the exams or have not taken them within the five-year mandatory period, the Alliance helps them prepare for exams and overcome test anxiety. In the first four years of the Alliance, approximately 3,000 employees, who otherwise would have been laid off, passed the Alliance qualifying exam course and located new jobs at AT&T. The Alliance exam preparation course raised the pass rates from a 20–25 percent level to a 75–80 percent level.

Consistent with this bottom-up approach to training, the Alliance gives primary responsibility for developing and administering the program to labor-management worksite committees. By contract, three representatives appointed by the union and three appointed by management make up the local training committee. As with most decentralized systems, this structure opens up the advantages associated with participation and local initiative but increases the risks of uneven development and access to programs by union members.

One way that the Alliance has decreased these risks is by hiring highly trained national staff to advise local committees. Alliance staff train the committee members to survey employees, develop proposals, and subcontract with vendors to provide on-site services. The training for committee members includes orientation in basic human resource management as well as direction on how to gather and assess local labor-market information.

An example of a local effort is AT&T's largest manufacturing plant, Merrimack Valley Works in Massachusetts. This plant produces transmission equipment and components with a work force of about 8,000 employees from the Merrimack Valley region of northern Massachusetts and southern New Hampshire.

Approximately 3,500 union members participated in Alliance training programs in its first four years of operation. Training programs included courses in career planning, personal computers, financial planning, English as a second language, technical math, materials management, welding, basic skills, small-business start-up, and conversational Spanish.

Another example is the materials management certificate program developed by the Alliance and community college staff in response to new requirements at AT&T that lower-grade employees be college certified to move to a higher grade. Rather than replace unqualified existing workers, the company agreed to retain employees who attended the Alliance-sponsored program and to allow half the classroom attendance on company time. Two hundred employees have attended materials management courses under this program, with approximately 40 percent of the group pursuing an associate degree.

Employee involvement in the Alliance at this site is considerable. Employees initiated a quarterly newsletter and several new courses, including a study skills course for those returning to school and conversational Spanish for English-speaking workers. In addition to increased worker involvement, the Alliance has recruited forty union members as volunteers to serve as Alliance representatives in their respective work areas.

Source: Rosemary Batt and Paul Osterman, "Workplace Training Policy: Case Studies of State and Local Experiments," Case Studies for *A National Policy for Workplace Training: Lessons from State and Local Experiments* (Washington, D.C.: Economic Policy Institute, 1993), pp. 43–55.

The Alliance also illustrates how labor-management efforts of this kind offer lessons for nonunion workplaces and publicly funded programs. In particular, this case documents the importance of worksite committees for identifying and responding to the training needs of employers and workers, the effectiveness of employee-driven programs for increasing participation in training activities, and the utility of union and employee involvement for improving accountability. Local committee oversight increases the likelihood that training dollars will be spent for quality services and reduces the likelihood that external funds will supplant corporate training budgets.

In nonunion settings, worksite committees, a core element of this model, could survey employee training needs, encourage participation in skill development and upgrading, access public funds for training through grant proposals, and subcontract with public or private training vendors for services. They could similarly undertake oversight functions of monitoring quality and substitution of funds. The evidence from the experience of the Alliance is that worksite committees are essential for building an ongoing commitment to education and training on the part of employers and workers alike.

Additional Program Initiatives

Beyond direct training assistance to firms, there are a number of other ways in which creative public policy can foster adoption of mutual gains systems. One widely discussed idea is using a training tax, or grant/levy scheme, to accomplish twin goals: to encourage firms to provide more training to their incumbent workers and to finance government training programs. Under these programs, firms are taxed a certain percentage of their payroll for training. If the firm actually provides that level of training, the tax is refunded. If the firm does not provide the required level of training, the tax—or the difference between the actual level and the required level—is paid into a government fund, and the resources are used to support public training policies. This policy has been implemented in England, Australia, Singapore, Korea, and France.

The great attraction of a scheme along these lines is its simplicity. If firms for which the constraint is binding (i.e., which spend less than the threshold) comply, the nation's training is enhanced without the usual problems of a government program. Furthermore, one might expect that most firms would comply because if they do not, they lose the funds. Finally, since there will inevitably be some form of tax collection, the plan becomes a convenient financing mechanism for the kind of programs we discuss here.

These arguments are powerful yet have drawbacks. The most central problem is whether such a scheme can adequately address the relative lack of training in small and medium-size firms. Another issue is how to link the tax scheme with workplace reform. Any training tax scheme will have to specify the kinds of expenditures that qualify, i.e., meet the standard. It seems almost certain that informal on-the-job training will not count because it is impossible to monitor. In France, for example, only formal training delivered by trainers is counted as meeting the expenditure target. This, however, immediately introduces a bias to large firms, since smaller firms tend not to have the staff or resources to provide formal training. Consequently, small firms are more likely to have to pay the tax. The gap between the number of small and large firms using the program is exacerbated because government usually finds it easier to administer relatively few large grants than numerous small ones. Therefore, small firms are less likely to receive grants.[10]

The experience overseas convinces us that the costs of a grant/levy scheme outweigh its potential benefits. Of additional concern is the potential of the program for stimulating creative tax avoidance. Either the government establishes a substantial bureaucracy to monitor compliance or it accepts the firms' word for their accounting of training costs. Even with the exclusion of on-the-job training, this is a murky area.[11]

Although we are skeptical of the grant/levy system, it may be possible to develop other, less objectional means of deploying the tax system. One idea worth considering is to provide firms with tax credits for investments in human resources that go beyond a baseline level. This is analogous to the investment tax credit for machinery. We also believe that firms which wish to receive these credits should be required to establish an employer-employee training committee to oversee the allocation of the additional investments. In unionized settings, members of this committee would be selected from the established labor organization, in nonunion settings from the total work force in a fair and democratic way. Chapter 8 goes into more detail on how such employee committees might work.

Employer Networks or Consortia

Employer networks or consortia are institutional arrangements that work well in some settings. Using employer associations as brokers for training programs responds to the need to build institutions that outlive particular projects. These associations can serve as effective intermediaries between the state and employers, particularly small ones, both to expand training and to accomplish other important human resource objectives. Hence a project grant to an association has an institution-building impact that helps solidify the aims of training programs.

Employer consortia are effective because their member firms trust one another and because they meet the needs of both the state and independent small firms. State bureaucracies generally do not have the resources to administer thousands of small contracts and small firms usually do not have the resources necessary to apply for complex state grants. Thus public administrators solve problems related to the equitable distribution of funds to small firms and small firms gain access to programs in which they would otherwise be unlikely to participate. In addition, the better employer associations house considerable expertise regarding training and technology, and they can combine training assistance with assistance in other fields (for example, marketing) and hence have the need for training taken more seriously.

Our case studies suggest that there are two types of training consortia. In the first model, employer associations develop and initiate training programs and the government plays a largely passive funding role. The Los Angeles chapter of the National Machining and Tooling Association is an illustration, since it builds on the prior experience of active and well-organized associations in addressing the needs of its many small members. The state of California has also sought to address the problem of lack of small-firm participation in its Employer Training Program by actively seeking the involvement of the building trades and sheetmetal workers associations.

Such associations, however, are difficult to find. In general, small business is not organized. To extend this model, state agencies would have to become more involved. The second model is built on the assumption that public agencies must play a more active role in facilitating the development of employer and other associations. The model also involves broadening the participation of local organizations, including not only firms but community groups, unions, and educational institutions. This approach is considerably more difficult to execute than the first, but it offers the possibility for building a broader political base to weather funding crises and for serving a broader constituency.

With these considerations in mind, we believe that program funds should, in large part, be expended to build the role of these associations and networks, either to strengthen existing ones or establish new ones.

Dislocated Worker Programs

We have emphasized repeatedly that it is unreasonable to expect employees to cooperate in organizational change if their economic livelihood is at risk. Enhanced training inside the firm provides employees with the skills to move about in the enterprise and, should the need arise, to find jobs in the labor market.

Obviously, this solution will not work for everyone. It is therefore important to develop well-funded training programs for adults who lose their jobs. Research demonstrates that this group faces substantial economic losses, on the order of 20 percent of prior earnings, if they are lucky enough to find new jobs.[12]

In the past, dislocated worker programs have been run on a number of different models ranging from simple assistance in job search to more extensive skills training. Today a number of states are experimenting with more innovative models. For example, in New Jersey dislocated workers are eligible for a training voucher (funded by a small state training tax levied on payroll) as well as extended unemployment insurance while in training.

We cannot argue that there is a single best way of delivering training to this group and thereby hasten their re-employment at their old wages. It is important, however, to ensure that adequate funding be made available to experiment with various models since, absent a credible dislocated worker program, it will be hard to sell employees on the need to move away from traditional forms of job protection.

A final piece of the puzzle is to link training and human resource initiatives to broader efforts of economic development and modernization. The Clinton administration has proposed expanding the manufacturing modernization centers, which are currently funded on a small scale by the National Institute of Standards and Technology. These centers advise small and medium-size firms about how best to introduce new technology. It will be important for these centers to address human resource considerations more explicitly.

Programs for Youth

In the end, the way to improve the skill base of the labor force is to improve the education and training of youth. As already noted, this is a long-term policy because, for many years to come, employed workers will constitute the bulk of the labor force. Nonetheless, no comprehensive human resource development policy can overlook the importance of providing a strong entry-level work force.

At the core of any policy along these lines is school improvement. Numerous states have launched reform initiatives, there is considerable discussion of national standards, both political parties have proposed education reform agendas, and in many cities business-school partnerships have proliferated. All this is very much to the good. We, however, focus on programs that link youth more effectively to the labor market.

Most federal youth-training policy emphasizes income-targeted programs aimed at the disadvantaged. Although it merits high priority, the evaluation evidence suggests that narrow programs aimed exclusively at this group will not do well. This is not the place to review these findings in great detail, but such a review does suggest that we should consider broader interventions in the structure of the school-to-work transition. Such broader interventions—if adequately funded—will assist disadvantaged youth by linking programs that involve them to a broader constituency.[13]

There has recently been an explosion of interest in this subject, inspired in part by growing awareness of the German system. The German dual model is attractive because it represents a balance between firm- and school-based training. In addition, all observers agree that the quality of training is high. For these reasons, and because there appears to be a correlation between the dual system and German productivity, recent American discussion has centered on efforts to transplant the German model here.

There is considerable irony in this interest in the German model. In the first two decades of the twentieth century a heated debate raged in the United States concerning the desirability of establishing separate vocational schools. The rationale for a dual system was that technologies were changing, the U.S. labor force lacked adequate skills, the role of schools was to prepare youth for work, and efficiency and equality of opportunity required separate tracks for the "vocationally inclined." The irony is that then, as now, Germany was the model. The Chicago superintendent of schools, who was the major advocate of the plan, had developed his ideas after a trip to Germany, and business support for the effort was also derived from the German model. Consider the following comments by a Chicago businessman, comments that could easily be mistaken as excerpts from the current debate:

> There is perhaps no greater object lesson of the possibilities
> of vocational training than the phenomenal industrial advance

of Germany during the last generation. . . . This has been accomplished primarily because forty years ago German statesmen were sufficiently farsighted and progressive to inaugurate the comprehensive system of vocational education by which German youth acquire a better training for their life's work than youth of any other nation.[14]

The Chicago proposal led to a bitter battle as unions and progressive reformers fought the plan on the grounds that it would enshrine class distinctions, remove education from democratic control, and place it in the hands of business. The plan was defeated and, indeed, the very struggle over the proposal to create a dual system was a key event in the formation of the current structure of American education. Perhaps ironically, unions did nonetheless support establishment of vocational tracks (or lines) within comprehensive high schools, and in the end these lines became both ineffective and stigmatizing.

Irony aside, there has been a flurry of activity intended to set the stage for new forms of apprenticeship in this country. Numerous national conferences have been held, and roughly thirty demonstration programs have been established by the federal government and several national foundations. Most important, the Clinton administration and the Congress are moving toward school-to-work transition legislation that encompasses apprenticeships.

The typical structure proposed under these models is that high school students spend a portion of their school time in job placements designed to impart both skills and a mature sense of the world of work. It is crucial that these placements not be simply make-work. In addition, the proposals envision that the school curriculum be revised to build on the lessons at the workplace and to use the work experience to motivate academic learning. Finally, the programs often involve a connection with further higher education in the same general area as the work experience.

What should we make of these efforts? At the broadest level they are attractive because they speak directly to the inadequate skills that American youth bring to the workplace; they do so in a way that promises a structural reform of the school-to-work transition. It is for these compelling reasons that the ideas caught on so fast. Nonetheless, it is important to probe a little deeper into their principles and practicality.

As noted, there are only a few apprenticeship demonstration programs and these have yet to be evaluated. Other related efforts, such as career academies, are organized on a "school within a school" basis; their curriculum centers around an occupational field like health care or electronics. Students receive some work experience in appropriate settings although not at the same level of intensity as envisioned in the apprenticeship model. Evaluation results suggest that these programs keep young people in school longer and increase the chances of their continuing on to college, but the economic payoff is as yet uncertain.[15]

The relative paucity of past experience and the modest results of these efforts are cause for some caution as we move toward substantial expansion of apprenticeship models. Another important concern is how quickly programs can be moved to scale. At the core of the apprenticeship model is quality job placements, but to date there is no broad commitment by American firms to provide them. If the placements are, by default, in youth labor-market jobs and those jobs are not enriched, not much will be learned and the initiative will end up no different from past youth-employment initiatives. In Germany, by contrast, society demands provision of training slots. Furthermore, firms have geared their production systems around these slots, with large firms having training staffs and small firms counting on apprentices to help with production. The staff of employers have themselves gone through the program and hence are committed to the system and to quality training. Virtually none of the above applies in the United States. Employer motivations would be either public service or perceived labor shortages. Both are weak foundations on which to build a fundamental transformation: imagine what the current status of a program in New England would be if, eight years ago, apprenticeships had been set up to meet expected labor shortages in real estate and financial services!

Such concerns do not lead us to conclude that the model is unworthy of support. We favor funding and expansion of these programs but at a pace that permits quality to be maintained. Considerable effort must be devoted to making youth labor-market jobs learning experiences. We also believe that the programs must embody several principles to make them acceptable in an American context.

First, the program must avoid tracking. One of the strengths of the American entry system is the opportunities it gives young people to experiment and to change their minds. A second strength is its lack of tracking relative to European systems. Both these advantages are at risk in a German model. It is hard to imagine Americans willing to accept a system that requires most youth to select occupations in the tenth or eleventh grade. To complicate matters further, even if such a selection were made, the system would have to be designed to accommodate the enormous amount of mind-changing that would ensue (such second thoughts are not a central part of the German system). This means that it is important not to overly specialize the occupational training or the classroom elements since everything would have to be transferable.

Second, the program must ensure portability. Americans are mobile, and any apprenticeship program must lead to credentials that are recognized countrywide. This difficulty is exacerbated by the highly decentralized structure of American education, which means that the apprenticeships have to be organized on a district-by-district basis. We are a long way from the German uniformity of 400 recognized occupations and standard national examinations. Current efforts to create occupational skill standards are a commendable start.

Third, apprenticeship must be part of a broader strategy for school reform. By bringing the workplace into the classroom and by providing an arena for schools, local employers, and other interested parties to interact around curriculum and jobs, we are moving the schools in the direction of higher-quality preparation.

Fourth, school-to-work transition programs must be designed and administered by, or at least with, active business and labor leadership. This is one opportunity in which business and labor at a local level share many interests and can leverage their experiences and mutual gains in tackling other labor-management and economic development issues.

Summary and Conclusions

In this chapter we have described what we see as the central elements for a national employment and training policy directed both at employed adults and at youth. Although we have not discussed it in the same detail, we believe that such a policy must be combined with school reform initiatives and meet the needs of the economically disadvantaged youth and adults who have been the traditional targets of federal policy.

Our arguments run counter to recent history in which employment and training policy has been marginalized. It has not been seen as an integral part of the country's national economic strategy. Labor market policies have been treated as subservient to macroeconomic strategies for regulating the cyclical fluctuations in the economy, not, as they should be, as an important determinant of long-term economic performance.

We argue that training is central for several reasons. It provides the skill base that transformed employment systems require; it helps ameliorate the problems of dislocation; it provides an entry for public policy to address larger issues of work organization and labor-management relations. Given the weak national infrastructure, a credible national training policy will not be built overnight, but we believe that considerable progress is possible.

In the next chapter we turn to the second broad policy theme: how to reconstitute our labor laws and industrial relations framework in order to facilitate workplace transformation.

chapter eight

TOWARD A MUTUAL GAINS LABOR-MANAGEMENT POLICY

Most of the reports and recommendations of competitiveness policy commissions end where our last chapter left off. After proposing comprehensive new initiatives for linking public and private training and human resource development practices, they include the mandatory boilerplate statement that to make this new approach work we must have greater labor-management cooperation at the workplace. But few if any of these commissions seriously explore how to do so. Yet, as we have seen throughout this book, involving employees and their representatives is essential to sustaining innovation over time and ensuring that the mutual gains are both realized and shared equitably.

This issue is usually avoided because it is so divisive. Consensus on how to reform our labor relations policies simply does not exist in American society. Therefore, it is easier to stop short of risking an impasse over this issue when business, labor, and employment policy experts can agree on broad policy objectives and, in some cases, on more specific policy initiatives or tools for increasing investment in training and development. Effective implementation of such training and human resource development initiatives, however, languishes for lack of viable workplace institutions to carry them out.

In this chapter we carry the policy discussion a step further and discuss how U.S. labor-management policies can be updated to support the transformation processes under way in American workplaces. Indeed, we show that significant changes in labor law and the broader environment in which labor-management relations take place are essential to diffusing and sustaining workplace innovations. We start by reviewing the history of policy making in this area, emphasizing developments from 1960 to the present.

The Historical Legacy of Labor Politics

Why has it been so difficult to enact labor-management policies? One explanation stems from the limited role the government plays in the economic and social affairs of individuals and organizations. Among advanced industrialized democracies, the United States has been known historically for having what political scientists call a weak state, i.e., a government that stays out of the affairs of private enterprise. Nowhere is this more true than in the domain of labor policy. Individualism, free enterprise, and property rights have pre-empted worker rights to full employment and a voice in the workplace.

As a result, labor policy advocates have found it difficult to articulate a coherent theoretical and analytical justification for creating strong worker institutions lest they impinge on the free play of market forces, constrain the autonomy of entrepreneurs and individual corporations, or, at most, go beyond "free collective bargaining."[1] In contrast, Germany and other European countries more readily accept labor as one of society's partners, as long as labor's role is market enhancing and encourages cooperation among the parties rather than promoting adversarial relations.[2] Even the New Deal labor legislation came well after comparable rights for union organizing were enacted in most of Europe. Moreover, the National Labor Relations Act, which came late in the New Deal policy agenda, was sponsored by Senator Robert F. Wagner, not President Franklin D. Roosevelt.[3]

Another argument for why labor policy changes are so difficult to achieve is that we view labor and employment policy as a contest *between* two monolithic groups: organized labor and big business.[4] Labor policy therefore has become special-interest politics, a test of the power of these two groups. Despite the best efforts of labor policy experts in or outside government, the outcome of policy debates is dictated by the group that holds the dominant position in national political affairs. Moreover, these parties' interests are seen as fixed and entrenched; analytical or rational argument or quiet negotiation and mediation will modify neither party's views that a change in policy will do anything more than alter the balance of power between labor and management. Therefore, this argument holds that only a rather dramatic change in the balance of political power, one that occurs as a result of, say, a depression or war, will produce a change in labor-management policy.

By conceiving of labor policy making in this narrow fashion, Americans have ignored the diversity of the labor force and missed opportunities to build the broader coalitions needed to enact and sustain support for policies that promote high employment standards and improvements in productivity and organizational performance. While the need to balance power and regulate conflicting interests in employment relations remains, so too does the need to design labor policies that support mutual gains strategies.

Although we recognize the obvious importance of interest-group politics, we believe that the key to breaking out of interest-group gridlock lies in proposing changes in labor-management policy as a part of larger systemic reform of government's role in employment relations. Instead of partial or incremental reforms in labor legislation that will easily be seen as benefiting labor or management at the expense of the other, the new policy must broaden and reconfigure the alignment among the parties affected, promise some potential mutual gains to them and the country, and be driven by well-grounded ideas that neither labor nor management would espouse on its own.

There is historical precedent for the impact of ideas on labor policy in the United States. The New Deal legislation was, for example, largely derived from ideas advocated for many years by such scholars as John R. Commons and his students at the University of Wisconsin. At first, neither the craft union–dominated AFL nor the business community were strong advocates for these ideas. Similarly, the intellectual arguments and practical legislative proposals that broke with the time-honored view that the right to strike was essential to making collective bargaining work and opened the door to public sector bargaining legislation in the 1960s were developed by the leading academic experts of that era. Indeed, the "Taylor Law" passed in the state of New York was named for George Taylor, the chairman of the commission of outside experts who proposed a new approach to dispute resolution that neither labor nor management had advocated at the time.[5] Several years later, another creative and widely heralded new idea about public sector collective bargaining policies was "final offer arbitration," a concept proposed by Professor Carl Stevens of Reed College.[6] If proposed first to labor or management practitioners, this idea would have been deemed too radical a departure from accepted collective-bargaining practice to be taken seriously. Yet within a decade the idea became accepted public policy in ten states and in as visible and high stakes an arena as major league baseball! Even Congress adopted this approach in 1992, when it intervened to end a national work stoppage in the railroad industry.

But unfortunately, there has been no similar adoption of new ideas by labor policy makers over the past decade. Industrial relations scholars have been hesitant to openly press labor leaders to rethink their strategies for fear of losing influence, access, and acceptability. Similarly, human resource management professors or consultants have been unwilling to challenge the dominant managerial ideology and world views concerning labor unions or the role of the government for fear of losing access to research sites and resources.

Ideas, therefore, need to be put forward with more vigor and independence so that labor and management can see their worlds differently. Otherwise, employment and human resource policy will continue to suffer from the conservatism of incremental interest-group politics. But ideas uninformed by recent history and experience are unlikely to have a significant impact either. A brief overview of the recent history of labor relations and employment policy making and administration is therefore in order.

Labor Relations Policy: 1960 to the Present

The election of President John F. Kennedy in 1960 ushered in a new era for labor policy. The labor movement was near the pinnacle of its membership and influence in Washington. Arthur Goldberg, the former chief counsel to the United Steelworkers union and a major figure in drafting the 1955 merger agreement between the AFL and the CIO, was appointed secretary of Labor. Goldberg became an activist secretary, using his broad experience in labor-management relations to form a President's Advisory Committee on Labor Management Relations, thereby elevating discussion of these issues to national prominence. He, more than any other secretary of Labor in recent history, also put his considerable experience to work in resolving collective-bargaining disputes, for example, his intervention in a strike at the New York Metropolitan Opera (folklore says at the behest of President Kennedy because the president didn't want Jackie to miss the opera season!).

Goldberg was perhaps the last of the great interveners in collective bargaining and labor-management relations. Secretaries after him tended to follow a course of intervening only as a last resort. When George Shultz became secretary in 1968, he acted on the recommendations of a report he commissioned, which concluded that the emergency dispute procedures in the Taft-Hartley Act (a strike-ending "cooling off period," government-sponsored fact finding, and so forth) had probably been overused; few disputes constituted a threat to national health or safety and did not comprise a national emergency. Shultz left the resolution of labor disputes to the private parties and the quiet mediation efforts of the professionals at the Federal Mediation and

Conciliation Service. Shultz's view reflected a long and deeply held tradition in American industrial relations: the parties themselves know best how to shape employment practices to meet their needs. So it is better for government to promote "free collective bargaining" or let market forces determine employment practices rather than try to change the behaviors of the parties closest to workplace problems.[7] This view still holds. The lesson is that any effort to impose substantive rules on labor or management or to intervene in collective bargaining in ways deemed inconsistent with the rights of a free labor movement or free enterprise will be strongly resisted.

It was not until John Dunlop, the nation's leading expert in labor-management relations, became secretary of Labor in 1975 under President Gerald Ford that the government's role in labor relations once again took center stage. Dunlop's long experience in construction industry labor relations had convinced him of the need for more regional, centralized bargaining structures in that industry. Consequently, he quietly negotiated with labor and management a compromise bill that provided for more centralized bargaining in return for something labor had wanted for years—the right to picket whole construction sites even when a dispute involved only one contractor working on the site. Congress passed the bill mainly because of the negotiated consensus Dunlop had achieved between business and labor and the promise of President Ford's support. But pressure from conservative Republicans—particularly the threat of Ronald Reagan as a potential rival to President Ford for the 1976 Republican nomination—led President Ford to rescind his support and veto the bill. Secretary Dunlop resigned and that chapter in labor policy was closed. Once again, the politics of ideology reigned over ideas, and in this case over professional expertise and experience. The promise of improved labor relations was not important enough on its own to overcome such formidable political obstacles.

William Usery, another of the nation's premier labor mediators and most respected authorities on labor-management relations, then became secretary of Labor and continued to explore ways to improve both the climate and the practice of labor relations. He also spoke out forcefully for "free collective bargaining" and warned against, as did his immediate predecessor, the growing role of government regulations in the workplace.[8] However, his efforts were cut short by President Ford's defeat in 1976.

Labor-management relations policy under President Jimmy Carter was largely stymied by the failed debate over labor law reform (see

Exhibit 8-1) and unsuccessful efforts to develop a national accord over wage policies. Secretary of Labor Ray Marshall, one of the country's leading labor-market economists, was most effective in expanding and strengthening employment and training policies and in establishing a steel industry tripartite (government, industry, and labor) structure and process for negotiating a new trade and worker adjustment policy

Exhibit 8-1
The Case of Failed Labor Law Reform

In 1977–1978, Congress debated a labor law reform bill that was designed to overcome obstacles to union organizing that the labor movement and its supporters in Congress argued restricted workers' rights to make a fair choice of whether or not they wanted to be represented by a union. The bill would have reduced delays in the election certification process and strengthened penalties imposed on labor law violators. At the time, these issues had attracted a great deal of attention from lawyers and union organizers but little empirical research had been done on this issue. Despite the fact that the changes would have had no effect on most large employers or on the balance of power in existing bargaining relationships, the business community coalesced in uniform opposition to the bill and narrowly defeated it (actually the bill died in the Senate because Democrats could not find the one additional vote needed to break a filibuster). This defeat of a modest set of reforms proved to have enormous symbolic impact. Labor leaders took it as a sign of management's deep ideological opposition to unions and as evidence that cooperative efforts were doomed as long as management failed to accept labor's right to exist. The business community interpreted its victory as a sign of labor's political vulnerability and as a signal that its "union-free" ideology could come out of the closet. As a result, employers increased their use of consultants and of legal maneuvers to defeat union organizing drives after the defeat of the labor law reform bill.

For years after that defeat labor leaders have argued that business cannot be trusted and therefore many held back in their support of labor-management cooperation, saying that this is impossible until a "level playing field" exists in which workers' basic rights to organize are adequately protected and enforced. The net result of this legislative debate was therefore to chill the climate for labor-management cooperation and to escalate adversarial tensions and behavior for more than a decade and a half following defeat of the bill!

---

to deal with the rise of imports in that industry. Marshall's basic problem was that some saw the Department of Labor as simply the labor movement's conduit to national policy making, a captive of "special interests." The key lesson here is that although the labor movement is an important external constituent of the Labor Department, the department, or any other group proposing changes in labor policies, must reach out to a broader work force and business constituency if it is to be a major player in national economic and social policy making.

In the Reagan-Bush years, labor-management relations were downgraded and eventually ignored within the department. The assistant secretary for Labor-Management Relations position was downgraded and later eliminated. In its place a small Bureau of Labor Management Relations and Cooperative Programs was created with the mission to work with business and labor to promote labor-management cooperation and innovation. The bureau gained considerable visibility and recognition for its work with those in the labor-management and research communities who shared the view that workplace innovations were necessary. But it never had significant influence within the department, the administration, or Congress and was unable to mobilize the support of the broad business or labor communities. As a result, the bureau slowly declined in status, influence, and size until it was dismantled in 1992 when the president's Office of Management and Budget (OMB) refused to continue its funding.

A similar small program housed within the FMCS, supporting innovative labor-management committees in industries, regions, and firms, struggled to survive throughout the 1980s. Each year OMB rejected the FMCS request for this activity and each year, until 1992, Congress restored the budget. In 1992 OMB again rejected the budget for this program and, unfortunately, Congress failed to reinstate it. So the last remaining government initiative supporting innovative efforts was suspended. By the time the Bush administration left office, no policy, research, or outreach services in contemporary labor-management relations existed in the U.S. Department of Labor or, for that matter, anywhere else in the federal government.

Repeating History: 1930s and 1990s

The parallels between the current state of labor policy and that of the 1930s are quite remarkable. In 1932 an administration took office with a mandate to bring the country out of the depression; union representation had experienced a decade of decline partly because its craft mode of organizing and representing workers no longer fit the growing number of semiskilled and unskilled workers in the manufacturing sector and partly because employers had introduced management-led practices for employee involvement. But the economic pressures of the depression proved too powerful for these management-initiated innovations to be sustained. It was therefore left to the new administration and Congress to fashion a New Deal employment and labor relations policy that could provide the microeconomic and institutional foundation for sustained commitment to practices needed to support long-term economic growth. This meant institutionalizing collective bargaining and minimum standards for wages, working hours, and other conditions so that the intense conflicts between workers and employers could be resolved, firms could expand domestic markets, and employees could share in the prosperity that they helped to produce. Achieving the new paradigm envisioned in the New Deal model required fundamental shifts in ideology and strategy on the part of labor, business, and above all, government.

The same is still true. The only difference is that today's challenge is to design basic principles and policy instruments that encourage the parties to pursue the mutual gains strategies discussed throughout this book.

Principles for a Mutual Gains Labor-Management Policy

Our review of the past thirty-four years of labor policy making suggests that to promote mutual gains practices, national labor-management policy needs, at a minimum, to rest on the following broad substantive and procedural principles.

First, labor-management policy should be a catalyst for innovation and transformation of American workplaces by encouraging adoption and sustainability of mutual gains practices. To do this it will need to strengthen the role of human resources within firms and provide workers with opportunities to participate and be represented at the workplace in ways that promote continuous improvements in productivity *and* an equitable sharing of the gains achieved.

Second, to avoid having the government set the substantive terms and conditions of employment, labor-management policy should encourage the private sector to take greater responsibility for administering and adapting the full range of employment policies to its particular needs and circumstances.

Third, we must recognize that collective bargaining continues to be the most widely used and, in many situations, still the most appropriate form of worker representation. It must, therefore, be effective in resolving conflicting interests and encouraging the parties to find mutual gains solutions in areas where the potential for such gains exists. A comprehensive transformation of labor-management policy must ensure that the labor law and its administration fulfill these objectives.

These principles are gaining support among current government policy makers and experts in this field. For example, the "Mission Statement" of a Commission on the Future of Worker-Management Relations established jointly by the secretaries of Commerce and Labor early in 1993 evolved out of considerable quiet discussion and debate among leaders in the administration, policy analysts, and business and labor representatives. Essentially, the commission, composed of former cabinet members, academics, and leaders from the business and labor communities, is charged with developing the specific strategies and policies needed to address the substantive objectives outlined above.

Our review also suggests three principles that have to be embedded in the administration of labor-management policies. First, these policies must be *integrated* with and be a part of the nation's overall economic strategies and the training and development policies outlined in Chapter 7. Labor-management policy can no longer be viewed as a stand-alone domain. Second, they must rest on a strong *analytical foundation*—clear theoretical ideas supported by equally clear empirical evidence that sets the terms of debate about these policies and keeps the debate from becoming a test of political power between organized labor and management. Third, these policies must be *practical.* This can best be achieved by building on the experiences of the firms and unions that have led the way in introducing workplace innovations described throughout this book. In this way, public policy will be grounded in reality—how organizations administer their human resource strategies and practices and how government can facilitate the diffusion of those practices that have already proven their value.

Specific Policy Alternatives

If labor policy is to promote mutual gains, it must promote continuous improvements in productivity. Most productivity-enhancing strategies call for tax or other incentives to encourage greater investment in research and development, physical capital, or human capital. This is the first point where labor-management institutions at the workplace could be linked to broader macroeconomic and employment policies.

We earlier presented evidence that capital investments are more likely to pay off when combined with investments in human resources and integrated with changes in organizational practices designed to speed the implementation and utilization of new equipment. Incentives should encourage investment in both hardware and human resources and the participatory practices needed for these investments to realize their full potential. This is one way to encourage adoption and support diffusion of employee-driven training and human resource development programs discussed in the previous chapter.

A variety of specific policy instruments could be used to implement such a policy. Central to their success, however, would be employee participation adapted to a particular workplace setting. For example, firms receiving investment tax credits or other incentives or public funds could be required to demonstrate that their employees have a voice in the design and use of new equipment. Evidence of employee participation could similarly be required of firms receiving tax credits or grants for training and human resource development. In fully unionized enterprises, union participation and support could be required; where unions represent only a portion of the work force, evidence that nonunion employees have a voice could also be required; and where there is no union, evidence that a council is representative of and chosen by the full work force could be required.

This approach would require modifications of the National Labor Relations Act (NLRA) since it calls for forms of employee participation and representation that clearly are not encouraged or protected and, indeed, may be illegal under current law. But, as we suggested in Chapter 6, there are sound reasons to open our law and practice to include a wider variety of participation and representation processes. We now turn to how this might be done, and to the other difficult and controversial issues associated with the performance of the NLRA.

Transforming National Labor Relations Policy

The NLRA and related policies such as the Railway Labor Act, which governs the airline and railway industries, will need to be fundamentally transformed if the government is to play a positive facilitating role in promoting adoption and diffusion of mutual gains practices across the economy. Passed as part of the New Deal effort to lift the country out of the Great Depression, the NLRA served the American work force and economy well in an era when the challenge was to build a stable collective-bargaining process that could resolve peacefully the deep and often violent conflicts between workers and employers. It also provided a means for workers to increase their purchasing power as the overall economy improved. The law did a good job of resolving *conflicting interests* of labor and management. It has not, however, been as successful in encouraging *joint problem solving,* where the potential for mutual gains exists. Further, over time, the law has lost its ability to provide workers a voice in workplace decisions that have the greatest impact on their long-run economic security. A brief review of a 1992 decision of the National Labor Relations Board (NLRB) illustrates this problem.

The Electromation case. This was a dispute in which a company was found to have a "company-dominated" labor organization, an illegal practice under the NLRA. Fear of company-dominated unions dates back to the 1920s and early 1930s just prior to the passage of the NLRA. As noted in Chapter 4, to thwart organization of independent trade unions, many large firms established company-specific employee representation plans.[9] These generally provided a structure for employees within each firm to advise and in some cases negotiate personnel practices with management. But because the rules governing their structure, authority, and scope were established and controlled by management, they generally barred association with outside trade unions and could be disbanded by management at will. So the framers of the NLRA included a provision outlawing company unions by making it illegal for employers to dominate or support labor organizations. Instead, the law provided that employees have the right to decide if they wish to be represented by a labor organization of their choosing.

Electromation, a nonunion shop, had established a number of employee committees to provide input on its absenteeism policy, pay and bonus arrangements, and several other employment practices. Under the NLRA it is an unfair labor practice for employers to control the selection of people on such committees, provide financial or other in-kind support for committees, or control their agenda if they are found to be labor organizations as defined in the law. In this case the definition clearly fit and the board therefore ruled Electromation's participation process in violation of labor law. Although each member of the board sought to limit the scope of this decision by pointing out ways in which employers could, in effect, get around the law by carefully structuring the selection, content, and role of employee participation processes, from a practical standpoint the legal arguments can only serve to discourage participatory arrangements in nonunion settings. *Business Week's* report on this case outlines the parameters of relevance (see Exhibit 8-2) and shows that the conditions employers need to avoid are essentially those which make teams worth having in the first place.

The use of teams and other forms of employee participation can be and are abused as union avoidance devices by some employers. So the legal issues here are not trivial. But the major point that *Electromation* illustrates is just how outdated the current law is and how badly a new one is needed. Janice Bellace, a labor law professor at the Wharton School, has outlined changes in the NLRA that would address most of our concerns and update the law to provide for employee participation at the workplace and consultation at higher levels of management (see Exhibit 8-3). We do not present her recommendations as the last word or as the only way to update the law, but her proposal is one of the more comprehensive and thoughtful outlines of a new strategy to date.[10]

Exhibit 8-2
When Teams Are Illegal

A mid-December [1992] ruling by the National Labor Relations Board (NLRB) held that employee teams created by Electromation Inc. were illegal. Experts say that many companies have similar teams. Here are the primary factors to look for that could mean a team violates national labor law.

Representation:	Does the team address issues affecting non-team employees—i.e., does it represent other workers?
Subject Matter:	Do these issues involve matters such as wages, grievances, hours of work, or working conditions?
Management Involvement:	Does the team "deal with" any supervisors, managers, or executives on any issue?
Employer Domination:	Did the company create the team or decide what it would do and how it would function?

Source: Aaron Bernstein, "Making Teamwork Work—And Appeasing Uncle Sam," *Business Week,* January 25, 1993, p. 101.

Exhibit 8-3
Updating the National Labor Relations Act to Legalize Employee Participation and Consultation

Sec. 7:	Amend to state that employees have a right to receive information regarding the state of the company and that employees have a right to collectively express their views to their employer.
Sec. 8(a)(2)	Amend to allow creation of independent employee consultative committees whose members can discuss terms and conditions of employment with the employer. Further amend this section to allow the employer to pay for items needed to support the functioning of these committees regardless of whether it is a union or nonunion committee.
Sec. 8(a)(3)	Amend to protect members of employee committees from discrimination; require the employer to prove just cause for discharging a committee member.
Sec. 8(a)(5)	Amend to declare it to be an unfair labor practice for an employer to refuse to disclose information when the employer knew the information was relevant to employees' interests.
Sec. 9	Amend to provide for the formation and membership structure of a committee when unions are present and when no union is present. (Here the objective would be to both insure the committee represents the full diversity of the work force and to allow a union present on the work site to elect to exercise the functions of a consultative committee.) Twenty percent of the employees in an establishment would be required to sign forms indicating they want a committee created. Then elections for committee members would be held.
Sec. 8(d)	Amend to define the scope of issues and the rights of the committee to information and to prohibit committee members from divulging confidential information.
New Sections	Add a provision prohibiting the committee from engaging in or promoting a work stoppage and defining the term "consultation" to mean "an exchange of views based on relevant information."

Source: Janice R. Bellace, "Electromation: The Dilemma of Employee Participation under the NLRA," in Bruno Stein, ed., *Proceedings of the Forty-fifth Annual National Conference on Labor* (Boston: Little, Brown, 1993), pp. 225–244.

Opening the NLRA to allow for workplace participation and team systems is only the first step. In Chapter 5 we discussed the role of European-style works councils and representation on boards of directors. In Chapter 7 we discussed the value of consultative committees or enterprise councils that administer joint training programs and, as we suggest later in this chapter, policies governing safety and health, and perhaps other public and private human resource policies within individual enterprises. The question is how best to encourage experimentation in and adoption of these alternatives in settings where they can add the most value.

New Participation Forums

As suggested above, options should include more than just employee participation teams at the workplace. They should allow for, among other things, more experimentation with an American equivalent of works councils that reflect the full diversity of an enterprise's work force. Employee representation on company boards of directors and in other corporate strategic decision-making and governance structures should be encouraged so that experience is gained in cases other than those of extreme economic duress. This could be done by simply eliminating such legal restrictions as the illusive doctrine that directors must consider only the interests of shareholders even if employees are significant shareholders or stakeholders

There are other options to consider as well. By opening labor law to more varied forms of participation, we would accomplish three important objectives: (1) empower the full diversity of the work force, (2) allow the parties themselves to address and resolve a broader array of workplace issues, and (3) allow the parties to adopt and combine these forms to fit their particular circumstances.

How might this be done? One simple option would be to follow the German approach and require works councils in all establishments over a certain size. The German cutoff is a firm with five or more employees. In the United States a cutoff of perhaps fifty employees might be more realistic, as this would conform to the approach taken in the Family and Medical Leave Act in 1993. This option has the virtue of being a one-time political decision that would produce the most rapid diffusion of an *institutional form and structure* of participation that enfranchises the total work force in an enterprise. Moreover, it would have the desirable secondary effect of elevating human resource issues to a higher level of decision making and over time would give all managers direct, practical experience with employee participation and representation. Richard Freeman and Edward Lazear also present a strong theoretical argument for making works councils mandatory. They argue that employers will not voluntarily cede enough power to employee councils to make them effective while employees or unions will give these councils too much power for them to produce mutual gains. They believe that only a uniform law which carefully specifies the rights and duties of such councils will make them effective in the United States.[11]

Thus, there is a great deal to be said for this approach, but there are two serious drawbacks to it. First, although it may produce a rapid diffusion of new *structures* for employee representation, mandating new institutional forms may antagonize managers and employee representatives who are not ready to adopt the more cooperative approach needed to make these councils produce mutual gains. Second, this option is probably the least feasible from a political standpoint. American business is adamantly opposed to more government regulations, especially of this broad a nature, for an institution that has yet to demonstrate its fit or value in an American setting.

A second option would be simply to open labor law to *allow* firms and employees to create voluntarily any new form of participation. Firms might choose to set up councils for advisory purposes and keep their agendas open to whatever issues are of greatest concern to the parties. The advantage of this approach is that it requires little more than elimination of the restrictions in the NLRA to such things as employee participation teams in nonunion workplaces, nonexclusive representation, and limitations on the scope of bargaining, or supervisory and managerial exclusions from coverage under the law. This voluntary and open-ended approach has the further advantage of encouraging the parties to experiment with new types of participation and representation in the labor movement, in other employee groups that provide support for these councils, or in the business community.

The disadvantages of this approach are quite obvious—slow diffusion to the point where few macroeconomic benefits and little or no integration with other macroeconomic or labor policy objectives will be achieved. But it is an option worthy of consideration to get the ball rolling.

A third option would be to go a step farther than option two by encouraging workplace councils to address one or more issues now regulated by the government and enforced through litigation. These councils would have an active role in an overall strategy of decentralizing and internalizing responsibility for administering or enforcing government policies. As suggested above, such an approach might be feasible, for example, in the occupational safety and health or training areas. The parties could also be given incentives for taking greater responsibility for resolving issues or disputes over other labor standards, such as those covering discrimination, diversity, work-family issues, and so on.

Where bona fide employee participation and representation forums are in place, the parties could be given the authority to administer, enforce, and resolve issues that are now enforced through inspections or legal proceedings before a regulatory agency or court. This expanded role would require the parties to develop effective dispute resolution procedures that can stand the test of judicial review by the courts for fairness, due process, and consistency with the rights embodied in the specific laws and regulations involved. With this approach both public and private resources could be shifted from litigation to building institutions that can deliver more efficient and effective problem solving and conflict resolution on the full range of issues of relevance to today's work force.

The benefit of this approach is that it allows for a certain amount of mutual self-selection by firms and employees. Those inclined to believe they have the climate, management style, and labor-management relationships ready to take this mutual gains approach to workplace issues will opt for it. Those where either management or employees—or the unions that represent them—do not believe this approach workable will opt for more conventional relationships and enforcement regimes, diffusing the process more naturally. If combined with an active information, research, evaluation, and dissemination program, this approach allows others to learn from the experiences of the early adopters. Because these lessons have broad social and economic value (i.e., externalities in the economic sense), government can justify using its resources to support these early efforts. Although the task of evaluating and generalizing the results of such self-selected programs is a challenge to social scientists, it is this type of data and evidence that practitioners learn from best. This is the approach of the Baldrige Award for TQM and it is worth extending to other employment and labor management practices.

One serious drawback of the approach is that the macroeconomic benefits of these innovations will accrue more slowly because diffusion will be gradual. But it does have the advantage of helping reduce enforcement and administrative costs in the critical areas of labor and human resource policy.

Regardless of which option is chosen, all new committees or councils for employee participation and representation need to be guided by a common set of broad principles.

1. There must be an equivalent to the German "peace obligation." That is, councils or committees should not be allowed to call a strike or other form of work stoppage since their primary function is to serve as an integrative mechanism.

2. Council membership should reflect the occupational distribution of the enterprise or establishment. Although it would be a mistake to set fixed proportional representation rules, both exempt and nonexempt workers should be on the council. Members should be elected by employees for fixed—perhaps two-year—terms.

3. Discrimination against individuals for exercising their rights to run for or serve on a council should be prohibited.

4. Once a council is established, neither management nor employee representatives should be able to abolish it unilaterally without due notice. Alternatively, a vote of the work force to terminate the council could be required.

5. Council members should not only have access to the information needed to perform their functions but also an obligation to respect the proprietary nature of information that, if made public, might harm the organization.

6. Alternative dispute resolution procedures need to be established, especially for those councils with responsibility for enforcing public policies or regulations.

It is important to keep the requirements as simple as possible so that these new institutions do not bog down in legal tangles that prevent them from realizing the mutual gains they are charged with pursuing.

Fixing the Problems of the Current Law

Although the policies we have proposed are aimed at creating a climate that encourages mutual gains strategies, employment policy cannot continue to ignore the basic right of employees to join the employee organization of their choice. Not all employers will choose to compete or manage in ways that are consistent with the types of institutional arrangements proposed here. More important, distributive issues will remain a central part of employment relationships, even in those firms which do choose to adopt a mutual gains strategy. This means that we must remedy the law's demonstrated deficiencies regarding union representation and collective bargaining.

We have not focused on the documented weaknesses and inequities that in current law and the enforcement of the provisions of the law govern union organizing. But the results of many empirical studies conducted since the labor law reform debate of 1978 suggest that the law no longer provides effective access to collective bargaining for most workers.[12]

An employer determined to avoid unionization or discourage organizing drives can do so through a variety of legal delaying tactics and illegal practices that seldom result in enforcement actions quick or expensive enough to deter such conduct. Frustration with this aspect of the law and its effects on workers and unions has been the single argument used by some union leaders for opposing labor-management cooperation. This aspect of the law must be changed if we are to improve the climate for labor-management cooperation.

Minor reforms of union recognition procedures are unlikely to do anything more than encourage the parties to use new tactics and escalate their rhetorical attacks on each other's motives and integrity, which will not serve anyone's long-term interests. Effective reforms would include changes in the recognition process that:

1. Encourage the parties to establish their own procedures for extending recognition voluntarily when new facilities or work sites are being designed and planned.
2. Reduce delays in elections and certification decisions where elections are held.
3. Strengthen the penalties imposed on violators so as to eliminate the economic incentives that now exist to violate the labor law.
4. Provide for effective mediation, other alternative dispute resolution techniques, and, if necessary, first contract arbitration in situations where the parties are unable to conclude these negotiations on their own.

There are other aspects of the current law that no longer reflect the diversity found in the current labor force or in organizational practices and needs. For example, supervisors and middle managers are excluded from coverage under the NLRA, and although professional workers are allowed to organize, they are generally segregated into separate bargaining units, further dividing the labor force in an enterprise into narrow interest groups.

Supervisors and managers. The NLRA excludes supervisors and managers from coverage under the law under the theory that a clear line of demarcation must be and can be drawn between those who perform managerial duties and therefore should be loyal to the company and those who execute those duties. Both the theory of behavior and the notion of who does "managerial work" are outmoded, especially in firms that encourage employee participation and semi-autonomous work teams and push authority down to the lowest possible level in the organization. In team-based organizations, rank-and-file employees perform much of what was traditionally supervisory and managerial work. This has led to rather perverse effects. In a decision involving Yeshiva University, the faculty union was ruled to be outside the scope and protection of the law because the faculty was found to have a significant role in the governance and management of the university! Clearly it is not in the national interest to exclude employees from the protection of labor law for taking on greater responsibilities and participating in organizational governance.

Supervisors and middle managers also face significant employment security risks in the current environment, and they hold the keys to implementing the organizational reforms needed to sustain mutual gains practices. To leave them disenfranchised is to continue to encourage their subtle but effective resistance to innovation. They need to be brought under the participatory umbrella but in a way that addresses their concerns as employees and builds their support for mutual gains practices.

Professional and technical workers. Although not legally excluded from coverage under the law, the vast majority of professional, technical, and office workers are, for all practical purposes, left out. The kind of participation these workers want and need cannot be satisfied by formal collective-bargaining rights wielded by separate bargaining units. Recall that in the results of the Gallup poll summarized in Table 6-1, employees indicated a strong preference for an "association" mechanism. Moreover, to extend problem solving organizationwide, these groups must be part of cross-functional teams working with each other and with production workers to design and implement new products, technologies, and organizational practices. To require engineers, technicians, and other professionals or office workers to form separate bargaining units and petition for exclusive representation so that they can bargain over wages, hours, and working conditions only increases the functional barriers that organizations are trying desperately to remove in order to improve the innovation process. These groups must also be included in a policy that supports and facilitates mutual gains practices. This is another reason why experimentation with an American equivalent to the European-style works council is in order.

It is important to note that new opportunities for employee participation and representation are not a substitute for a cure for the deficiencies of current labor and employment policy and practice. But they do offer a means of empowering employees and giving them the tools to make a positive contribution to the transformation of workplace practices in ways that generate and sustain mutual gains. However, as we suggest below, more than simple legal changes are necessary. We also need a government that sees itself as a facilitator, catalyst, and enabler of private initiatives rather than as an enforcer, arbiter, or regulator of private practice. We now turn to specific actions that would shift the role of the government in this direction.

Government as a Catalyst for Innovation

Although government must continue to enforce national labor and employment policy, it has a historic opportunity to be a catalyst for innovation, if policy makers have the vision and determination to do so. Indeed, we already see positive steps in this direction. In 1993, for the first time, the secretaries of Commerce and Labor, with the active support and involvement of the president, jointly hosted a showcase national conference on workplace innovation. Most of the companies and labor unions mentioned in this book participated. The participation of President Bill Clinton in this conference served as a highly visible symbol of the administration's support for the type of mutual gains practices we have discussed. It also provided top government officials with an opportunity to listen to and learn from the managers, labor leaders, and workers who have direct experience in implementing various innovative practices. Such meetings are useful symbolic and motivational events; however, they tend to attract only the "converted." The challenge is to widen the circle of believers.

One tool for following up on these public events is to use the field offices of the Federal Mediation and Conciliation Service (FMCS), the nation's agency charged with responsibility for mediating labor negotiations and strikes, to provide technical assistance to firms and employees interested in, but inexperienced at, establishing employee participation efforts. The FMCS has played this role sporadically over the years. It has administered a provision of the Labor Management Cooperation Act of 1978 to support formation of various industry, community, and in-plant labor-management committees. Its resources have also been put into programs such as "relations by objectives" or "interest-based" bargaining to help labor and management develop problem-solving approaches to the issues facing them. Unfortunately, these programs have received only intermittent support from the FMCS, Congress, and OMB and only a small fraction of professional mediators have been active promoters of these efforts. Meanwhile the traditional mediation functions of the agency have declined in importance, demand, and effectiveness. One mediator who tracked his cases over a four-year period found, for example, that only a third of them used the traditional bargaining process and responded to the traditional mediation intervention.[13] This suggests that the FMCS needs to broaden the array of services and skills it offers to help implement these new approaches and show that better alternatives are available.

These services could be provided not only to union-management relationships but, with appropriate authorization, FMCS could also offer its technical services to the full range of workplaces in the private sector, union and nonunion. In this respect the mission of the FMCS is similar to that of the War Labor Board (WLB) in the 1940s—to help the parties develop the principles and practices needed to make these new participatory forms work, just as the WLB mediators helped labor and management develop the principles and practices that made collective bargaining work well then and in the decades that followed. Like the government-training initiatives suggested in Chapter 7, these new facilitation efforts are probably most needed by and therefore best targeted at small firms and employee groups that lack the technical and financial resources to build or hire this expertise.

The government can also serve an important function by providing the data, knowledge, and interactive learning opportunities derived from the parties' own experiences needed to deepen both the analysis and the understanding of the benefits of workplace innovations. Recently Congress authorized funding for a National Center for the Workplace, a consortium of universities charged with responsibility for producing the data, analysis, and communication programs needed to support wider adoption of workplace innovations. This, too, is a positive example of how the government can work in partnership with universities and other private agents to facilitate learning and innovation. The Labor Department has established a new Office of the American Workplace and charged it with responsibility to promote workplace innovation. These are all good examples of how the government can serve as a catalyst in the adoption and sustainability of mutual gains practices.

Summary and Conclusions

Although the state has historically played a limited role in human resource and labor-management practices governing private sector firms and employees, at critical junctures the government has been an important and successful catalyst for positive change in employment practices. We are now at such a historic juncture. Indeed, our analysis suggests that the government has both a rare opportunity and an obligation to design a new, mutual gains labor and human resource policy that can serve as a positive framework for sustaining the innovative momentum begun by leading firms, employee groups, and unions.

The stakes involved are high. Failure to act decisively risks allowing the momentum to dissipate into yet another business fad. But any attempt to transform current labor law and employment policies may increase the regulatory burdens and adversarial proceedings that will destroy the innovative momentum. However, with the right mix of changes in law, incentives, and administrative support, the government can be the catalyst needed to diffuse mutual gains practices broadly enough to benefit the macroeconomy and society.

chapter nine

BUILDING THE MUTUAL GAINS COALITION

The key point we make in this book is that no single actor in the labor market can implement the changes in employment practices needed to achieve a high-productivity/high-wage economy. Nor can this result be achieved simply by urging business, labor, and government to work together. Yet each of these parties can block or slow the pace of innovation and each has important contributions to make if the rate of change is to be accelerated and innovation sustained. But if debates on these issues remain locked in traditional interest-group politics, little progress will be made. Instead, a broader coalition of voices that reflect the full diversity of the work force and broader society will need to be mobilized if the mutual gains systems discussed are to diffuse widely enough to produce observable benefits to the American economy and society.

Moreover, rather than in emphasizing the uniformity of interests of the actors and the differences that separate them, progress lies in recognizing their internal diversity and the common interests that are shared across at least some segments of these groups. To make this possible the coalition must be as well grounded at the grassroots as it is at the establishment, firm, industry, or national policy-making levels.

There are a number of positive signs that a new coalition is beginning to take shape. In 1992 American voters sent a message to Washington that the status quo was no longer acceptable. The message of President Bill Clinton's campaign, that the economy must create "good jobs with good wages," captured the basic concerns of the American public. Moreover, voters did not seem to be looking to the government to solve their economic problems. Instead, the message was that voters

213

want each sector—government, business, labor, and individual workers—to do its part to solve the country's problems and safeguard the future for their children. Perhaps for this reason it was politically safe for all the candidates to discuss the need to improve productivity, a term that until recently was viewed by most workers as either a threat to job security or an abstract concept with little perceived relationship to employee welfare. The most hopeful sign is that the American work force appears to be willing to contribute to the pursuit of mutual gains, given the opportunities and the tools to do so.

The general consensus about the need to promote greater investment in training and innovations at the workplace provides a potentially sustainable foundation on which to build a broad coalition. Even traditional business and labor protagonists such as the National Association of Manufacturers and the AFL-CIO are working together to encourage new private sector training initiatives. Organizations such as the Council on Competitiveness, the Collective Bargaining Forum, and the National Planning Association are promoting mutual gains concepts, encouraging joint efforts, and studying options for funding and delivering more training and development opportunities and supporting labor-market services to the work force. So a window of opportunity for innovation that has been closed for some time is opening.

New institutions that hold promise for diffusing mutual gains practices are also being created at state and local levels. A business-labor-government coalition in the state of Kentucky has been working together for more than a decade to promote economic development by improving the labor-management climate in that state. In Louisville a similar coalition of leaders formed a Workforce Institute in the mid-1980s to improve the quality of the public school system, and these leaders are developing new apprenticeship and school-to-work transition programs. In Wisconsin a Manufacturing Training Consortium was formed, with the help of several faculty members at the University of Wisconsin, which has now attracted the support of a group of firms to develop common skill standards and training programs. Within each participating firm, labor-management committees are responsible for adapting work practices to ensure that these new skills are fully utilized on the job. In California's Silicon Valley, firms and local government officials have formed Joint Ventures Silicon Valley, which, among other things, studies the nexus between productivity growth and job creation to provide better data on the changing nature of employment in that industry and area.

Each example represents the type of broad-based and diverse coalition that can harness the mixture of resources and support needed to make progress on a local level. Each has union and nonunion firms, business and labor representatives, and community and educational leaders working together on a broad array of human resource development, work organization, and labor-management issues. Each is a microcosm of the kind of local institution that will be needed in large numbers across the country.

Warning Signals

Despite such hopeful signs, there is no guarantee that the efforts will overcome the distrust which has built up among these parties over the past two decades. The managerial culture that believes it can socially engineer mutual gains practices without the other parties still dominates in too many circles. There is a strong risk of a worker backlash if the economy fails to create a sufficient number of new good-paying jobs. Union leaders could easily misread the change in the political environment as an opportunity to simply reinforce the existing collective-bargaining and government regulatory system and return to traditional arm's-length relationships. At the workplace, internal union or management politics could overwhelm champions of mutual gains practices. The financial community could throw cold water on the whole effort by continuing to press for short-term rewards for shareholders at the expense of long-term investment or improvements in worker wages. Partisan conflicts over macroeconomic policies could continue to eat up time and political resources so that the more micro employment issues never rise to the top of the national agenda.

All these countervailing forces are real, strong, and have held back the formation of a new coalition for decades. We end our book, therefore, by outlining the actions required of each member of this new coalition if we are to take advantage of this window of opportunity.

Managing for Mutual Gains

In the past decade management led the way in innovations in the American workplace, largely because of a pragmatic recognition that traditional practices no longer work in a world that requires flexibility, continuous improvements in productivity, problem solving, and cost

215

reduction. The problem is that the champions of innovation in American management have not been influential or numerous enough to win over their skeptical colleagues and, therefore, have had difficulty sustaining their own commitment to these principles. The advocates face not only the opposition of managers who do not share their views but also an economic and capital-market environment in which pressures for short-term cost reduction, profits, and layoffs dominate strategic decision making. A new strategy is needed to overcome the obstacles.

The new approach must start with managers of individual enterprises realizing that, acting alone, they cannot create sustainable mutual gains relationships. This is true for two reasons. As noted throughout the book, individual firms fail to convince other employers to match their investments in human resources and to compete on the basis of high quality and continuous innovations and improvement. Coordinated efforts of managers working together across firms in labor markets, communities, and industries are needed. But management has another limitation: acting alone without the involvement and commitment of a firm's total work force, management lacks the credibility, trust, and political support required to avoid having its programs considered just another passing fad. This means managers must share information, power, and responsibility for promoting mutual gains with the entire work force.

Having said this, we believe that top management values and commitment remain as critical, necessary conditions for innovation. Put simply, top executives and business leaders control the resources needed to fund innovations and have the capacity to act on their personal convictions. Unless they are personally convinced of the value and long-term viability of mutual gains strategies, all other efforts will be for naught. For this reason those business leaders who believe in the value of mutual gains practices have to make special efforts to convince more of their colleagues to become visible champions for those practices.

Because individual firms acting alone cannot sustain a commitment to innovation, managers must become even more externally focused and work to build support and commitment to these principles among their colleagues in other firms in their industry, customer and supplier communities, and labor markets. This is one of the most positive features of the TQM movement, namely, the recognition that customers and suppliers must match any given firm's commitment to quality if these efforts are to pay off.

But more than individual firm-to-firm efforts are needed. Industry and community employer associations must be strengthened if efforts to develop more effective skill certification standards and school-to-work transition programs and institutions are to bear fruit. As noted in Chapter 7, U.S. employer associations tend to be weaker than those in other countries. Where they are strongest is in their political lobbying roles. If the cost to an individual firm of implementing mutual gains practices is to be lowered, the circle of committed firms must be widened. Community- and industry-based employer associations must be part of the solution.

Business leaders must also rein in their colleagues who resist any new employee or union rights to participation. In the 1970s the business community closed ranks in opposition to labor law reform and promoted a new organization called the Council for a Union-Free Environment. It is essential not only to avoid a repetition of this experience but also for those who believe in mutual gains practices to demonstrate their convictions by helping form the type of coalition suggested here. The toughest part of most coalition negotiations lies in one's own member group. This is no exception to that rule.

Managers of individual enterprises need not stand idly by, waiting for cross-firm and cross-group coalitions to form. Indeed, the same kind of mutual gains coalition is just as necessary in firms as in local communities and in national policy making. In the past, the argument has been that front-line employees must be empowered and involved. Where these employees were represented by a union, it was generally recognized that the union leaders should be involved as joint partners.

These approaches are necessary, but they are not sufficient. Other groups are left out—middle managers, the group most often cited as resistant to organizational change, and the groups that have specialized technical knowledge need to be brought into the coalition. Neglecting them will only invite their continued opposition and resistance and result in keeping the mutual gains principles from spreading to the white-collar, office, and service portions of American firms.

Representing Workers for Mutual Gains

Labor unions lack the power and the diversity of leadership and membership to drive the process of change on their own. Yet unions are a critical voice for innovation and for upgrading employment standards and practices. American society suffered in the 1980s because of the lack of a strong and progressive voice for the American work force in political and social affairs. Labor's voice was weakened both by its lack of access to those in power in Washington and by its declining membership. As a result it fell into a largely defensive stance, holding the line against further erosion of worker rights and interests until the political pendulum swung back in its favor. Although it is too early to tell how far the pendulum has swung, it is clear that the labor movement has a new opportunity to articulate the interests of American workers to audiences eager for new ideas and progressive strategies.

Therefore labor has to be engaged in the coalition. We believe that the labor movement could *lead* the coalition if it articulates a vision that reflects the deep concerns of the work force and translates this vision into a sound and feasible strategy for promoting mutual gains.

But the labor movement has more than just a role to play in Washington or in state capitals or in community forums. At the workplace unions must deliver tangible benefits and services to their current and potential members. This is one of the reasons that unions can and do help make mutual gains practices work! Without local union leaders' interest in achieving concrete results, workplace innovations can easily get stuck at a surreal rhetorical level—managers can say they are doing the right thing but in reality many of their efforts will be seen as cosmetic programs or limited to a small subset of the organization's work force.

Democratically elected worker representatives cannot get away with symbolic or partially diffused innovations; they will be thrown out of office. They will demand that the program be either abandoned or institutionalized and spread to cover more of their constituents. This is one reason why we observe a higher rate of sustainability of mutual gains practices where labor leaders are joint partners in the innovation process and a higher rate of attrition where unions are present but not active partners.

Although union participation is crucial, no single institutional arrangement for worker representation dominates or fits all situations in the American economy today. A variety of participatory and representative forms must be available for workers, their representatives, and employers. In addition to traditional collective bargaining, among the options should be those discussed in previous chapters, such as employee representation on corporate boards of directors, Americanized versions of works councils, labor-management consultative committees, and jointly administered employee involvement programs at the workplace. Combinations of these or other participatory and representative processes may be appropriate in different settings. Advocating their adoption and providing the expertise and leadership required to make them work for employees and other stakeholders should be part of the full-service capacity of the unions of the future. Above all, the advocates of worker interests must insist on adequate private and public investment in the training needed to build and sustain workers' earning power over the full course of their careers.

This new model of representation paradoxically requires that unions become more centralized and more decentralized.[1] Centralization is necessary to provide the technical services and leadership training necessary to develop new forms of participation and representation within specific enterprises. Centralization is also necessary to set the broad parameters around wages, human capital investment, and working hours as the German unions do in regional- and industry-level negotiations or as Japanese unions do for wage movements in their annual spring offensive. Decentralization is necessary to allow individual enterprises and workplaces to develop the participatory processes suitable to their particular environment. As our report on the new unions at Saturn and at Harvard suggests, this structural and political realignment of roles, power, and internal processes is, like any other organizational innovation or structural change, difficult and itself subject to significant internal conflicts.

Mutual gains strategies at the workplace cannot hope to succeed without the labor movement's making them a priority on its political and social agenda. This is a controversial and somewhat risky issue for today's labor leaders because there is no guarantee that the organizations which support worker participation and representation and facilitate mutual gains will necessarily be part of the existing labor movement. But the risk of not championing innovation is equally clear. Other new employee advocacy groups or organizations may fill the void. This is the story of the rise of the CIO in response to a lethargic AFL in the 1930s and the rise of public sector employee associations and then unions in the 1960s because private sector unions did not believe it was possible to organize public employees.

The innovations of the past decade produced a major debate in the labor movement about whether to endorse new forms of participation or to press for labor law reforms to strengthen traditional collective bargaining once a more friendly president and Congress returned to office. Although the number of supporters of workplace innovations has expanded somewhat in recent years, the pent-up frustrations of what labor leaders see as twelve years of neglect of labor law leads some of them to favor lobbying hard for a series of individual legislative initiatives such as a striker replacement bill, reform of the Occupational Safety and Health Administration, improvements in unemployment compensation, and so forth. Those favoring this approach agree that changes in union strategies are needed but argue that a level playing field for labor relations must be achieved first. Only then will labor leaders be able to cooperate with management.

If this approach dominates labor's political agenda, it will sour the political and labor-management environment and face stiff opposition from a Congress that will see the labor movement as promoting its special interests. If the advocates of a return to traditional approaches dominate, we can also expect a continuation of the cycle of conflict at the workplace as progressive managers lose confidence in the ability of union leaders to support innovation.

Indeed, unless labor becomes a more positive and visible champion for a new approach and demonstrates its determination to lead efforts to achieve it, the American work force, management, and public policy makers will continue to view labor as a largely negative or, at best, irrelevant force at the workplace and in economic and social affairs.

Government as a Facilitator

Government cannot force innovation or develop initiatives that are not supported by the private sector. This was the lesson learned by the failure of the National Commission on Productivity and the Quality of Work in the 1970s. But times have changed. Now the private sector has shown government what works, what doesn't, and has pointed out the obstacles to further innovation that only the government can help overcome. This is why we believe that government policy makers have a window of opportunity open to them to break the logjam and facilitate broad-scale diffusion of mutual gains practices. Its role is to overcome the market, institutional, legal, and political obstacles that block the path of innovation or make it difficult for these changes to be sustained through good times and bad.

But this means that the government must adopt a new role, one as mediator, facilitator, and enabler of change. Clearly, traditional enforcement functions remain important in many areas of employment policy. But the momentum that has built up in the private sector requires government to become a partner in encouraging investment in human resources and diffusing innovative practices throughout the American workplace.

The specific policies we believe would help movement in this direction were laid out in detail in the previous chapters and need not be repeated here. But the toughest challenge for government lies not in formulating the details of a specific policy or regulation but in demonstrating its ability to work as an effective partner with the private sector. In some cases, as in the area of labor law or occupational safety and health, government must be prepared to take the lead in building the new coalition. It must use the full power of its position as regulator and facilitator. In other settings, such as assisting small businesses by expanding training, providing access to modern technologies and expertise on human resource innovations, the government must be seen as a trusted expert, rather like the agricultural extension agent of the past. In still other cases, the government must be an effective listener, funder, and problem solver for coalitions of private parties who need government resources and services to meet their specific needs. These then are the multiple roles state and federal government officials will have to play if they are to help facilitate and diffuse mutual gains practices.

The Academic Community

The academic community has too long been either split into disciplinary camps that see only part of the challenge or intellectual puzzle, or too quick to jump on the bandwagon of the latest fad without doing the deep analysis required to help the parties see what works and what doesn't. Moreover, U.S. academics have until recently failed to provide the international perspective needed to help identify practices from around the world that, with appropriate modifications, could be adapted to fit the American workplace. But university faculty are supposed to be the source of new theories and empirical findings as well as outside critics and facilitators. All these roles are especially vital during a time of transformation.

The academics who teach and study employment issues need to reconstruct the multidisciplinary networks first envisioned in the charter of the Industrial Relations Research Association. Consider the relevance today of the 1947 comments by Edwin Witte, the first president of that organization:

There is need in the study of industrial relations for the approaches of all academic disciplines represented in this Association and those practical minded people who must deal daily with these problems. But it is highly desirable that there should be cross-fertilization between these workers in their differing approaches and points of view and that all people who undertake research in industrial relations should have ready access to what has been done by others. Improvement of the situation in these respects is one of the major objectives of the Industrial Relations Research Association.[2]

Some of this cross-disciplinary and researcher-practitioner dialogue is beginning to happen again. For example, in recent years the Sloan Foundation has supported industry-based research projects designed to build a better understanding of the determinants of industry performance. Teams of researchers from such leading universities as Stanford, Berkeley, Cornell, Wharton, Carnegie-Mellon, Columbia, Pittsburgh, Harvard, and MIT are working on both the technical and the human resource and organizational issues associated with performance in industries as diverse as pharmaceuticals, steel, clothing, semiconductors, autos, financial services, telecommunications, and computers. The idea is to build a generation of researchers who have deeper industry-specific knowledge and to strengthen the contacts between universities and industry representatives. Out of these efforts should come better data and empirical evidence on the effects of various workplace innovations and practices that, if broadly communicated, should help diffuse and apply mutual gains principles.

Business school faculties have a special obligation to adapt the teaching of organizational theory and human resources to address these issues. Again, this is occurring in some schools. For example, at MIT's Sloan School of Management we require first-year students to take an organization perspectives course. The emphasis is on the organizations of the future and the management of organizational transformations consistent with the mutual gains perspective and on building the personal, managerial, and leadership skills needed to support mutual gains practices. This course is followed by a more focused one on human resources and industrial relations that takes up the issues discussed in this book and by a course on operations management, which treats both the traditional technical issues associated with production and service delivery (e.g., scheduling, inventory management, statistical process control, and so forth) and teamwork, TQM, and many of the other issues that intersect with mutual gains practices.

At MIT we bring these issues together most effectively in our Leaders for Manufacturing Program, a joint management and engineering master's degree program. Participants in this program—a mix of students on leave from industrial companies that are partners in funding and managing the program and students who apply on their own—take these and other management courses as well as a complement of engineering requirements and electives. The students also spend six months in a manufacturing setting, getting hands-on experience applying these concepts, then write a thesis based on their experience.

Such courses and new programs are beginning to appear in most other major business schools in the country. Nonetheless, a great deal still needs to be done to break down the traditional disciplinary barriers that limit integration of this knowledge into a systemic view of organizational transformations and provide the skills and perspectives needed to manage for mutual gains. As TQM enters operations management and operations research courses, there is an opportunity, indeed an obligation, for faculty to bring in material relevant to mutual gains practices. More attention to the role of corporate finance, governance, and public policy needs to find its way into organizational behavior and human resource courses. In turn, behavioral issues need to be taken up in the finance, accounting, and economics disciplines where these issues are normally taught.

Perhaps the key to opening the eyes of current managers in executive education programs and future managers in MBA programs is to take an international perspective in teaching such issues. Using international cases and, even better, having international students and executives in class, are excellent ways to help American students recognize the exceptional nature of the ideology of American management toward labor and institutions of worker participation and representation.

Academics must interact with practitioners on the front line to experience directly the difficulty of implementing innovations at the workplace. Research networks that involve business and labor representatives are useful means to provide this real-world grounding. But ultimately, the long-run value-added of the research community comes from maintaining sufficient independence to offer critical, objective analysis and creative new ideas. It is this balance of involvement with and learning from the parties and the independence to challenge the parties to do better that has been the hallmark of previous generations of scholars in the broad field of employment relations. A similar mix of independence and involvement will be needed in the future.

Throughout this book we have emphasized the need for a new perspective on the role of human resource management practice. If this is to materialize, a similarly new and expanded theoretical and analytical framework must guide research on these topics. By now the outlines of the new framework should be clear. We need only summarize its key components here.

First, human resource studies must expand their horizons beyond the boundaries of the individual firm and the perspectives of either the functional specialist (as in the old personnel management field) or line management (as in the strategic human resource management approach). Both these perspectives are important but far from sufficient. The personnel management perspective provides the technical foundation and specialized expertise needed to add value in managerial decision making and public policy processes. The strategic perspective broadens the lens to speak to the basic competitive strategies and performance objectives of the firm. But the employment relationship consists of multiple interests. To support a mutual gains paradigm, multiple interests must be seen as legitimate outcomes in human resource models. Moreover, these interests do not always neatly divide into "labor" versus "management." The diversity of today's labor force is mirrored in employment relationships and needs to be incorporated more fully into the theories and perspectives of human resource management scholars.

Modern human resource theory must also take an international perspective and develop a deeper and more realistic theory of the firm, its governance, sources of capital, internal politics, and its linkages to other institutions. Moreover, a theory of organizational change that is grounded in this broader theoretical perspective is also needed. But this theory needs not just to take into account models of change within a given enterprise but also to speak to the diffusion and sustainability of change and innovation across enterprises. Thus, the process of institutional change must be addressed in the updated human resources paradigm. The next generation of human resource researchers and teachers will have to relearn the lessons of institutional economics, political science, and sociology that were at the heart of the field in the 1940s and 1950s but were lost in recent decades as the field retreated into its microtechnical niche.

Seizing the Initiative: The Mutual Gains Work Force

None of the strategies, policies, or expenditures of time, money, and effort will succeed in fulfilling the promise of mutual gains practices unless American workers are solidly behind these efforts and demand access to training and development at each stage of their careers and the opportunities to put these skills to work on their jobs.

Most workers will act in their own self-interest if given the opportunity to do so. They will recognize the premium that the mutual gains enterprise puts on education and cognitive and problem-solving skills, and see continuous or lifelong learning as the way to enhance and protect their lifelong earning power. They will make the personal investments and commitments needed to get ahead. But they must not just wait for managers, union leaders, or the government to ask, encourage, or allow them to do so. Workers at all levels of the enterprise must demand access to the resources, tools, and learning opportunities they will need to get ahead in today's economy and labor markets.

American voters issued a wake-up call in the election of 1992. Now American workers have to issue the same wake-up call to themselves, and to their employers, labor or professional associations, and educational institutions so that they are equipped to participate effectively in and help fulfill the promise of mutual gains employment systems.

notes

Chapter 1

[1]The concept of mutual gains labor-management relationships was first developed by Edward Cohen-Rosenthal and Cynthia Burton in *Mutual Gains—A Guide to Union-Management Cooperation* (New York: Praeger, 1987). This term has also been adopted in the negotiations literature to describe bargaining strategies that promise win-win outcomes, i.e., results that address the key interests of all the parties to the negotiations. See, for example, Roger Fisher and William Ury, *Getting to Yes: Negotiating Agreement without Giving In* (New York: Penguin Books, 1983).

[2]The most popular of these was Thomas Peters and Robert H. Waterman, Jr., *In Search of Excellence: Lessons from America's Best-Run Companies* (New York: Harper & Row, 1982). Another example is David T. Kearns and David A. Nadler, *Prophets in the Dark: How Xerox Reinvented Itself and Beat Back the Japanese* (New York: Harper Business, 1992).

[3]See, for example, Bryan Burrough and John Helyar, *Barbarians at the Gate* (New York: Harper & Row, 1990).

[4]An early example of this type of account is Noel Tichy and Stratford Sherman, *Control Your Destiny or Someone Else Will: How Jack Welch Is Making General Electric the World's Most Competitive Company* (New York: Doubleday, 1993).

Chapter 2

[1]These productivity numbers are calculated as a compound annual rate of gross domestic product (GDP) per hour. As such they are not strictly comparable with Figure 2-1 because the nonfarm business sector consists of the total GDP reduced by the rental value of owner-occupied real estate and by the output of government, nonprofit, domestic, and farm sectors. However, our analysis is not affected by this discrepancy as nonfarm business still comprises the bulk of the economy and the numbers are essentially stable: GDP per hour worked in the United States averaged 2.5 percent from 1950 to 1973 and 1 percent between 1973 and 1984. See Angus Maddison, "Growth and Slowdown in Advanced Capitalist Economies: Techniques of Quantitative Assessment," *Journal of Economic Literature* 25 (June 1987): 649–698.

[2]William J. Baumol, Sue Anne Batey Blackman, and Edward N. Wolff, *Productivity and American Leadership: The Long View* (Cambridge, Mass.: MIT Press, 1989).

[3]Arthur Neef and Christopher Kask, "Manufacturing Productivity and Labor Costs in 14 Economies," *Monthly Labor Review,* December 1991, 29–30.

[4]Christopher Heye, "Five Years After: A Preliminary Assessment of U.S. Industrial Performance Since Made in America," paper presented at the World Economic Forum Industry Summit Conference, Cambridge, Mass., September 1993.

[5]This decline in earnings remains true even when only full-time employees are considered. Also, it remains true within sectors: see Table 2-2 on manufacturing wages.

[6]John Bound and George Johnson, "Wages in the US During the 1980's and Beyond," in Marvin H. Kosters, ed., *Workers and Their Wages: Changing Patterns in the US* (Washington, D.C.: AEI Press, 1991); Frank Levy and Richard Murnane, *US Earnings Levels and Earnings Inequality: A Review of Recent Trends and Proposed Explanations,* mimeo, Harvard University, July 1991; Lawrence Katz and Kevin Murphy, *Changes in Relative Wages, 1963–1987: Supply and Demand Factors,* mimeo, Harvard University, April 1990.

[7]David Bloom and Richard Freeman, "The Fall in Private Pension Coverage in the United States," *American Economic Review,* May 1992, 539–542.

[8]Robert S. Smith, "Have OSHA and Workers' Compensation Made the Workplace Safer?" in D. Lewin, O. Mitchell, and P. Sherer, eds., *Research Frontiers in Industrial Relations and Human Resources,* Industrial Relations Research Association Series (Madison, Wis.: Industrial Relations Research Association, 1992). Smith controls for incentives to misreport injuries and finds that the upward trend survives his corrections.

[9]The data in this paragraph are taken from Richard Wokutch, *Cooperation and Conflict in Occupational Safety and Health: A Multinational Study of the Automotive Industry* (New York: Praeger, 1990). Comparability problems result from divergent reporting requirements and methods of data collection, particularly between countries but also within countries over time. Currently the United States and Germany both report injuries per full-time worker, while the United Kingdom reports injuries per worker and Sweden focus on injuries per million hours worked.

[10]The help wanted index is a tool of business cycle analysis constructed by The Conference Board. It provides information on employment trends by tracking the volume of help wanted advertising.

[11]Mary Ellen Kelley, "Unionization and Job Design under Programmable Automation," *Industrial Relations* 28, no. 2 (Spring 1989): 174–187.

[12]Keith Camhi, "The Effective Integration of Statistical Quality Control, Cross-Training and Employee Empowerment for Achieving High Performance in Manufacturing Work Teams," M.S. thesis, MIT, 1991, and Augustus Tai, " Effects of Manufacturing Process Design on a Work Team's Ability to Continuously Improve," M.S. thesis, MIT, 1991.

[13]These patterns remain after more sophisticated controls for other factors. See ibid.

[14]UNESCO, *Statistical Yearbook, 1989* (Geneva: UNESCO, 1990).

[15]National Assessment of Vocational Education, "Second Interim Report of the National Assessment of Vocational Education" (Washington, D.C.: U.S. Department of Education, 1988), pp. 1–4.

[16]Paul Osterman, *In the Midst of Plenty* (Boston, Mass.: The Boston Foundation, 1990).

[17]Lisa Lynch, "Private Sector Training and Its Impact on the Earnings of Young Workers," rev. NBER Working Paper No. 2060-88, June 1990.

[18]John Bishop, "Work Force Preparedness," in Lewin, Mitchell, and Sherer, *Research Frontiers in Industrial Relations and Human Resources,* pp. 447–486.

[19]National Assessment of Vocational Education, "Second Interim Report," pp. 1–6.

[20]W. Norton Grubb, "The Varied Economic Returns to Postsecondary Education," *Journal of Human Resources* 28, no. 2 (Spring 1993): 365–382.

[21]National Assessment of Vocational Education, "Second Interim Report," pp. 1–20, and the Bureau of Apprenticeship and Training, June 29, 1993.

[22]Data provided by the Bureau of Apprenticeship and Training, June 29, 1993. The last period for which complete data are available on trade breakdowns within apprenticeship programs is 1978–1979. See Robert W. Glover, "American Apprenticeship and Disadvantaged Youth," in Robert E. Taylor, Howard Rosen, and Frank C. Pratzner, eds., *Job Training for Youth: The Contributions of the US Employability Development System* (Columbus: Ohio State University, 1982), pp. 165–201.

[23]James Rosenbaum and Takehiko Kariya, "From High School to Work: Market and Institutional Mechanisms in Japan," *American Journal of Sociology* 94, no. 6 (May 1989): 1334–1365.

[24]Paul Osterman, *Getting Started: The Youth Labor Market* (Cambridge, Mass.: MIT Press, 1980).

[25]This figure is based on analysis of the National Longitudinal Survey of Youth. See Paul Osterman, "Is There a Problem in the Youth Labor Market and If So What Should We Do About It? Lessons for the U.S. from American and European Experiences," in Roger Lawson, Katherine McFate, and William J. Wilson, eds., *Poverty, Inequality, and the Crisis of Social Policy: Western States in the New World Order* (New York: Russell Sage, forthcoming).

[26]Robert E. Cole, *Strategies for Learning: Small-Group Activities in American, Japanese, and Swedish Industry* (Berkeley: University of California Press, 1989), pp. 8–11.

[27]Ronald Dore and David Cairncross, *Employee Training in Japan* (Washington, D.C.: Office of Technology Assessment, 1989), p. 9.

[28]D. E. Westney and K. Sakakibara, "The Role of Japan-based R&D in Global Technology Strategy," in M. Horwitch, ed., *Technology in the Modern Corporation* (New York: Pergamon Press, 1985), p. 14.

[29]Dore and Cairncross, *Employee Training in Japan*, p. 12.

[30]The results of this study are presented in more detail in John Paul MacDuffie and John Krafcik, "Integrating Technology and Human Resources for High-Performance Manufacturing: Evidence from the International Auto Industry," in T. Kochan and M. Useem, eds., *Transforming Organizations* (New York: Oxford University Press, 1992), 209–226; and in John Paul MacDuffie, "Beyond Mass Production, Flexible Production Systems and Manufacturing Performance in the World Auto Industry," Ph.D. diss., MIT Sloan School of Management, 1991.

[31]John Paul MacDuffie and Thomas A. Kochan, "Do U.S. Firms Underinvest in Training? Determinants of Training in the World Auto Industry," unpublished manuscript, MIT Sloan School of Management, 1993.

[32]Ibid.

[33]*The Wall Street Journal*, March 30, 1993.

[34]Paul S. Adler, "The 'Learning Bureaucracy': New United Motor Manufacturing, Inc.," in Barry M. Staw and Larry L. Cummings, eds., *Research in Organizational Behavior*, vol. 15 (Greenwich, Conn.: JAI Press, 1993), pp. 111–194.

[35]MacDuffie and Krafcik, "Integrating Technology."

[36]Haruo Shimada and John Paul MacDuffie, "Industrial Relations and Humanware: Japanese Investments in Automobile Manufacturing in the United States," working paper, MIT Sloan School of Management, 1987.

[37]It should be noted that the negative responses of layoff survivors are conditioned by the perceived fairness of the cause and the implementation process of the layoff, and by the perceived threats and opportunities in the workplace after the work force reduction. However, it is also true that the sharpest declines in organizational commitment are likely where employees with high levels of prior commitment perceive downsizing to be unfair. See Joel Brockner et al., "Threat of Future Layoffs, Self-esteem, and Survivors' Reactions: Evidence from the Laboratory and the Field," *Strategic Management Journal* 14 (Summer 1993): 153–166; Joel Brockner, "Managing the Effects of Layoffs on Survivors," *California Management Review* 34, no. 2 (Winter 1992): 9–26; Joel Brockner, Tom R. Tyler, and Rochelle Cooper-Schneider, "The Influence of Prior Commitment to an Institution on Reactions to Perceived Unfairness: The Higher They Are, the Harder They Fall," *Administrative Science Quarterly* 37, no. 2 (June 1992): 241–261.

[38]Lee Dyer and Donna Blancero, "Workplace 2000: Pieces and Patterns," in Lee Dyer, Donna Blancero, and Linda Gasser, eds., *Workplace 2000: A Human Resource Perspective* (Ithaca, N.Y.: ILR Press, forthcoming).

Chapter 3

[1]Richard Walton, "Toward a Strategy of Eliciting Employee Commitment Based on Policies of Mutuality," in Richard E. Walton and Paul R. Lawrence, eds., *HRM Trends and Challenges* (Boston: Harvard Business School Press, 1985), pp. 35–65.

[2]Thomas J. Peters and Robert H. Waterman, Jr., *In Search of Excellence: Lessons from America's Best-Run Companies* (New York: Harper & Row, 1982).

[3]Michael L. Dertouzos, Richard K. Lester, and Robert M. Solow, *Made in America* (Cambridge, Mass.: MIT Press, 1989).

[4]See Edward E. Lawler III, *High Involvement Management: Participative Strategies for Improving Organizational Performance* (San Francisco: Jossey-Bass, 1986).

[5]Paul Osterman, *Employment Futures; Reorganization, Dislocation, and Public Policy* (New York: Oxford University Press, 1988).

[6]Thomas A. Kochan, Harry C. Katz, and Robert B. McKersie, *The Transformation of American Industrial Relations* (New York: Basic Books, 1986).

[7]Edward Cohen-Rosenthal and Cynthia Burton, *Mutual Gains—A Guide to Union-Management Cooperation* (New York: Praeger, 1987).

[8]Kochan, Katz, and McKersie, *The Transformation of American Industrial Relations.*

[9]Peter Cappelli, "Is the Skills Gap Really about Attitudes?" working paper, University of Pennsylvania, National Center on the Education Quality of the Work Force, 1993.

[10]McKinley L. Blackburn, David E. Bloom, and Richard B. Freeman, *The Declining Economic Position of Less-skilled American Males* (Cambridge, Mass.: National Bureau of Economic Research, 1989).

[11]Richard J. Murnane, John B. Willett, and Frank Levy, "The Growing Importance of Cognitive Skills in Wage Determination," unpublished paper, MIT, 1992.

[12]Michael Useem, "Management Culture, Corporate Restructuring, and Company Policies on Education and Training," working paper, Wharton School of Management, University of Pennsylvania, 1992.

[13]See, for example, Charles L. Hulin and Milton R. Blood, "Job Enlargement, Individual Differences, and Worker Responses," *Psychological Bulletin* 69 (1968): 41–55.

[14]See Richard E. Walton, "Establishing and Maintaining High Commitment Work Systems," in J. R. Kimberly, Robert H. Miles, and Associates, eds., *The Organizational Life Cycle: Issues in the Creation, Transformation, and Decline of Organizations* (San Francisco: Jossey-Bass, 1980), pp. 208–290, and Thomas A. Kochan and Thomas A. Barocci, *Human Resource Management and Industrial Relations* (Boston: Little, Brown, 1985), pp. 425–435.

[15]Lawler, *High Involvement Management.*

[16]See Edward E. Lawler III, Susan Albers Mohrman, and Gerald E. Ledford, Jr., *Employee Involvement and Total Quality Management: Practices and Results in Fortune 1000 Companies* (San Francisco: Jossey-Bass, 1992).

[17]Paul S. Adler, "The 'Learning Bureaucracy': New United Motor Manufacturing, Inc.," in Barry M. Staw and Larry L. Cummings, eds., *Research in Organizational Behavior,* vol. 13 (Greenwich, Conn.: JAI Press, 1993).

[18]Alan Fox, *Beyond Contract: Work, Authority, and Trust Relations in Industry* (London: Macmillan, 1974).

[19]Robert McKersie, research notes of October 1990.

[20]Lee Dyer, George Milkovich, and Felician Foltman, "Contemporary Employment Stabilization Practices," in Kochan and Barocci, *Human Resource Management and Industrial Relations,* pp. 203–214.

[21]Fred Leiseur, *The Scanlon Plan* (Cambridge, Mass.: MIT Press, 1957).

[22]See Harry C. Katz, Thomas A. Kochan, and Kenneth Gobeille, "Industrial Relations Performance, Economic Performance, and QWL Programs: An Interplant Analysis," *Industrial and Labor Relations Review* 37 (1983): 3–17, Harry C. Katz, Thomas A. Kochan, and Mark Weber, "Assessing the Effects of Industrial Relations Systems and Efforts to Improve the Quality of Working Life on Organizational Effectiveness," *Academy of Management Journal* 28 (1986): 509–526, and Harry C. Katz, Thomas A. Kochan, and Jeffrey Keefe, "Industrial Relations and Productivity in the U.S. Automobile Industry," *Brookings Papers on Economic Activity* 3 (1987): 685–715.

[23]See John Krafcik, "Triumph of the Lean Production System," *Sloan Management Review* 30 (Fall 1988): 41–52, and John Paul MacDuffie and John Krafcik, "Integrating Technology and Human Resources for High Performance Manufacturing: Evidence from the International Auto Industry," in Thomas A. Kochan and Michael Useem, eds., *Transforming Organizations* (New York: Oxford University Press, 1992), pp. 209–226.

[24]James Womack, Daniel Jones, and Daniel Roos, *The Machine That Changed the World* (New York: Rawson, 1990).

[25]Casey Ichniowski, Kathryn Shaw, and Giovanna Prennushi, "The Effects of Human Resource Management Practices on Productivity," draft manuscript, Carnegie-Mellon, June 1993.

[26]Ibid., p. 35.

[27]See Joel Cutcher-Gershenfeld, *Tracing a Transformation in Industrial Relations* (Washington, D.C.: U.S. Department of Labor, Bureau of Labor Management Relations and Cooperative Programs, 1988), and Joel Cutcher-Gershenfeld, "The Impact on Economic Performance of a Transformation in Workplace Relations," *Industrial and Labor Relations Review* 44, no. 2 (January 1991): 241–260.

[28]Eileen Appelbaum and Rose Batt, "Transforming the Production System in U.S. Firms," report to the Alfred P. Sloan Foundation (Washington, D.C.: The Economic Policy Institute, January 1993).

[29]Ellen Rosen, *Bitter Choices: Blue-collar Women in and out of Work* (Chicago: University of Chicago Press, 1987).

[30]See Edward E. Lawler III, Daniel J. B. Mitchell, and David Lewin, "Alternative Pay Systems, Firm Performance, and Productivity," in Alan Blinder, ed., *Paying for Productivity* (Washington, D.C.: Brookings Institution, 1990), pp. 15–94.

[31]John Abowd, "Does Performance-based Managerial Compensation Affect Corporate Performance?" *Industrial and Labor Relations Review* 43, no. 3, special issue (February 1990): 52–73.

[32]Jonathan Leonard, "Executive Pay and Firm Performance," *Industrial and Labor Relations Review* 43, no. 3, special issue (February 1990): 13–29.

[33]In fact, there are several alternative gain-sharing plans. The Scanlon Plan is based on a reduction in the ratio of labor costs to sales volume; the Rucker plan is based on increases in value-added production; and the Improshare plan is based on the ratio of units produced to hours worked. However, the principles underlying these plans are the same.

[34]Roger T. Kaufman, "The Effects of Improshare on Productivity," *Industrial and Labor Relations Review* 45 (January 1992): 311–322.

[35]Lawler, Mitchell, and Lewin, "Alternative Pay Systems," p. 67.

[36]See Ronald G. Ehrenberg and George Milkovich, "Compensation and Firm Performance," in Morris Kleiner, Richard Block, Myron Roomkin, and Sidney Salsverg, eds., *Human Resources and the Performance of the Firm* (Madison, Wis.: Industrial Relations Research Association, 1987), pp. 87–122.

[37]Michael H. Schuster, *Union-Management Cooperation: Structure, Process, Impact* (Kalamazoo, Mich.: W. E. Upjohn Institute for Employment Research, 1984).

[38]Martin Weitzman and Douglas Kruse, "Profit Sharing and Productivity," in Blinder, *Paying for Productivity,* pp. 95–139.

[39]In answering this question it is important to distinguish between individual and social returns. We know that the earnings of individuals grow as training increases, but this does not necessarily imply that there is a social gain. We may simply be observing a game of musical chairs as the best trained displace others but output does not rise. It is, however, difficult to distinguish these effects with the kind of individual survey data commonly available. Two alternative strategies are available. One approach is to introduce the education and training of the labor force directly into a production function to see if there is an increase in output associated with skill. The second strategy is to compare matched samples of firms that produce the same product using the same technology to observe whether firms with better trained labor forces outperform others. This latter approach can

understate the impact of training since one effect of having a trained labor force may be to provide a firm with the opportunity to shift to a different technology. Hence holding technology constant eliminates one gain from training.

[40]See, for example, Ann P. Bartel and Frank Lichtenberg, "The Comparative Advantage of Educated Workers in Implementing New Technology," *Review of Economics and Statistics* 64 (February 1987): 1–11; Charles Brown and James Medoff, "Trade Unions in the Production Process," *Journal of Political Economy* 86 (June 1978): 335–378; Anne Daly, "Education and Productivity: A Comparison of Great Britain and the United States," *British Journal of Industrial Relations,* July 1986, 251–266; R. Jaikumar, "Postindustrial Manufacturing," *Harvard Business Review,* November–December 1986, 69–76; M. Maurice, A. Sorge, and M. Warner, "Societal Differences in Organizing Manufacturing Units: A Comparison of France, West Germany, and Great Britain," *Organization Studies* 1 (1980): 59–86; G. Hartmann, I. Nicholas, A. Sorge, and M. Warner, "Computerized Machine-tools, Manpower Consequences and Skill Utilization: A Study of British and West German Manufacturing Firms," *British Journal of Industrial Relations* 21, no. 2 (1983): 221–231; MacDuffie and Krafcik, "Integrating Technology and Human Resources for High Performance Manufacturing," pp. 209–226; H. Steedman and K. Wagner, "A Second Look at Productivity, Machinery and Skills in Britain and Germany," *National Institute Economic Review,* no. 122 (November 1987): 84–96; A. Daly, D. M. Hitchens, and K. Wagner, "Productivity, Machinery and Skills in a Sample of British and German Manufacturing Plants," *National Institute Economic Review,* no. 11 (February 1985): 48–61; Marcie Tyre, "Managing the Introduction of New Process Technology: International Differences in a Multi-Plant Network," working paper #3004-89-BPS, MIT, 1990.

[41]Mark A. Huselid, "Human Resource Management Practices and Firm Performance," draft paper, Institute of Management and Labor Relations, Rutgers University, 1993.

[42]Barry Macy et al., "A Meta Analysis of Organizational Innovations," draft paper, Center for Quality of Work Life, Texas Tech University, 1993.

Chapter 4

[1]Sanford Jacoby, *Employing Bureaucracies* (New York: Columbia University Press, 1985); Thomas A. Kochan and Peter Cappelli, "The Transformation of the Industrial Relations and Personnel Function," in Paul Osterman, ed., *Internal Labor Markets* (Cambridge, Mass.: MIT Press, 1984), pp. 133–162; James Baron, Frank R. Dobbin, and P. Devereaux Jennings, "War and Peace: The Evolution of Modern Personnel Administration in U.S. Industry," *American Journal of Sociology* 92, no. 2 (September 1986): 350–383.

[2]See Keith Sisson, "Change and Continuity in UK Industrial Relations: 'Strategic Choice' or 'Muddling Thru'?" Paper prepared for International IR/HR Research Network, Paris, June 22–24, 1992. See also John Storey, "HRM in Action: The Truth Is Out at Last," *Personnel Management,* April 1992, 28–31.

[3]After eliminating cases with missing variables and a few establishments that slipped into the survey inappropriately, we used a final sample size of 694. For a more complete description and analysis of this survey, see Paul Osterman, "How Common Is Workplace Transformation and How Can We Explain Who Adopts It? Results from a National Survey," *Industrial and Labor Relations Review,* January 1994, 175–188.

[4]We wish to thank Joshua Hammond of the American Quality Foundation and Stephen Yearout of Ernst & Young for making these data available to us and for their comments on the results of our analysis of these data. For a complete report on this work, see Thomas A. Kochan, Jody Hoffer Gittell, and Brenda A. Lautsch, "Adoption, Institutionalization, and Sustainability of Total Quality Management Practices," working paper, MIT Sloan School of Management, 1993.

[5]The core job was defined as "the largest group of nonsupervisory, nonmanagerial workers at this location who are directly involved in making the product or providing the service at your

location. We want you to think of the various groups directly involved in making the product or providing the service and then focus on the largest group. For example, these might be assembly line workers at a factory or computer programmers in a software company, or sales or service representatives in an insurance company." The distribution of responses was as follows: (a) professional/technical 14.3%, (b) sales 19.0%, (c) clerical 6.0%, (d) service 18.3%, and (e) blue-collar 42.3%.

⁶For the skeptical view of TQM, see M. Beer, B. Spector, and R. Eisenstadt, "Why Change Programs Don't Produce Change," *Harvard Business Review,* November–December 1990, 158–166, and G. Fuchsberg, "Baldrige Awards May Be Losing Their Luster," *The Wall Street Journal,* April 19, 1993, B-1. For the optimistic view, see J. M. Juran, *Juran on Planning for Quality* (New York: Free Press, 1988), and W. E. Deming, *Out of the Crisis* (Cambridge, Mass.: MIT Center for Advanced Engineering Study, 1986).

⁷The most widely cited statistic to date is the one used by the Commission on the Skills of the American Workforce. Its report argues that only about 5 percent of American firms can be considered to be significant adopters of workplace innovations that produce what the commission terms "high-performance workplaces." The empirical basis for this estimate apparently comes from an informal survey and the estimates of the experts on the commission rather than from a representative survey. See *America's Choice: High Skills or Low Wages* (Rochester, N.Y.: The National Center on Education and the Economy, 1991).

⁸This is calculated as an average of the percentage employee usage of each of the twenty-one quality tools.

⁹Canadian banking and autos prove to be somewhat exceptional; 12 percent of firms in the Canadian auto industry involve a majority of employees in quality functional deployment, while a full 25 percent of financial institutions report a similar level of employee involvement in experimental design.

¹⁰Edward E. Lawler III, Susan Albers Mohrman, and Gerald E. Ledford, *Employee Involvement and Total Quality Management: Practices and Results in Fortune 1000 Companies* (San Francisco: Jossey-Bass, 1992), p. 22.

¹¹This point is vividly illustrated in Shoshana Zuboff, *In the Age of the Smart Machine: The Future of Work and Power* (New York: Basic Books, 1988).

¹²Frederick W. Taylor, *The Principles of Scientific Management* (New York: W. W. Norton, 1911).

¹³See, for example, the various papers in Paul S. Adler, *Technology and the Future of Work* (New York: Oxford University Press, 1992).

¹⁴Robert J. Thomas, *What Machines Can't Do* (Berkeley: University of California Press, 1993).

¹⁵Benjamin Whipple, "Organizing Information for Team-based Manufacturing," unpublished paper, MIT Sloan School of Management, 1993.

¹⁶Haruo Shimada and John Paul MacDuffie, "Industrial Relations and Humanware," working paper, MIT Sloan School of Management, 1986.

¹⁷Michael Cusumano, *The Japanese Automobile Industry* (Cambridge, Mass.: Harvard University Press, 1985).

¹⁸See John F. Krafcik, "Triumph of the Lean Production System," *Sloan Management Review* 30 (1988): 41–52, and John Paul MacDuffie and John F. Krafcik, "Integrating Technology and Human Resources for High-Performance Manufacturing: Evidence from the International Auto Industry," in Thomas A. Kochan and Michael Useem, eds., *Transforming Organizations* (New York: Oxford University Press, 1992), pp. 209–225. These results are also summarized in James Womack, Daniel Jones, and Daniel Roos, *The Machine That Changed the World* (New York: Rawson, 1990).

¹⁹Sociotechnical theorists focused on enriching job content through such innovations as team-based work organization and extensive employee involvement in task-related problem solving. See Thomas A. Kochan, Harry C. Katz, and Robert B. McKersie, *The Transformation of American Industrial Relations* (New York: Basic Books, 1986).

[20]See Kim Clark, W. Bruce Chew, and Takahiro Fujimoto, "Product Development in the World Auto Industry," *Brookings Papers on Economic Activity,* no. 3 (1987): 729–771. See also Deborah Ancona, "Outward Bound: Strategies for Team Survival in the Organization," *Academy of Management Journal* 33: 334–365.

[21]Marcie Tyre, "Managing the Introduction of New Process Technology: International Differences in a Multi-Plant Network," working paper #3004-89-BPS, MIT, 1990.

[22]For the U.S. establishment survey, see Paul Osterman, "How Common Is Workplace Transformation and How Can We Explain Who Adopts It?" *Industrial and Labor Relations Review,* January 1994, 175–188. For the international quality survey results, see Thomas A. Kochan, Jody Hoffer Gittell, and Brenda A. Lautsch, "Adoption, Institutionalization, and Sustainability of Total Quality Management Practices," working paper, MIT Sloan School of Management, 1993.

[23]Gary Jacobson and John Hillkirk, *Xerox: American Samurai* (New York: College Books, 1986).

[24]Jeffrey B. Arthur, "The Link Between Business Strategy and Industrial Relations Systems in American Steel Minimills," *Industrial and Labor Relations Review* 45 (April 1992): 488–506.

[25]Kochan, Katz, and McKersie, *The Transformation of American Industrial Relations.*

[26]Specifically, the question was, "In general, what is your establishment's philosophy about how appropriate it is to help increase the well-being of employees with respect to their personal or family situations?" The distribution of responses was: 1.7% "Not Appropriate," 9.4% "A Little Appropriate," 33.0% "Moderately Appropriate," 42.8% "Very Appropriate," and 12.8% "Extremely Appropriate."

[27]The history of these plans is well documented in Harry A. Millis and Royal E. Montgomery, *Organized Labor* (New York: McGraw-Hill, 1945); Sanford Jacoby, *Employing Bureaucracy: Managers, Unions, and the Transformation of Work in American Industry* (New York: Columbia University Press, 1985); and David Brody, *Workers in Industrial America: Essays on the Twentieth-Century Struggle* (New York: Oxford University Press, 1980).

[28]Paul S. Goodman, "Quality of Work Life Projects in the 1980s," Industrial Relations Research Association, Proceedings of the 1980 Spring Meeting, Philadelphia, 1980.

[29]Edward E. Lawler III and Susan Albers Mohrman, "Quality Circles after the Honeymoon," *Organizational Dynamics* 15 (Spring 1987): 42–54, and Robert Drago, "Quality Circle Survival: An Exploratory Analysis," *Industrial Relations* 27, no. 3 (Fall 1988): 336–351.

[30]Gordon Betcherman and Anil Verma, "Follow-up to the New Technology Survey," paper presented to the Canadian Industrial Relations Research Association, June 1993.

[31]An establishment was defined as having sustained the mutual gains system if two of the four work innovations had been in place with 50 percent of the core work force involved for five or more years. To test the relationship between a particular human resource practice and whether the mutual gains system was sustained, a regression was estimated in which the dependent variable was the human resource practice in question, and the independent variables included a dummy variable that took on the value of one if the establishment had sustained the mutual gains system and zero otherwise, as well as controls for industry and occupation.

[32]See Thomas A. Kochan, Harry C. Katz, and Nancy R. Mower, *Worker Participation and American Unions: Threat or Opportunity?* (Kalamazoo, Mich.: W. E. Upjohn Institute for Employment Research, 1984), pp. 123–124.

[33]Fred Kofman, Nelson Repenning, and John Sterman, "Can Successful Quality Programs Hurt the Firm? A Paradox of Organizational Improvement," working paper, MIT Sloan School of Management, 1993.

[34]As indicated in Table 4-6, the significant training variable measured the percentage of core employees who receive cross-training.

[35]David Levine and Laura D'Andrea Tyson, "Participation, Productivity, and the Firm's Performance," in Alan S. Blinder, ed., *Paying for Productivity: A Look at the Evidence* (Washington, D.C.: Brookings Institution, 1990).

[36]For early documentation of this finding, see Kochan, Katz, and Mower, *Worker Participation and American Unions.*

[37]For a report on the project, see Malcolm Lovell, Robert B. McKersie, and Thomas A. Kochan, "Making It Together: The Modern Operating Agreement," final report to the U.S. Department of Labor, 1991.

[38]Drago, "Quality Circle Survival."

[39]Mary Ellen Kelley's results were reported at a meeting of the HR Network working group at the MIT Sloan School of Management, July 8, 1993.

Chapter 5

[1]Susan Antilla, "Most Admired—By Short Sellers, Too," *New York Times,* February 14, 1993.

[2]Quoted in "How to Succeed in Business When Your Company Doesn't," *Business Week,* February 15, 1993, 34.

[3]A summary of these arguments is found in Michael Porter's synthesis chapter in M. Porter, ed., *Capital Choices: Changing the Way America Invests in Industry* (Boston: Harvard Business School Press, forthcoming).

[4]Ibid.

[5]Jeremy Stein, Kenneth Froot, and André Perold, "Shareholder Trading Practices and Corporate Investment Horizons," in Porter, *Capital Choices.*

[6]Michael T. Jacobs, *Short-Term America: The Causes and Cures of Our Business Myopia* (Boston: Harvard Business School Press, 1991), p. 36.

[7]Dan L. Worrell, Wallace N. Davidson III, and Varinder M. Sharma, "Layoff Announcements and Stockholder Wealth," *Academy of Management Journal* 34 (1991): 662–678.

[8]The material for this case was compiled from a review of the business and academic articles reporting on Cummins between 1979 and 1993. We thank Jody Hoffer Gittel for preparing this material.

[9]"Mr. Rust Belt," *Business Week,* October 17, 1988, 72–82.

[10]Paul A. Branstad, "Toward Common Ground," *Outlook* 15 (1991): 25–32.

[11]"The Twelve Labors: To Hell and Back with Henry Schacht of Cummins Engine," *Financial World,* June 9, 1992, 60–61.

[12]Timothy T. Baldwin, Richard J. Wagner, and Charles Chasteen, "A Real Commitment to Training," *Training and Development Journal,* September 1989, 60–64.

[13]Ibid., 60.

[14]"Mr. Rust Belt," 73.

[15]Branstad, "Toward Common Ground," 26.

[16]"Turning Cummins into the Engine Maker That Could: Why Kubota Hitched Its Tractor to Cummins," *Business Week,* July 30, 1990, 20–21.

[17]Eric J. Savitz, "True Believers: To This Research Boutique, Graham & Dodd Is Still the Investment Bible," *Barron's* 70, iss. 51 (December 17, 1990): 14–15, 30, 38.

[18]Branstad, "Toward Common Ground," 31.

[19]"Humming on All Cylinders," *New York Times,* February 18, 1993, D3.

[20]See, for example, Jeffrey Pfeffer, *Managing with Power* (Boston: Harvard Business School Press, 1992).

[21]Thomas A. Kochan, "Determinants of Power of Boundary Units in an Inter-Organizational Bargaining Relationship," *Administrative Science Quarterly* 20 (September 1975): 434–452.

[22]See Sanford Jacoby, *Employing Bureaucracy Managers, Unions, and the Transformation of Work in American Industry* (New York: Columbia University Press, 1985); Thomas A. Kochan and Peter Cappelli, "The Transformation of the Industrial Relations and Personnel Function," in Paul Osterman, ed., *Internal Labor Markets* (New York: Oxford University Press, 1983); and James Baron, Frank R. Dobbin, and P. Devereaux Jennings, "War and Peace: The Evolution of Modern Personnel Administration in U.S. Industry," *American Journal of Sociology* 92, no. 2 (September 1986): 350–383.

[23]*Priorities for Competitive Advantage: A Worldwide Human Resource Study* (New York: Towers Perrin, 1992), p. 30.

[24]For an argument in support of this view, see Randall Shuler, *World Class HR Departments: Six Critical Issues,* Stern Graduate School of Business, New York University, 1992.

[25]*Priorities for Competitive Advantage,* pp. 20–22 and Exhibit 7.

[26]"GE's Doyle Urges HR to Embrace a World of Change," *Work in America* 18, no. 3 (March 1993): 3.

[27]Michael Useem, *Executive Defense: Shareholder Power and Corporate Reorganization* (Cambridge, Mass.: Harvard University Press, 1993).

[28]Masahiko Aoki, *Information, Incentives, and Bargaining in the Japanese Economy* (New York: Cambridge University Press, 1988).

[29]An excellent analysis of this aspect of the governance structure of Japanese firms is provided in W. Carl Kester, *Japanese Takeovers: The Global Contest for Corporate Control* (Boston: Harvard Business School Press, 1991), pp. 53–81.

[30]German financial markets and governance arrangements are summarized in Christopher S. Allen, "Domestic Politics and Private Investment: Financial Regulation in West Germany and the United States," Research Report No. 2, American Institute for Contemporary Studies, Johns Hopkins University, 1990; Peter Katzenstein, *Politics and Policy in the Federal Republic: The Semi-Sovereign State* (Philadelphia: Temple University Press, 1987); Jacobs, *Short-Term America,* pp. 69–71; and Kirsten S. Wever and Christopher S. Allen, "Change and Innovation in Germany and the U.S.: Internal versus External Flexibility," unpublished paper, Northeastern University, School of Business Administration, 1992.

[31]Quoted in Kathleen A. Thelen, *Union of Parts: Labor Politics in Postwar Germany* (Ithaca, N.Y.: Cornell University Press, 1991), p. 49.

[32]Katharine G. Abraham and Susan N. Houseman, *Job Security in America: Lessons from Germany* (Washington, D.C.: Brookings Institution, 1993).

[33]For two comparative case studies of industrial restructuring in Germany and Japan that make the same point, namely, that working out a plan for meeting the interests of all the stakeholders involved enhances rather than constrains the adjustment process, see Robert Reich, "Bailout: A Comparative Study in Law and Industrial Structure," in A. Michael Spence and Heather Hazard, eds., *International Competitiveness* (Cambridge, Mass.: Ballinger, 1988), pp. 301–372, and Ronald Dore, *Flexible Rigidities Industrial Policy and Structural Adjustment in the Japanese Economy, 1970–80* (London: Athlone Press, 1986).

[34]See, for example, Richard B. Freeman and Edward P. Lazear, "An Economic Analysis of Works Councils," and Richard B. Freeman and Joel Rogers, "Who Speaks for Us? Employee Representation in a Non-Union Labor Market." Both papers are part of a National Bureau of Economic Research comprehensive study of the role of works councils in European firms. We thank the authors for allowing us to draw on this work in progress. See also Thelen, *Union of Parts.*

[35]Case studies of the role of works councils in the auto and metalworking sectors are found in Wolfgang Streeck, *Industrial Relations in the West German Car Industry* (London: Heinemann, 1984), and in Lowell Turner, *Democracy at Work: Changing World Markets and the Future of Labor Unions* (Ithaca, N.Y.: Cornell University Press, 1991). Case studies outside metalworking are included in Kirsten Wever, "Learning from Works Councils: Five Unspectacular Cases for Germany," *Industrial Relations,* forthcoming.

[36]Here too we draw on the work of Kirsten Wever, "What German Employers Think about Employee Representation and Competitiveness," unpublished manuscript, Northeastern University, 1993, and the interviews with German managers reported in Freeman and Rogers, "Who Speaks for Us?"

[37]Wever, "What German Employers Think."

[38]Freeman and Rogers, "Who Speaks for Us?" p. 42.

[39]Turner, *Democracy at Work.*

[40]Thelen, *Union of Parts.*

[41]For a review of the relevant labor and corporate law doctrines affecting corporate governance, see Marleen O'Connor, "The Human Capital Era: Reconceptualizing Corporate Law to Facilitate Labor-Management Cooperation," *Cornell Law Review* 78 (1993): 901–965.

[42]*Daily Labor Report* No. 206 (Washington, D.C.: Bureau of National Affairs, 1986), p. A-2.

[43]For two books describing the world of mergers and deal making in the 1980s, see Bryan Burrough and John Helyar, *Barbarians at the Gate: The Fall of RJR Nabisco* (New York: Harper & Row, 1990), and Michael Lewis, *Liar's Poker* (New York: W. W. Norton, 1989).

[44]Larry W. Hunter, "Is Joint Governance Possible? What Happens When Unions Enter American Boardrooms," unpublished manuscript, Wharton School of Management, 1993.

[45]Michael A. Conte and Jan Svejnar, with a comment by Joseph R. Blasi, "The Performance Effects of Employee Ownership Plans," in Alan S. Blinder, ed., *Paying for Productivity: A Look at the Evidence* (Washington, D.C.: Brookings Institution, 1990), pp. 143–182.

[46]Edwin H. Land, Polaroid Handbook, 1947, p. 1.

Chapter 6

[1]For the most recent review of the state of unions and the causes of their decline in the United States, see George Strauss, Daniel G. Gallagher, and Jack Fiorito, eds., *The State of Unions* (Madison, Wis.: Industrial Relations Research Association, 1991).

[2]Douglas V. Brown and Charles A. Myers, "The Changing Industrial Relations Philosophy of American Management," *Proceedings of the Ninth Annual Winter Meeting of the Industrial Relations Research Association* (Madison, Wis.: Industrial Relations Research Association, 1957), p. 92.

[3]See, for example, Derek C. Bok and John T. Dunlop, *Labor and the American Community* (New York: Simon & Schuster, 1970), or Thomas A. Kochan, "How American Workers View Unions," *Monthly Labor Review* 102 (April 1979): 15–22.

[4]Joel Rogers and Richard Freeman, "Who Speaks for Us? Employee Representation in a Non-Union Labor Market," in *Employee Representation: Alternatives and Future Directions,* Bruce E. Kaufman and Morris M. Kleiner, eds. (Madison, Wis.: Industrial Relations Research Association, 1993), pp. 13–80.

[5]As reported by Leonard Silk, *New York Times,* December 13, 1992, D-2.

[6]See James Weinstein, *The Corporate Ideal in the Liberal State, 1900–1918* (Boston: Beacon Press, 1968).

[7]Richard B. Freeman and James B. Medoff, *What Do Unions Do?* (New York: Basic Books, 1984).

[8]Sumner H. Slichter, James J. Healy, and E. Robert Livernash, *The Impact of Collective Bargaining on Management* (Washington, D.C.: Brookings Institution, 1960).

[9]See Harry C. Katz, Thomas A. Kochan, and Kenneth Gobeille, *Industrial Relations Performance, Economic Performance and the Effects of Quality of Working Life Efforts: An Inter-Plan Analysis,* MIT, Sloan School of Management, 1981.

[10]See, for example, Freeman and Medoff, *What Do Unions Do?;* Brian Becker and Craig Olson, "Labor Relations and Firm Performance," in Morris M. Kleiner et al., eds., *Human Resources and the Performance of the Firm* (Madison, Wis.: Industrial Relations Research Association, 1987).

[11]See Thomas A. Kochan, Harry C. Katz, and Robert B. McKersie, *The Transformation of American Industrial Relations* (New York: Basic Books, 1986), p. 252.

[12]Barry Bluestone and Irving Bluestone, *Negotiating the Future: A Labor Perspective on American Business* (New York: Basic Books, 1993).

[13]Harry C. Katz, Thomas A. Kochan, and Kenneth Gobeille, "Industrial Relations Performance, Economic Performance and Quality of Working Life Efforts: An Inter-Plant Analysis," *Industrial and Labor Relations Review* 37 (October 1983): 13–17; Harry C. Katz, Thomas A. Kochan, and Mark Weber, "Assessing the Effects of Industrial Relations Systems and Efforts to Improve the Quality of Working Life on Organizational Effectiveness," *Academy of Management Journal* 28 (1986): 509–526.

[14]For the earliest report using actual productivity and quality data from NUMMI, see John Krafcik, "World Class Manufacturing: An International Comparison of Automobile Assembly Plant Performance," *Sloan Management Review* 30: 41–52. For a more recent and deeper anthropological account of the reaction of the work force over the course of NUMMI's first nine years, see Paul Adler, "The Learning Bureaucracy: New United Motors Manufacturing, Inc.," in Barry Staw and Larry L. Cummings, eds., *Research in Organizational Behavior,* vol. 13 (Greenwich, Conn.: JAI Press, 1992).

[15]Mike Parker and Jane Slaughter, *Choosing Sides: Unions and the Team Concept* (Boston: South End Press, 1988); Lowell Turner, *Democracy at Work: Changing World Markets and the Future of Labor* (Ithaca, N.Y.: Cornell University Press, 1991); Adler, "The Learning Bureaucracy."

[16]See Saul Rubinstein, Michael Bennett, and Thomas A. Kochan, "Reinventing the Local Union: The Partnership between Saturn and UAW Local 1853," in Bruce Kaufman and Morris Kleiner, eds., *Employee Representation: Alternatives and Future Directions* (Madison, Wis.: Industrial Relations Research Association, 1993), pp. 339–370.

[17]*New Patterns of Labor-Management Relations* (Washington, D.C.: The Collective Bargaining Forum, 1988). Distributed by the U.S. Department of Labor.

[18]In "Quality of Work Life: AT&T and CWA Examine Process after Three Years" (Washington, D.C.: U.S. Department of Labor, Bureau of Labor-Management Relations and Cooperative Programs, 1985), p. 49.

[19]"Workplace of the Future." The 1993 Collective Bargaining Agreement between AT&T and the Communications Workers of America and the International Brotherhood of Electrical Workers.

[20]*The Wall Street Journal,* January 7, 1993, 3.

[21]See Joel Cutcher-Gershenfeld, *Tracing a Transformation in Industrial Relations* (Washington, D.C.: U.S. Department of Labor, Bureau of Labor-Management Relations and Cooperative Programs, 1988).

[22]John T. Dunlop and David Weil, "Human Resource Innovations in the Apparel Industry: An Industrial Relations System Perspective," unpublished paper, Harvard University/Boston University, October 1992.

[23]The material in this section is drawn from John Hoerr, "Unionism at Harvard," *The American Prospect,* forthcoming, and from Susan Eaton, "Stories Make Things Real: A Reflection on Union Activism and Personal Change for Five 'Clerical Workers Union' Activists," unpublished paper, Harvard Graduate School of Education, 1993. We wish to thank them for making this material available.

[24]See, for example, Thomas A. Kochan, "Crossroads in Employment Relations: Approaching a Mutual Gains Paradigm," *Looking Ahead* 14, no. 4 (January 1993): 8–14.

[25]See Roy Adams, "Should Works Councils Be Used as Industrial Relations Policy?" *Monthly Labor Review,* July 1985, 25–29; Thomas A. Kochan and Robert B. McKersie, "Future Directions for Labor and Human Resource Policy," *Relations Industrielles* 44 (1989): 224–243; Paul Weiler,

Governing the Work Place: The Future of Labor and Employment Law (Cambridge, Mass.: Harvard University Press, 1990); Turner, *Democracy at Work;* Kirsten Wever, Peter Berg, and Thomas A. Kochan, "Employee Skills Development in Institutional Context: Comparing the United States and Germany," report for the Economic Policy Institute, June 15, 1993; Richard Freeman and Edward Lazear, "An Economic Analysis of Works Councils" (Cambridge, Mass.: National Bureau of Economic Research Working Paper, 1992); Rogers and Freeman, "Who Speaks for Us?"; and Joel Rogers and Barbara Wootton, "Works Councils in the United States: Could We Get There from Here?" prepared for Works Councils Project Conference, Geneva, 1993.

Chapter 7

[1]Richard E. Walton, *Innovating to Compete: Lessons for Diffusing and Managing Change in the Workplace* (San Francisco: Jossey-Bass, 1987).

[2]Robert Cole, *Strategies for Learning: Small-Group Activities in American, Japanese, and Swedish Industry* (Berkeley: University of California Press, 1989).

[3]Bureau of National Affairs, *Personnel Policies Forum Survey No. 140* (Washington, D.C.: Bureau of National Affairs, 1985), p. 22.

[4]The problem is that graduates of income-targeted programs can be stigmatized and employers may avoid them. For evidence on this point, see Paul Osterman, "Rethinking the American Training System," *Social Policy* 19, no. 1 (Summer 1988): 28–35.

[5]Paul Osterman and Rosemary Batt, "Employer-Centered Training Programs for International Competitiveness: Lessons from State Programs," *Journal of Policy Analysis and Management* 12, no. 3 (Summer 1993): 456–477.

[6]This section is based on ibid.

[7]As a concrete example in the Illinois project to develop standards, one occupation under development is general production technician in metalworking. The proposed standard sets forth a description of the job's duties, a relatively detailed skill-performance standard (relating to blueprint reading, use of measuring tools, and measurement of accuracy), a demonstrated knowledge standard (relating to the nature and uses of different tools), and a list of competency levels to be achieved in reading, math, and written communication. See Robert Sheets, "Building a World-Class Workforce in the United States: The Need for a National-State System of Industry Skill Standards for State Workforce Preparation Programs," paper prepared for the National Center for the Educational Quality of the Workforce, University of Pennsylvania, 1991.

[8]Ibid.

[9]This case, written by Rosemary Batt, is in Osterman and Batt, "Employer-Centered Training Programs."

[10]In France the grant/levy scheme, in operation since 1971, currently requires training expenditure of 1.1 percent of payroll (it began at 0.5 percent), and has been the subject of careful evaluations.

The good news in the French experience is that the average amount spent per firm on training grew a great deal over the period since the tax was implemented. It is certain that not all the credit goes to the tax: first, many firms spent a good deal more than the tax required, so the tax was not a constraint. Second, in other nations (for example, the United States) that lacked such a tax, average firm spending on training also increased over the period (New York: Conference Board, *Trends in Corporate Education and Training*, 1985). Nonetheless, the tax deserves some credit. Just over 20 percent of firms with between 500 and 1,999 employees and just under 20 percent of firms of 2,000 and more spend between 1.1 and 1.5 percent of their payroll on training. One might speculate that many of these were pushed over the limit by the program. In addition, just under 30 percent of the 500–1,999-size firms and just under 15 percent of the largest firms spend less than 1.1 percent and presumably pay into the training funds.

The bad news is that the gap between training expenditures of large and small firms did not change in this period. In 1972, firms with between 20 and 49 employees spent, on average, 0.62 percent of their payroll on training, while firms with 2,000 or more employees spent 2.5 percent. By 1984 the gap had widened, with the figures 1.22 percent and 3.45 percent, respectively. In the large firms 38.3 percent of employees received training, while in small firms the rate was 9.7 percent.

Not only has the French system not closed the gap between the large and small firms but it also became a transfer system from small to large because small firms paid more in taxes but received less in grants, for the reasons cited above. Hence for every 100 francs deposited into the fund, small and medium-size firms received 50 francs back, while large firms received 120.

The British program, initiated in 1964, was abolished by Prime Minister Margaret Thatcher in the late 1970s. It was different from the French plan in that the levy/grant scheme was administered on an industry-by-industry basis by industrial training boards. However, with respect to the impact on small firms, the experience seems to parallel that in France. The Bolton Committee evaluated the program in 1971 and concluded that "the cost of claiming grants, the drain imposed by the levy on small firms . . . are in our view fundamental difficulties which . . . will always prevent making a worthwhile economic impact on the needs of small firms under the levy/grant system." For documentation, see Jean-Paul Gehin, "La Formation Continue dans les Petites et Moyennes Enterprises: Spécificietés et Paradoxes," *Formation Emploi*, no. 16 (Octobre–Décembre 1986): 80, and Peter Senker, "Policy Implications of the EITB's History," Social Science Policy Unit, University of Sussex, December 1990.

[11]The Senate legislation speaks of "organized instruction" but the meaning of this phrase is unclear, to say the least.

[12]Christopher J. Ruhm, "Are Workers Permanently Scarred by Job Displacements?" *American Economic Review* 81 (March 1991): 319–323; Lori Gladstein Kletzer, "Returns to Seniority After a Permanent Job Loss," *American Economic Review* 79 (June 1989): 536–543; Louis S. Jacobson, Robert J. LaLonde, and Daniel G. Sullivan, "Earnings Losses of Displaced Workers," *American Economic Review* 83, no. 4 (September 1993): 685–709.

[13]Osterman and Batt, "Employer-Centered Training Programs."

[14]The quotation, from Theodore Robinson, first vice president of the Illinois Steel Company, was delivered in 1913 to the American Steel Institute. Cited in Julia Wrigley, *Class Politics and Public Schools: Chicago, 1900–1950* (New Brunswick, N.J.: Rutgers University Press, 1982), p. 69.

[15]Paul Osterman and Maria Iannozzi, "Youth Apprenticeships and School-to-Work Transition: Current Knowledge and Legislative Strategy," Center for the Educational Quality of the Workforce Working Paper, University of Pennsylvania, January 1993.

Chapter 8

[1]See William E. Forbath, "The Shaping of the American Labor Movement," *Harvard Law Review* 102 (1991): 1,109. See also Victoria C. Hattam, *Labor Visions and State Power: The Origins of Business Unionism in the United States* (Princeton: Princeton University Press, 1993).

[2]See Andrei Markovitz, *The Politics of the West German Trade Unions: Strategies of Class and Interest Representation in Growth and Crisis* (New York: Cambridge University Press, 1986).

[3]Christopher L. Tomlins, "The New Deal, Collective Bargaining and the Triumph of Industrial Pluralism," *Industrial and Labor Relations Review* 39 (1985): 19–34.

[4]Margaret Weir, Ann Shola Orloff, and Theda Skocpol, "Understanding American Social Politics," in Weir, Orloff, and Skocpol, eds., *The Politics of Social Policy in the United States* (Princeton: Princeton University Press, 1988), pp. 3–35.

[5]See *Final Report of the Governor's Committee on Public Employee Relations* (Albany: State of New York, 1966). For some of the intellectual issues regarding the right to strike that influenced

this legislation, see George W. Taylor, "Public Employment: Strikes or Procedures," *Industrial and Labor Relations Review* 20 (July 1967): 617–636, and John T. Dunlop, "The Functions of the Strike," in John T. Dunlop and Neil W. Chamberlain, eds., *Frontiers of Collective Bargaining* (New York: Harper & Row, 1967), pp. 103–121.

[6]Carl Stevens, "Is Compulsory Arbitration Compatible with Collective Bargaining?" *Industrial Relations* 5 (February 1966): 38–52.

[7]For a discussion of the political and moral traditions that give rise to the importance traditionally attached to "free collective bargaining," see "The Values of Free Collective Bargaining," in Thomas A. Kochan, *Collective Bargaining and Industrial Relations: From Theory to Policy and Practice* (Homewood, Ill.: Richard D. Irwin, 1980), pp. 235–239.

[8]See the remarks of William J. Usery, Jr., in Abraham J. Siegel and David B. Lipsky, eds., *Unfinished Business: An Agenda for Labor, Management and the Public* (Cambridge, Mass.: MIT Press, 1978), pp. 37–40.

[9]See Harry A. Millis and Royal E. Montgomery, *Organized Labor* (New York: McGraw-Hill, 1945).

[10]Another comprehensive proposal is presented in William Gould IV, *Agenda for Reform: The Future of Employment Relationships and the Law* (Cambridge, Mass.: MIT Press, 1993).

[11]Richard B. Freeman and Edward P. Lazear, "An Economic Analysis of Works Councils" (Cambridge, Mass.: National Bureau of Economic Research, 1992).

[12]See Paul Weiler, *Governing the Workplace: Employee Representative in the Eyes of the Law* (Cambridge, Mass.: Harvard University Press, 1990).

[13]See Donald Powers, Joel Cutcher-Gershenfeld, and Pat McHugh, "Collective Bargaining in Small Firms: Preliminary Evidence of Fundamental Change," unpublished paper, Michigan State University, 1993.

Chapter 9

[1]Harry C. Katz and Charles Sabel, "Industrial Relations and Industrial Adjustment in the Car Industry," *Industrial Relations* 24, no. 3 (Fall 1985): 295–315.

[2]Edwin E. Witte, "Where We Are in Industrial Relations," in Milton Derber, ed., *Proceedings of the First Annual Meeting of the Industrial Relations Research Association* (Champaign, Ill.: Industrial Relations Research Association, 1949), p. 7.

name index

subject index

CWA/AT&T experiment,
153–154
UAW/GM experiment, 147–149
QWL. *See* Quality of work life

Railway Labor Act, 200
Rath Meatpacking, 132–133
Reagan-Bush administrations
Bureau of Labor Management Relations and Cooperative Programs, 197
labor-management relations
downgraded, 197
Real wages, 19, 23, 25
"Relations by objectives," 211
Representation gap, in labor force, 17
Rohm & Haas Bayport, Inc., effect
of mutual gains practices at, 65
Role of labor and worker representation, 141–168. *See also* Unions
alternative forms of worker representation, 165–167, 219–220
Amalgamated Clothing and Textile Workers Union, 157–161
Communication Workers of
America, 153–156
decline of unions, 141–147, 218
Harvard Union of Clerical and
Technical Workers, 161–163
new AFL-CIO strategy, 164–165,
166
toward a new model: union efforts,
147–165, 219–220
United Auto Workers, 148–153
United Steelworkers, 156–157
Rucker plan, 231n.33

Saturn Corporation
Committee of 99, union-management planning, 151
employee participation program
at, 50, 51
mutual gains system at, 39, 61

new governance model, 152
new information system for teams,
91
self-managing work teams, 91,
152
Strategic Action Council, 51
training policy, 30
UAW's role at, 30, 51, 106,
151–153
workplace innovations at, 70
Scanlon plan, 54
School-to-work transition programs,
186–189, 214, 217
Scientific management, 90. *See also*
Taylorism
Sears Roebuck, layoffs at, 29
Second International Math Study,
34
Second International Science Study,
34
Self-managed work teams, 33, 89,
91, 173
definition of, 108
Shareholder interests
and emphasizing short-term gain,
9–10, 13, 112, 131
as obligation of corporation, 9,
131, 204
supremacy of, 122
vs. employee interests, 8, 112
Shenandoah Life Insurance Company, effect of mutual gains
practices at, 64
Skilled labor
and education, 33–35
increased demand for, 26, 29–33
international comparison: auto industry, 37–38
skill certification standards, 217
supply of, 33–35
and training, 30–31, 34, 37–38
white- vs. blue-collar, 31–33
Sloan Foundation, 222
Small-lot production, 92